Redburn
His First Voyage

by

Herman Melville

Redburn
His First Voyage
by Herman Melville

Copyright © 2024

All Rights reserved.

No part of this publication may be reproduced, stored in a retrieval system, or transmitted in any form or by any means, electronic, mechanical, photocopying or Otherwise, without the written permission of the publisher.
The author/editor asserts the moral right to be identified as the author/editor of this work.

ISBN: 978-93-68099-63-5

Published by

DOUBLE 9 BOOKS

2/13-B, Ansari Road
Daryaganj, New Delhi – 110002
info@double9books.com
www.double9books.com
Tel. 011-40042856

This book is under public domain

ABOUT THE AUTHOR

Herman Melville was an American Renaissance novelist, poet, and short story writer who lived from August 1, 1819, to September 28, 1891. His most well-known pieces are Typee (1846), a romanticized narrative of his experiences in Polynesia; Moby-Dick (1851); and Billy Budd, Sailor, a novella that was released after his death. Although Melville was no longer well-known to the general public at the time of his death, a Melville renaissance began in 1919, the year of his birth. In the end, Moby-Dick was regarded as one of the best American novels. The third child of a wealthy merchant who died in 1832, leaving the family in terrible financial shape, Melville was born in New York City. He sailed as a common sailor in 1839, first as a whaler Acushnet and subsequently as a merchant ship. However, he abandoned ship in the Marquesas Islands. His first work, Typee, and its follow-up, Omoo (1847), were travelogues inspired by his interactions with the island peoples. He was able to marry Elizabeth Shaw, the daughter of Boston lawyer Lemuel Shaw, because to their prosperity. His debut novel not drawn from personal experience, Mardi (1849), was not well received.

CONTENTS

CHAPTER I
HOW WELLINGBOROUGH REDBURN'S TASTE FOR
THE SEA WAS BORN AND BRED IN HIM 11

CHAPTER II
REDBURN'S DEPARTURE FROM HOME 18

CHAPTER III
HE ARRIVES IN TOWN 22

CHAPTER IV
HOW HE DISPOSED OF HIS FOWLING-PIECE 26

CHAPTER V
HE PURCHASES HIS SEA-WARDROBE, AND ON
A DISMAL RAINY DAY PICKS UP HIS
BOARD AND LODGING ALONG THE WHARVES 30

CHAPTER VI
HE IS INITIATED IN THE BUSINESS OF
CLEANING OUT THE PIG-PEN, AND
SLUSHING DOWN THE TOP-MAST 34

CHAPTER VII
HE GETS TO SEA AND FEELS VERY BAD 39

CHAPTER VIII
HE IS PUT INTO THE LARBOARD WATCH;
GETS SEA-SICK; AND RELATES SOME
OTHER OF HIS EXPERIENCES 44

CHAPTER IX
THE SAILORS BECOMING A LITTLE SOCIAL,
REDBURN CONVERSES WITH THEM 50

CHAPTER X
HE IS VERY MUCH FRIGHTENED;
THE SAILORS ABUSE HIM; AND HE
BECOMES MISERABLE AND FORLORN 55

CHAPTER XI
HE HELPS WASH THE DECKS, AND THEN
GOES TO BREAKFAST 58

CHAPTER XII
HE GIVES SOME ACCOUNT OF ONE OF
HIS SHIPMATES CALLED JACKSON 61

CHAPTER XIII
HE HAS A FINE DAY AT SEA, BEGINS TO
LIKE IT; BUT CHANGES HIS MIND 68

CHAPTER XIV
HE CONTEMPLATES MAKING A SOCIAL
CALL ON THE CAPTAIN IN HIS CABIN 72

CHAPTER XV
THE MELANCHOLY STATE OF HIS WARDROBE 77

CHAPTER XVI
AT DEAD OF NIGHT HE IS SENT UP TO LOOSE
THE MAIN-SKYSAIL 82

CHAPTER XVII
THE COOK AND STEWARD 85

CHAPTER XVIII
HE ENDEAVORS TO IMPROVE HIS MIND;
AND TELLS OF ONE BLUNT AND HIS DREAM BOOK 89

CHAPTER XIX
A NARROW ESCAPE 95

CHAPTER XX
IN A FOG HE IS SET TO WORK AS A BELL-TOLLER,
AND BEHOLDS A HERD OF OCEAN-ELEPHANTS 98

CHAPTER XXI
A WHALEMAN AND A MAN-OF-WAR'S-MAN 101

CHAPTER XXII
THE HIGHLANDER PASSES A WRECK 104

CHAPTER XXIII
AN UNACCOUNTABLE CABIN-PASSENGER,
AND A MYSTERIOUS YOUNG LADY 107

CHAPTER XXIV
HE BEGINS TO HOP ABOUT IN THE RIGGING
LIKE A SAINT JAGO'S MONKEY 114

CHAPTER XXV
  QUARTER-DECK FURNITURE 118

CHAPTER XXVI
  A SAILOR A JACK OF ALL TRADES 120

CHAPTER XXVII
  HE GETS A PEEP AT IRELAND, AND AT
  LAST ARRIVES AT LIVERPOOL 124

CHAPTER XXVIII
  HE GOES TO SUPPER AT THE SIGN OF
  THE BALTIMORE CLIPPER 130

CHAPTER XXIX
  REDBURN DEFERENTIALLY DISCOURSES
  CONCERNING THE PROSPECTS OF SAILORS 135

CHAPTER XXX
  REDBURN GROWS INTOLERABLY FLAT AND
  STUPID OVER SOME OUTLANDISH OLD GUIDE-BOOKS 140

CHAPTER XXXI
  WITH HIS PROSY OLD GUIDE-BOOK, HE TAKES
  A PROSY STROLL THROUGH THE TOWN 149

CHAPTER XXXII
  THE DOCKS 158

CHAPTER XXXIII
  THE SALT-DROGHERS, AND GERMAN
  EMIGRANT SHIPS 162

CHAPTER XXXIV
  THE IRRAWADDY 167

CHAPTER XXXV
  GALLIOTS, COAST-OF-GUINEA-MAN,
  AND FLOATING CHAPEL 171

CHAPTER XXXVI
  THE OLD CHURCH OF ST. NICHOLAS,
  AND THE DEAD-HOUSE 174

CHAPTER XXXVII
  WHAT REDBURN SAW IN LAUNCELOTT'S-HEY 177

CHAPTER XXXVIII
  THE DOCK-WALL BEGGARS 182

CHAPTER XXXIX
THE BOOBLE-ALLEYS OF THE TOWN 186

CHAPTER XL
PLACARDS, BRASS-JEWELERS, TRUCK-HORSES,
AND STEAMERS 189

CHAPTER XLI
REDBURN ROVES ABOUT HITHER AND THITHER 196

CHAPTER XLII
HIS ADVENTURE WITH THE *CROSS* OLD GENTLEMAN 203

CHAPTER XLIII
HE TAKES A DELIGHTFUL RAMBLE INTO
THE COUNTRY; AND MAKES THE ACQUAINTANCE
OF THREE ADORABLE CHARMERS 205

CHAPTER XLIV
REDBURN INTRODUCES MASTER HARRY BOLTON
TO THE FAVORABLE CONSIDERATION OF
THE READER 212

CHAPTER XLV
HARRY BOLTON KIDNAPS REDBURN, AND
CARRIES HIM OFF TO LONDON 220

CHAPTER XLVI
A MYSTERIOUS NIGHT IN LONDON 223

CHAPTER XLVII
HOMEWARD BOUND 233

CHAPTER XLVIII
A LIVING CORPSE 239

CHAPTER XLIX
CARLO 242

CHAPTER L
HARRY BOLTON AT SEA 247

CHAPTER LI
THE EMIGRANTS 253

CHAPTER LII
THE EMIGRANTS' KITCHEN 257

CHAPTER LIII
THE HORATII AND CURIATII 261

CHAPTER LIV
　SOME SUPERIOR OLD NAIL-ROD AND PIG-TAIL 264

CHAPTER LV
　DRAWING NIGH TO THE LAST SCENE IN
　JACKSON'S CAREER 268

CHAPTER LVI
　UNDER THE LEE OF THE LONG-BOAT, REDBURN
　AND HARRY HOLD CONFIDENTIAL COMMUNION 270

CHAPTER LVII
　ALMOST A FAMINE 276

CHAPTER LVIII
　THOUGH THE HIGHLANDER PUTS INTO NO
　HARBOR AS YET; SHE HERE AND THERE LEAVES
　MANY OF HER PASSENGERS BEHIND 278

CHAPTER LIX
　THE LAST END OF JACKSON 287

CHAPTER LX
　HOME AT LAST 290

CHAPTER LXI
　REDBURN AND HARRY, ARM IN ARM,
　IN HARBOR 294

CHAPTER LXII
　THE LAST THAT WAS EVER HEARD OF
　HARRY BOLTON 302

CHAPTER I
HOW WELLINGBOROUGH REDBURN'S TASTE FOR THE SEA WAS BORN AND BRED IN HIM

"Wellingborough, as you are going to sea, suppose you take this shooting-jacket of mine along; it's just the thing—take it, it will *save* the expense of another. You see, it's quite warm; fine long skirts, stout horn buttons, and plenty of pockets."

Out of the goodness and simplicity of his heart, thus spoke my elder brother to me, upon the *eve* of my departure for the seaport.

"And, Wellingborough," he added, "since we are both short of money, and you want an outfit, and I *Have* none to *give,* you may as well take my fowling-piece along, and sell it in New York for what you can get.—Nay, take it; it's of no use to me now; I can't find it in powder any more."

I was then but a boy. Some time previous my mother had removed from New York to a pleasant village on the Hudson River, where we lived in a small house, in a quiet way. Sad disappointments in several plans which I had sketched for my future life; the necessity of doing something for myself, united to a naturally roving disposition, had now conspired within me, to send me to sea as a sailor.

For months previous I had been poring over old New York papers, delightedly perusing the long columns of ship advertisements, all of which possessed a strange, romantic charm to me. Over and over again I devoured such announcements as the following:

FOR BREMEN.
The coppered and copper-fastened brig Leda, having nearly completed her cargo, will sail for the above port on Tuesday the twentieth of May.
For freight or passage apply on board at Coenties Slip.

To my young inland imagination every word in an advertisement like this, suggested volumes of thought.

A *brig!* The very word summoned up the idea of a black, sea-worn craft, with high, cozy bulwarks, and rakish masts and yards.

Coppered and copper-fastened! That fairly smelt of the salt water! How different such vessels must be from the wooden, one-masted, green-and-white-painted sloops, that glided up and down the river before our house on the bank.

Nearly completed her cargo! How momentous the announcement; suggesting ideas, too, of musty bales, and cases of silks and satins, and filling me with contempt for the vile deck-loads of hay and lumber, with which my river experience was familiar.

Will sail on Tuesday the 20th of May-and the newspaper bore date the fifth of the month! Fifteen whole days beforehand; think of that; what an important voyage it must be, that the time of sailing was fixed upon so long beforehand; the river sloops were not used to make such prospective announcements.

For freight or passage apply on board! Think of going on board a coppered and copper-fastened brig, and taking passage for Bremen! And who could be going to Bremen? No one but foreigners, doubtless; men of dark complexions and jet-black whiskers, who talked French.

Coenties Slip. Plenty more brigs and any quantity of ships must be lying there. Coenties Slip must be somewhere near ranges of grim-looking warehouses, with rusty iron doors and shutters, and tiled roofs; and old anchors and chain-cable piled on the walk. Old-fashioned coffeehouses, also, much abound in that neighborhood, with sunburnt sea-captains going in and out, smoking cigars, and talking about Havanna, London, and Calcutta.

All these my imaginations were wonderfully assisted by certain shadowy reminiscences of wharves, and warehouses, and shipping, with which a residence in a seaport during early childhood had supplied me.

Particularly, I remembered standing with my father on the wharf when a large ship was getting under way, and rounding the head of the pier. I remembered the *yo heave ho!* of the sailors, as they just showed their woolen caps above the high bulwarks. I remembered how I thought of their crossing the great ocean; and that that very ship, and those very sailors, so near to me then, would after a time be actually in Europe.

Added to these reminiscences my father, now dead, had several times crossed the Atlantic on business affairs, for he had been an importer in Broad-street. And of winter evenings in New York, by the well-remembered sea-coal fire in old Greenwich-street, he used to tell my brother and me of the monstrous waves at sea, mountain high; of the masts bending like twigs; and all about Havre, and Liverpool, and about going up into the ball of St. Paul's in London. Indeed, during my early life, most of my thoughts of the sea were connected with the land; but with fine old lands, full of mossy cathedrals and churches, and long, narrow, crooked streets without sidewalks, and lined with strange houses. And especially I tried hard to think how such places must look of rainy days and Saturday afternoons; and whether indeed they did have rainy days and Saturdays there, just as we did here; and whether the boys went to school there, and studied geography, and wore their shirt collars turned over, and tied with a black ribbon; and whether their papas allowed them to wear boots, instead of shoes, which I so much disliked, for boots looked so manly.

As I grew older my thoughts took a larger flight, and I frequently fell into long reveries about distant voyages and travels, and thought how fine it would be, to be able to talk about remote and barbarous countries; with what reverence and wonder people would regard me, if I had just returned from the coast of Africa or New Zealand; how dark and romantic my sunburnt cheeks would look; how I would bring home with me foreign clothes of a rich fabric and princely make, and wear them up and down the streets, and how grocers' boys would turn back their heads to look at me, as I went by. For I very well remembered staring at a man myself, who was pointed out to me by my aunt one Sunday in Church, as the person who had been in Stony Arabia, and passed through strange adventures there, all of which with my own eyes I had read in the book which he wrote, an arid-looking book in a pale yellow cover.

"See what big eyes he has," whispered my aunt, "they got so big, because when he was almost dead with famishing in the desert, he all at once caught sight of a date tree, with the ripe fruit hanging on it."

Upon this, I stared at him till I thought his eyes were really of an uncommon size, and stuck out from his head like those of a lobster. I am sure my own eyes must have magnified as I stared. When church was out, I wanted my aunt to take me along and follow the traveler home. But she said the constables would take us up, if we did; and so I never saw this wonderful Arabian traveler again. But he long haunted me; and several times I dreamt of him, and thought his great eyes were grown still larger and rounder; and once I had a vision of the date tree.

In course of time, my thoughts became more and more prone to dwell upon foreign things; and in a thousand ways I sought to gratify my tastes. We had several pieces of furniture in the house, which had been brought from Europe. These I examined again and again, wondering where the wood grew; whether the workmen who made them still survived, and what they could be doing with themselves now.

Then we had several oil-paintings and rare old engravings of my father's, which he himself had bought in Paris, hanging up in the dining-room.

Two of these were sea-pieces. One represented a fat-looking, smoky fishing-boat, with three whiskerandoes in red caps, and their browsers legs rolled up, hauling in a seine. There was high French-like land in one corner, and a tumble-down gray lighthouse surmounting it. The waves were toasted brown, and the whole picture looked mellow and old. I used to think a piece of it might taste good.

The other represented three old-fashioned French men-of-war with high castles, like pagodas, on the bow and stern, such as you see in Froissart; and snug little turrets on top of the mast, full of little men, with something undefinable in their hands. All three were sailing through a bright-blue sea, blue as Sicily skies; and they were leaning over on their sides at a fearful angle; and they must have been going very fast, for the white spray was about the bows like a snow-storm.

Then, we had two large green French portfolios of colored prints, more than I could lift at that age. Every Saturday my brothers and sisters used to get them out of the corner where they were kept, and spreading them on the floor, gaze at them with never-failing delight.

They were of all sorts. Some were pictures of Versailles, its masquerades, its drawing-rooms, its fountains, and courts, and gardens, with long lines of thick foliage cut into fantastic doors and windows, and towers and pinnacles. Others were rural scenes, full of fine skies, pensive cows standing up to the knees in water, and shepherd-boys and cottages in the distance, half concealed in vineyards and vines.

And others were pictures of natural history, representing rhinoceroses and elephants and spotted tigers; and above all there was a picture of a great whale, as big as a ship, stuck full of harpoons, and three boats sailing after it as fast as they could fly.

Then, too, we had a large library-case, that stood in the hall; an old brown library-case, tall as a small house; it had a sort of basement, with large doors, and a lock and key; and higher up, there were glass doors, through which might be seen long rows of old books, that had been printed in Paris, and London, and Leipsic. There was a fine library edition of the Spectator, in six large volumes with gilded backs; and many a time I gazed at the word "London" on the title-page. And there was a copy of D'Alembert in French, and I wondered what a great man I would be, if by foreign travel I should ever be able to read straight along without stopping, out of that book, which now was a riddle to every one in the house but my father, whom I so much liked to hear talk French, as he sometimes did to a servant we had.

That servant, too, I used to gaze at with wonder; for in answer to my incredulous cross-questions, he had over and over again assured me, that he had really been born in Paris. But this I never entirely believed; for it seemed so hard to comprehend, how a man who had been born in a foreign country, could be dwelling with me in our house in America.

As years passed on, this continual dwelling upon foreign associations, bred in me a vague prophetic thought, that I was fated, one day or other, to be a great voyager; and that just as my father used to entertain strange gentlemen over their wine after dinner, I would hereafter be telling my own adventures to an eager auditory. And I have no doubt that this presentiment had something to do with bringing about my subsequent rovings.

But that which perhaps more than any thing else, converted my vague dreamings and longings into a definite purpose of seeking my fortune on the sea, was an old-fashioned glass ship, about eighteen inches long, and of French manufacture, which my father, some thirty years before, had brought home from Hamburg as a present to a great-uncle of mine: Senator Wellingborough, who had died a member of Congress in the days of the old Constitution, and after whom I had the honor of being named. Upon the decease of the Senator, the ship was returned to the donor.

It was kept in a square glass case, which was regularly dusted by one of my sisters every morning, and stood on a little claw-footed Dutch tea-table in one corner of the sitting-room. This ship, after being the admiration of my father's visitors in the capital, became the wonder and delight of all the people of the village where we now resided, many of whom used to call upon my mother, for no other purpose than to see the ship. And well did it repay the long and curious examinations which they were accustomed to give it.

In the first place, every bit of it was glass, and that was a great wonder of itself; because the masts, yards, and ropes were made to resemble exactly the corresponding parts of a real vessel that could go to sea. She carried two tiers of black guns all along her two decks; and often I used to try to peep in at the portholes, to see what else was inside; but the holes were so small, and it looked so very dark indoors, that I could discover little or nothing; though, when I was very little, I made no doubt, that if I could but once pry open the hull, and break the glass all to pieces, I would infallibly light upon something wonderful, perhaps some gold guineas, of which I have always been in want, ever since I could remember. And often I used to feel a sort of insane desire to be the death of the glass ship, case, and all, in order to come at the plunder; and one day, throwing out some hint of the kind to my sisters, they ran to my mother in a great clamor; and after that, the ship was placed on the mantel-piece for a time, beyond my reach, and until I should recover my reason.

I do not know how to account for this temporary madness of mine, unless it was, that I had been reading in a story-book about Captain Kidd's ship, that lay somewhere at the bottom of the Hudson near the Highlands, full of gold as it could be; and that a company of men were trying to dive down and get the treasure out of the hold, which no one had ever thought of doing before, though there she had lain for almost a hundred years.

Not to speak of the tall masts, and yards, and rigging of this famous ship, among whose mazes of spun-glass I used to rove in imagination, till I grew dizzy at the main-truck, I will only make mention of the people on board of her. They, too, were all of glass, as beautiful little glass sailors as any body ever saw, with hats and shoes on, just like living men, and curious blue jackets with a sort of ruffle round the bottom. Four or five of these sailors were very nimble little chaps, and were mounting up the rigging with very long strides; but for all that, they never gained a single inch in the year, as I can take my oath.

Another sailor was sitting astride of the spanker-boom, with his arms over his head, but I never could find out what that was for; a second was in the fore-top, with a coil of glass rigging over his shoulder; the cook, with a glass ax, was splitting wood near the fore-hatch; the steward, in a glass apron, was hurrying toward the cabin with a plate of glass pudding; and a glass dog, with a red mouth, was barking at him; while the captain in a glass cap was smoking a glass cigar on the quarterdeck. He was leaning against the bulwark, with one hand to his head; perhaps he was unwell, for he looked very glassy out of the eyes.

The name of this curious ship was *La Reine,* or The Queen, which was painted on her stern where any one might read it, among a crowd of glass dolphins and sea-horses carved there in a sort of semicircle.

And this Queen rode undisputed mistress of a green glassy sea, some of whose waves were breaking over her bow in a wild way, I can tell you, and I used to be giving her up for lost and foundered every moment, till I grew older, and perceived that she was not in the slightest danger in the world.

A good deal of dust, and fuzzy stuff like down, had in the course of many years worked through the joints of the case, in which the ship was kept, so as to cover all the sea with a light dash of white, which if any thing improved the general effect, for it looked like the foam and froth raised by the terrible gale the good Queen was battling against.

So much for *La Reine*. We have her yet in the house, but many of her glass spars and ropes are now sadly shattered and broken,—but I will not have her mended; and her figurehead, a gallant warrior in a cocked-hat, lies pitching headforemost down into the trough of a calamitous sea under the bows—but I will not have him put on his legs again, till I get on my own; for between him and me there is a secret sympathy; and my sisters tell me, even yet, that he fell from his perch the very day I left home to go to sea on this *my first voyage*.

CHAPTER II
REDBURN'S DEPARTURE FROM HOME

It was with a heavy heart and full eyes, that my poor mother parted with me; perhaps she thought me an erring and a willful boy, and perhaps I was; but if I was, it had been a hardhearted world, and hard times that had made me so. I had learned to think much and bitterly before my time; all my young mounting dreams of glory had left me; and at that early age, I was as unambitious as a man of sixty.

Yes, I will go to sea; cut my kind uncles and aunts, and sympathizing patrons, and leave no heavy hearts but those in my own home, and take none along but the one which aches in my bosom. Cold, bitter cold as December, and bleak as its blasts, seemed the world then to me; there is no misanthrope like a boy disappointed; and such was I, with the warmth of me flogged out by adversity. But these thoughts are bitter enough even now, for they have not yet gone quite away; and they must be uncongenial enough to the reader; so no more of that, and let me go on with my story.

"Yes, I will write you, dear mother, as soon as I can," murmured I, as she charged me for the hundredth time, not fail to inform her of my safe arrival in New York.

"And now Mary, Martha, and Jane, kiss me all round, dear sisters, and then I am off. I'll be back in four months—it will be autumn then, and we'll go into the woods after nuts, an I'll tell you all about Europe. Good-by! good-by!"

So I broke loose from their arms, and not daring to look behind, ran away as fast as I could, till I got to the corner where my brother was waiting. He accompanied me part of the way to the place, where the steamboat was to leave for New York; instilling into me much sage advice above his age, for he was but eight years my senior, and warning me again and again to take care of myself; and I solemnly promised I would; for what cast-away will not promise to take of care himself, when he sees that unless he himself does, no one else will.

We walked on in silence till I saw that his strength was giving out,—he was in ill health then,—and with a mute grasp of the hand, and a loud thump at the heart, we parted.

It was early on a raw, cold, damp morning toward the end of spring, and the world was before me; stretching away a long muddy road, lined with comfortable houses, whose inmates were taking their sunrise naps, heedless of the wayfarer passing. The cold drops of drizzle trickled down my leather cap, and mingled with a few hot tears on my cheeks.

I had the whole road to myself, for no one was yet stirring, and I walked on, with a slouching, dogged gait. The gray shooting-jacket was on my back, and from the end of my brother's rifle hung a small bundle of my clothes. My fingers worked moodily at the stock and trigger, and I thought that this indeed was the way to begin life, with a gun in your hand!

Talk not of the bitterness of middle-age and after life; a boy can feel all that, and much more, when upon his young soul the mildew has fallen; and the fruit, which with others is only blasted after ripeness, with him is nipped in the first blossom and bud. And never again can such blights be made good; they strike in too deep, and leave such a scar that the air of Paradise might not erase it. And it is a hard and cruel thing thus in early youth to taste beforehand the pangs which should be reserved for the stout time of manhood, when the gristle has become bone, and we stand up and fight out our lives, as a thing tried before and foreseen; for then we are veterans used to sieges and battles, and not green recruits, recoiling at the first shock of the encounter.

At last gaining the boat we pushed off, and away we steamed down the Hudson. There were few passengers on board, the day was so unpleasant; and they were mostly congregated in the after cabin round the stoves. After breakfast, some of them went to reading: others took a nap on the settees; and others sat in silent circles, speculating, no doubt, as to who each other might be.

They were certainly a cheerless set, and to me they all looked stony-eyed and heartless. I could not help it, I almost hated them; and to avoid them, went on deck, but a storm of sleet drove me below. At last I bethought me, that I had not procured a ticket, and going to the captain's office to pay my passage and get one, was horror-struck to find, that the price of passage had been suddenly raised that day, owing to the other boats not running; so that I had not enough money to pay for my fare. I had supposed it would be but a dollar, and only a dollar did I have, whereas it was two. What was to be done? The boat was off, and there was no backing out; so I determined to say nothing to any body, and grimly wait until called upon for my fare.

The long weary day wore on till afternoon; one incessant storm raged on deck; but after dinner the few passengers, waked up with their roast-beef and mutton, became a little more sociable. Not with me, for the scent and savor of poverty was upon me, and they all cast toward me their evil eyes and cold suspicious glances, as I sat apart, though among them. I felt that desperation and recklessness of poverty which only a pauper knows. There was a mighty patch upon one leg of my trowsers, neatly sewed on, for it had been executed by my mother, but still very obvious and incontrovertible to the eye. This patch I had hitherto studiously endeavored to hide with the ample skirts of my shooting-jacket; but now I stretched out my leg boldly, and thrust the patch under their noses, and looked at them so, that they soon looked away, boy though I was. Perhaps the gun that I clenched frightened them into respect; or there might have been something ugly in my eye; or my teeth were white, and my jaws were set. For several hours, I sat gazing at a jovial party seated round a mahogany table, with some crackers and cheese, and wine and cigars. Their faces were flushed with the good dinner they had eaten; and mine felt pale and wan with a long fast. If I had presumed to offer to make one of their party; if I had told them of my circumstances, and solicited something to refresh me, I very well knew from the peculiar hollow ring of their laughter, they would have had the waiters put me out of the cabin, for a beggar, who had no business to be warming himself at their stove. And for that insult, though only a conceit, I sat and gazed at them, putting up no petitions for their prosperity. My whole soul was soured within me, and when at last the captain's clerk, a slender young man, dressed in the height of fashion, with a gold watch chain and broach, came round collecting the tickets, I buttoned up my coat to the throat, clutched my gun, put on my leather cap, and pulling it well down, stood up like a sentry before him. He held out his hand, deeming any remark superfluous, as his object in pausing before me must be obvious. But I stood motionless and silent, and in a moment he saw how it was with me. I ought to have spoken and told him the case, in plain, civil terms, and offered my dollar, and then waited the event. But I felt too wicked for that. He did not wait a great while, but spoke first himself; and in a gruff voice, very unlike his urbane accents when accosting the wine and cigar party, demanded my ticket. I replied that I had none. He then demanded the money; and upon my answering that I had not enough, in a loud angry voice that attracted all eyes, he ordered me out of the cabin into the storm. The devil in me then mounted up from my soul, and spread over my frame, till it tingled at my finger ends; and I muttered out my resolution to stay where I was, in such a manner, that the ticket man faltered back. "There's a dollar for you," I added, offering it.

"I want two," said he.

"Take that or nothing," I answered; "it is all I have."

I thought he would strike me. But, accepting the money, he contented himself with saying something about sportsmen going on shooting expeditions, without having money to pay their expenses; and hinted that such chaps might better lay aside their fowling-pieces, and assume the buck and saw. He then passed on, and left every eye fastened upon me.

I stood their gazing some time, but at last could stand it no more. I pushed my seat right up before the most insolent gazer, a short fat man, with a plethora of cravat round his neck, and fixing my gaze on his, gave him more gazes than he sent. This somewhat embarrassed him, and he looked round for some one to take hold of me; but no one coming, he pretended to be very busy counting the gilded wooden beams overhead. I then turned to the next gazer, and clicking my gun-lock, deliberately presented the piece at him.

Upon this, he overset his seat in his eagerness to get beyond my range, for I had him point blank, full in the left eye; and several persons starting to their feet, exclaimed that I must be crazy. So I was at that time; for otherwise I know not how to account for my demoniac feelings, of which I was afterward heartily ashamed, as I ought to have been, indeed; and much more than that.

I then turned on my heel, and shouldering my fowling-piece and bundle, marched on deck, and walked there through the dreary storm, till I was wet through, and the boat touched the wharf at New York.

Such is boyhood.

CHAPTER III
HE ARRIVES IN TOWN

From the boat's bow, I jumped ashore, before she was secured, and following my brother's directions, proceeded across the town toward St. John's Park, to the house of a college friend of his, for whom I had a letter.

It was a long walk; and I stepped in at a sort of grocery to get a drink of water, where some six or eight rough looking fellows were playing dominoes upon the counter, seated upon cheese boxes. They winked, and asked what sort of sport I had had gunning on such a rainy day, but I only gulped down my water and stalked off.

Dripping like a seal, I at last grounded arms at the doorway of my brother's friend, rang the bell and inquired for him.

"What do you want?" said the servant, eying me as if I were a housebreaker.

"I want to see your lord and master; show me into the parlor."

Upon this my host himself happened to make his appearance, and seeing who I was, opened his hand and heart to me at once, and drew me to his fireside; he had received a letter from my brother, and had expected me that day.

The family were at tea; the fragrant herb filled the room with its aroma; the brown toast was odoriferous; and everything pleasant and charming. After a temporary warming, I was shown to a room, where I changed my wet dress, and returning to the table, found that the interval had been well improved by my hostess; a meal for a traveler was spread and I laid into it sturdily. Every mouthful pushed the devil that had been tormenting me all day farther and farther out of me, till at last I entirely ejected him with three successive bowls of Bohea.

Magic of kind words, and kind deeds, and good tea! That night I went to bed thinking the world pretty tolerable, after all; and I could hardly believe that I had really acted that morning as I had, for I was naturally of an easy and forbearing disposition; though when such a disposition is temporarily roused, it is perhaps worse than a cannibal's.

Next day, my brother's friend, whom I choose to call Mr. Jones, accompanied me down to the docks among the shipping, in order to get me a place. After a good deal of searching we lighted upon a ship for Liverpool, and found the captain in the cabin; which was a very handsome one, lined with mahogany and maple; and the steward, an elegant looking mulatto in a gorgeous turban, was setting out on a sort of sideboard some dinner service which looked like silver, but it was only Britannia ware highly polished.

As soon as I clapped my eye on the captain, I thought myself he was just the captain to suit me. He was a fine looking man, about forty, splendidly dressed, with very black whiskers, and very white teeth, and what I took to be a free, frank look out of a large hazel eye. I liked him amazingly. He was promenading up and down the cabin, humming some brisk air to himself when we entered.

"Good morning, sir," said my friend.

"Good morning, good morning, sir," said the captain. "Steward, chairs for the gentlemen."

"Oh! never mind, sir," said Mr. Jones, rather taken aback by his extreme civility. "I merely called to see whether you want a fine young lad to go to sea with you. Here he is; he has long wanted to be a sailor; and his friends have at last concluded to let him go for one voyage, and see how he likes it."

"Ah! indeed!" said the captain, blandly, and looking where I stood. "He's a fine fellow; I like him. So you want to be a sailor, my boy, do you?" added he, affectionately patting my head. "It's a hard life, though; a hard life."

But when I looked round at his comfortable, and almost luxurious cabin, and then at his handsome care-free face, I thought he was only trying to frighten me, and I answered, "Well, sir, I am ready to try it."

"I hope he's a country lad, sir," said the captain to my friend, "these city boys are sometimes hard cases."

"Oh! yes, he's from the country," was the reply, "and of a highly respectable family; his great-uncle died a Senator."

"But his great-uncle don't want to go to sea too?" said the captain, looking funny.

"Oh! no, oh, no!— Ha! ha!"

"Ha! ha!" echoed the captain.

A fine funny gentleman, thought I, not much fancying, however, his levity concerning my great-uncle, he'll be cracking his jokes the whole voyage; and so I afterward said to one of the riggers on board; but he bade me look out, that he did not crack my head.

"Well, my lad," said the captain, "I suppose you know we haven't any pastures and cows on board; you can't get any milk at sea, you know."

"Oh! I know all about that, sir; my father has crossed the ocean, if I haven't."

"Yes," cried my friend, "his father, a gentleman of one of the first families in America, crossed the Atlantic several times on important business."

"Embassador extraordinary?" said the captain, looking funny again.

"Oh! no, he was a wealthy merchant."

"Ah! indeed;" said the captain, looking grave and bland again, "then this fine lad is the son of a gentleman?"

"Certainly," said my friend, "and he's only going to sea for the humor of it; they want to send him on his travels with a tutor, but he *will* go to sea as a sailor."

The fact was, that my young friend (for he was only about twenty-five) was not a very wise man; and this was a huge fib, which out of the kindness of his heart, he told in my behalf, for the purpose of creating a profound respect for me in the eyes of my future lord.

Upon being apprized, that I had willfully forborne taking the grand tour with a tutor, in order to put my hand in a tar-bucket, the handsome captain looked ten times more funny than ever; and said that *he* himself would be my tutor, and take me on my travels, and pay for the privilege.

"Ah!" said my friend, "that reminds me of business. Pray, captain, how much do you generally pay a handsome young fellow like this?"

"Well," said the captain, looking grave and profound, "we are not so particular about beauty, and we never give more than three dollars to a green lad like Wellingborough here, that's your name, my boy? Wellingborough Redburn!—Upon my soul, a fine sounding name."

"Why, captain," said Mr. Jones, quickly interrupting him, "that won't pay for his clothing."

"But you know his highly respectable and wealthy relations will doubtless see to all that," replied the captain, with his funny look again.

"Oh! yes, I forgot that," said Mr. Jones, looking rather foolish. "His friends will of course see to that."

"Of course," said the captain smiling.

"Of course," repeated Mr. Jones, looking ruefully at the patch on my pantaloons, which just then I endeavored to hide with the skirt of my shooting-jacket.

"You are quite a sportsman I see," said the captain, eying the great buttons on my coat, upon each of which was a carved fox.

Upon this my benevolent friend thought that here was a grand opportunity to befriend me.

"Yes, he's quite a sportsman," said he, "he's got a very valuable fowling-piece at home, perhaps you would like to purchase it, captain, to shoot gulls with at sea? It's cheap."

"Oh! no, he had better leave it with his relations," said the captain, "so that he can go hunting again when he returns from England."

"Yes, perhaps that *would* be better, after all," said my friend, pretending to fall into a profound musing, involving all sides of the matter in hand. "Well, then, captain, you can only give the boy three dollars a month, you say?"

"Only three dollars a month," said the captain.

"And I believe," said my friend, "that you generally give something in advance, do you not?"

"Yes, that is sometimes the custom at the shipping offices," said the captain, with a bow, "but in this case, as the boy has rich relations, there will be no need of that, you know."

And thus, by his ill-advised, but well-meaning hints concerning the respectability of my paternity, and the immense wealth of my relations, did this really honest-hearted but foolish friend of mine, prevent me from getting three dollars in advance, which I greatly needed. However, I said nothing, though I thought the more; and particularly, how that it would have been much better for me, to have gone on board alone, accosted the captain on my own account, and told him the plain truth. Poor people make a very poor business of it when they try to seem rich.

The arrangement being concluded, we bade the captain good morning; and as we were about leaving the cabin, he smiled again, and said, "Well, Redburn, my boy, you won't get home-sick before you sail, because that will make you very sea-sick when you get to sea."

And with that he smiled very pleasantly, and bowed two or three times, and told the steward to open the cabin-door, which the steward did with a peculiar sort of grin on his face, and a slanting glance at my shooting-jacket. And so we left.

CHAPTER IV
HOW HE DISPOSED OF HIS FOWLING-PIECE

Next day I went alone to the shipping office to sign the articles, and there I met a great crowd of sailors, who as soon as they found what I was after, began to tip the wink all round, and I overheard a fellow in a great flapping sou'wester cap say to another old tar in a shaggy monkey-jacket, "Twig his coat, d'ye see the buttons, that chap ain't going to sea in a merchantman, he's going to shoot whales. I say, maty—look here—how d'ye sell them big buttons by the pound?"

"Give us one for a saucer, will ye?" said another.

"Let the youngster alone," said a third. "Come here, my little boy, has your ma put up some sweetmeats for ye to take to sea?"

They are all witty dogs, thought I to myself, trying to make the best of the matter, for I saw it would not do to resent what they said; they can't mean any harm, though they are certainly very impudent; so I tried to laugh off their banter, but as soon as ever I could, I put down my name and beat a retreat.

On the morrow, the ship was advertised to sail. So the rest of that day I spent in preparations. After in vain trying to sell my fowling-piece for a fair price to chance customers, I was walking up Chatham-street with it, when a curly-headed little man with a dark oily face, and a hooked nose, like the pictures of Judas Iscariot, called to me from a strange-looking shop, with three gilded balls hanging over it.

With a peculiar accent, as if he had been over-eating himself with Indian-pudding or some other plushy compound, this curly-headed little man very civilly invited me into his shop; and making a polite bow, and bidding me many unnecessary good mornings, and remarking upon the fine weather, begged me to let him look at my fowling-piece. I handed it to him in an instant, glad of the chance of disposing of it, and told him that was just what I wanted.

"Ah!" said he, with his Indian-pudding accent again, which I will not try to mimic, and abating his look of eagerness, "I thought it was a better article, it's very old."

"Not," said I, starting in surprise, "it's not been used more than three times; what will you give for it?"

"We don't *buy* any thing here," said he, suddenly looking very indifferent, "this is a place where people *pawn* things." *Pawn* being a word I had never heard before, I asked him what it meant; when he replied, that when people wanted any money, they came to him with their fowling-pieces, and got one third its value, and then left the fowling-piece there, until they were able to pay back the money.

What a benevolent little old man, this must be, thought I, and how very obliging.

"And pray," said I, "how much will you let me have for my gun, by way of a pawn?"

"Well, I suppose it's worth six dollars, and seeing you're a boy, I'll let you have three dollars upon it"

"No," exclaimed I, seizing the fowling-piece, "it's worth five times that, I'll go somewhere else."

"Good morning, then," said he, "I hope you'll do better," and he bowed me out as if he expected to see me again pretty soon.

I had not gone very far when I came across three more balls hanging over a shop. In I went, and saw a long counter, with a sort of picket-fence, running all along from end to end, and three little holes, with three little old men standing inside of them, like prisoners looking out of a jail. Back of the counter were all sorts of things, piled up and labeled. Hats, and caps, and coats, and guns, and swords, and canes, and chests, and planes, and books, and writing-desks, and every thing else. And in a glass case were lots of watches, and seals, chains, and rings, and breastpins, and all kinds of trinkets. At one of the little holes, earnestly talking with one of the hook-nosed men, was a thin woman in a faded silk gown and shawl, holding a pale little girl by the hand. As I drew near, she spoke lower in a whisper; and the man shook his head, and looked cross and rude; and then some more words were exchanged over a miniature, and some money was passed through the hole, and the woman and child shrank out of the door.

I won't sell my gun to that man, thought I; and I passed on to the next hole; and while waiting there to be served, an elderly man in a high-waisted surtout, thrust a silver snuff-box through; and a young man in a calico shirt and a shiny coat with a velvet collar presented a silver watch; and a sheepish boy in a cloak took out a frying-pan; and another little boy had a Bible; and all these things were thrust through to the hook-nosed man, who seemed ready to hook any thing that came along; so I had no doubt he would gladly hook my gun, for the long picketed counter seemed like a great seine, that caught every variety of fish.

At last I saw a chance, and crowded in for the hole; and in order to be beforehand with a big man who just then came in, I pushed my gun violently through the hole; upon which the hook-nosed man cried out, thinking I was going to shoot him. But at last he took the gun, turned it end for end, clicked the trigger three times, and then said, "one dollar."

"What about one dollar?" said I.

"That's all I'll give," he replied.

"Well, what do you want?" and he turned to the next person. This was a young man in a seedy red cravat and a pimply face, that looked as if it was going to seed likewise, who, with a mysterious tapping of his vest-pocket and other hints, made a great show of having something confidential to communicate.

But the hook-nosed man spoke out very loud, and said, "None of that; take it out. Got a stolen watch? We don't deal in them things here."

Upon this the young man flushed all over, and looked round to see who had heard the pawnbroker; then he took something very small out of his pocket, and keeping it hidden under his palm, pushed it into the hole.

"Where did you get this ring?" said the pawnbroker.

"I want to pawn it," whispered the other, blushing all over again.

"What's your name?" said the pawnbroker, speaking very loud.

"How much will you give?" whispered the other in reply, leaning over, and looking as if he wanted to hush up the pawnbroker.

At last the sum was agreed upon, when the man behind the counter took a little ticket, and tying the ring to it began to write on the ticket; all at once he asked the young man where he lived, a question which embarrassed him very much; but at last he stammered out a certain number in Broadway.

"That's the City Hotel: you don't live there," said the man, cruelly glancing at the shabby coat before him.

"Oh! well," stammered the other blushing scarlet, "I thought this was only a sort of form to go through; I don't like to tell where I do live, for I ain't in the habit of going to pawnbrokers."

"You stole that ring, you know you did," roared out the hook-nosed man, incensed at this slur upon his calling, and now seemingly bent on damaging the young man's character for life. "I'm a good mind to call a constable; we don't take stolen goods here, I tell you."

All eyes were now fixed suspiciously upon this martyrized young man; who looked ready to drop into the earth; and a poor woman in a night-cap, with some baby-clothes in her hand, looked fearfully at the pawnbroker, as if dreading to encounter such a terrible pattern of integrity. At last the young man sunk off with his money, and looking out of the window, I saw him go round the corner so sharply that he knocked his elbow against the wall.

I waited a little longer, and saw several more served; and having remarked that the hook-nosed men invariably fixed their own price upon every thing, and if that was refused told the person to be off with himself; I concluded that it would be of no use to try and get more from them than they had offered; especially when I saw that they had a great many fowling-pieces hanging up, and did not have particular occasion for mine; and more than that, they must be very well off and rich, to treat people so cavalierly.

My best plan then seemed to be to go right back to the curly-headed pawnbroker, and take up with my first offer. But when I went back, the curly-headed man was very busy about something else, and kept me waiting a long time; at last I got a chance and told him I would take the three dollars he had offered.

"Ought to have taken it when you could get it," he replied. "I won't give but two dollars and a half for it now."

In vain I expostulated; he was not to be moved, so I pocketed the money and departed.

CHAPTER V
HE PURCHASES HIS SEA-WARDROBE, AND ON A DISMAL RAINY DAY PICKS UP HIS BOARD AND LODGING ALONG THE WHARVES

The first thing I now did was to buy a little stationery, and keep my promise to my mother, by writing her; and I also wrote to my brother informing him of the voyage I purposed making, and indulging in some romantic and misanthropic views of life, such as many boys in my circumstances, are accustomed to do.

The rest of the two dollars and a half I laid out that very morning in buying a red woolen shirt near Catharine Market, a tarpaulin hat, which I got at an out-door stand near Peck Slip, a belt and jackknife, and two or three trifles. After these purchases, I had only one penny left, so I walked out to the end of the pier, and threw the penny into the water. The reason why I did this, was because I somehow felt almost desperate again, and didn't care what became of me. But if the penny had been a dollar, I would have kept it.

I went home to dinner at Mr. Jones', and they welcomed me very kindly, and Mrs. Jones kept my plate full all the time during dinner, so that I had no chance to empty it. She seemed to see that I felt bad, and thought plenty of pudding might help me. At any rate, I never felt so bad yet but I could eat a good dinner. And once, years afterward, when I expected to be killed every day, I remember my appetite was very keen, and I said to myself, "Eat away, Wellingborough, while you can, for this may be the last supper you will have."

After dinner I went into my room, locked the door carefully, and hung a towel over the knob, so that no one could peep through the keyhole, and then went to trying on my red woolen shirt before the glass, to see what sort of a looking sailor I was going to make. As soon as I got into the shirt I began to feel sort of warm and red about the face, which I found was owing to the reflection of the dyed wool upon my skin. After that, I took a pair of scissors and went to cutting my hair, which was very long. I thought every little would help, in making me a light hand to run aloft.

Next morning I bade my kind host and hostess good-by, and left the house with my bundle, feeling somewhat misanthropical and desperate again.

Before I reached the ship, it began to rain hard; and as soon as I arrived at the wharf, it was plain that there would be no getting to sea that day.

This was a great disappointment to me, for I did not want to return to Mr. Jones' again after bidding them good-by; it would be so awkward. So I concluded to go on board ship for the present.

When I reached the deck, I saw no one but a large man in a large dripping pea-jacket, who was calking down the main-hatches.

"What do you want, Pillgarlic?" said he.

"I've shipped to sail in this ship," I replied, assuming a little dignity, to chastise his familiarity.

"What for? a tailor?" said he, looking at my shooting jacket.

I answered that I was going as a "boy;" for so I was technically put down on the articles.

"Well," said he, "have you got your traps aboard?"

I told him I didn't know there were any rats in the ship, and hadn't brought any "trap."

At this he laughed out with a great guffaw, and said there must be hay-seed in my hair.

This made me mad; but thinking he must be one of the sailors who was going in the ship, I thought it wouldn't be wise to make an enemy of him, so only asked him where the men slept in the vessel, for I wanted to put my clothes away.

"*Where's* your clothes?" said he.

"Here in my bundle," said I, holding it up.

"Well if that's all you've got," he cried, "you'd better chuck it overboard. But go forward, go forward to the forecastle; that's the place you'll live in aboard here."

And with that he directed me to a sort of hole in the deck in the bow of the ship; but looking down, and seeing how dark it was, I asked him for a light.

"Strike your eyes together and make one," said he, "we don't have any lights here." So I groped my way down into the forecastle, which smelt so bad of old ropes and tar, that it almost made me sick. After waiting patiently, I began to see a little; and looking round, at last perceived I was in a smoky looking place, with twelve wooden boxes stuck round the sides. In some of these boxes were large chests, which I at once supposed to belong to the sailors, who must have taken that method of appropriating their "Trunks," as I afterward found these boxes were called. And so it turned out.

After examining them for a while, I selected an empty one, and put my bundle right in the middle of it, so that there might be no mistake about my claim to the place, particularly as the bundle was so small.

This done, I was glad to get on deck; and learning to a certainty that the ship would not sail till the next day, I resolved to go ashore, and walk about till dark, and then return and sleep out the night in the forecastle. So I walked about all over, till I was weary, and went into a mean liquor shop to rest; for having my tarpaulin on, and not looking very gentlemanly, I was afraid to go into any better place, for fear of being driven out. Here I sat till I began to feel very hungry; and seeing some doughnuts on the counter, I began to think what a fool I had been, to throw away my last penny; for the doughnuts were but a penny apiece, and they looked very plump, and fat, and round. I never saw doughnuts look so enticing before; especially when a negro came in, and ate one before my eyes. At last I thought I would fill up a little by drinking a glass of water; having read somewhere that this was a good plan to follow in a case like the present. I did not feel thirsty, but only hungry; so had much ado to get down the water; for it tasted warm; and the tumbler had an ugly flavor; the negro had been drinking some spirits out of it just before.

I marched off again, every once in a while stopping to take in some more water, and being very careful not to step into the same shop twice, till night came on, and I found myself soaked through, for it had been raining more or less all day. As I went to the ship, I could not help thinking how lonesome it would be, to spend the whole night in that damp and dark forecastle, without light or fire, and nothing to lie on but the bare boards of my bunk. However, to drown all such thoughts, I gulped down another glass of water, though I was wet enough outside and in by this time; and trying to put on a bold look, as if I had just been eating a hearty meal, I stepped aboard the ship.

The man in the big pea-jacket was not to be seen; but on going forward I unexpectedly found a young lad there, about my own age; and as soon as he opened his mouth I knew he was not an American. He talked such a curious language though, half English and half gibberish, that I knew not what to make of him; and was a little astonished, when he told me he was an English boy, from Lancashire.

It seemed, he had come over from Liverpool in this very ship on her last voyage, as a steerage passenger; but finding that he would have to work very hard to get along in America, and getting home-sick into the bargain, he had arranged with the captain to work his passage back.

I was glad to have some company, and tried to get him conversing; but found he was the most stupid and ignorant boy I had ever met with. I asked him something about the river Thames; when he said that he hadn't traveled any in America and didn't know any thing about the rivers here. And when I told him the river Thames was in England, he showed no surprise or shame at his ignorance, but only looked ten times more stupid than before.

At last we went below into the forecastle, and both getting into the same bunk, stretched ourselves out on the planks, and I tried my best to get asleep. But though my companion soon began to snore very loud, for me, I could not forget myself, owing to the horrid smell of the place, my being so wet, cold, and hungry, and besides all that, I felt damp and clammy about the heart. I lay turning over and over, listening to the Lancashire boy's snoring, till at last I felt so, that I had to go on deck; and there I walked till morning, which I thought would never come.

As soon as I thought the groceries on the wharf would be open I left the ship and went to make my breakfast of another glass of water. But this made me very qualmish; and soon I felt sick as death; my head was dizzy; and I went staggering along the walk, almost blind. At last I dropt on a heap of chain-cable, and shutting my eyes hard, did my best to rally myself, in which I succeeded, at last, enough to get up and walk off. Then I thought that I had done wrong in not returning to my friend's house the day before; and would have walked there now, as it was, only it was at least three miles up town; too far for me to walk in such a state, and I had no sixpence to ride in an omnibus.

CHAPTER VI
HE IS INITIATED IN THE BUSINESS OF CLEANING OUT THE PIG-PEN, AND SLUSHING DOWN THE TOP-MAST

By the time I got back to the ship, every thing was in an uproar. The pea-jacket man was there, ordering about a good many men in the rigging, and people were bringing off chickens, and pigs, and beef, and vegetables from the shore. Soon after, another man, in a striped calico shirt, a short blue jacket and beaver hat, made his appearance, and went to ordering about the man in the big pea-jacket; and at last the captain came up the side, and began to order about both of them.

These two men turned out to be the first and second mates of the ship.

Thinking to make friends with the second mate, I took out an old tortoise-shell snuff-box of my father's, in which I had put a piece of Cavendish tobacco, to look sailor-like, and offered the box to him very politely. He stared at me a moment, and then exclaimed, "Do you think we take snuff aboard here, youngster? no, no, no time for snuff-taking at sea; don't let the 'old man' see that snuff-box; take my advice and pitch it overboard as quick as you can."

I told him it was not snuff, but tobacco; when he said, he had plenty of tobacco of his own, and never carried any such nonsense about him as a tobacco-box. With that, he went off about his business, and left me feeling foolish enough. But I had reason to be glad he had acted thus, for if he had not, I think I should have offered my box to the chief mate, who in that case, from what I afterward learned of him, would have knocked me down, or done something else equally uncivil.

As I was standing looking round me, the chief mate approached in a great hurry about something, and seeing me in his way, cried out, "Ashore with you, you young loafer! There's no stealings here; sail away, I tell you, with that shooting-jacket!"

Upon this I retreated, saying that I was going out in the ship as a sailor.

"A sailor!" he cried, "a barber's clerk, you mean; *you* going out in the ship? what, in that jacket? Hang me, I hope the old man hasn't been shipping any more greenhorns like you—he'll make a shipwreck of it if he has. But this is the way nowadays; to save a few dollars in seamen's wages, they think nothing of shipping a parcel of farmers and clodhoppers and baby-boys. What's your name, Pillgarlic?"

"Redburn," said I.

"A pretty handle to a man, that; scorch you to take hold of it; haven't you got any other?"

"Wellingborough," said I.

"Worse yet. Who had the baptizing of ye? Why didn't they call you Jack, or Jill, or something short and handy. But I'll baptize you over again. D'ye hear, sir, henceforth your name is *Buttons.* And now do you go, Buttons, and clean out that pig-pen in the long-boat; it has not been cleaned out since last voyage. And bear a hand about it, d'ye hear; there's them pigs there waiting to be put in; come, be off about it, now."

Was this then the beginning of my sea-career? set to cleaning out a pig-pen, the very first thing?

But I thought it best to say nothing; I had bound myself to obey orders, and it was too late to retreat. So I only asked for a shovel, or spade, or something else to work with.

"We don't dig gardens here," was the reply; "dig it out with your teeth!"

After looking round, I found a stick and went to scraping out the pen, which was awkward work enough, for another boat called the "jolly-boat," was capsized right over the longboat, which brought them almost close together. These two boats were in the middle of the deck. I managed to crawl inside of the long-boat; and after barking my shins against the seats, and bumping my head a good many times, I got along to the stern, where the pig-pen was.

While I was hard at work a drunken sailor peeped in, and cried out to his comrades, "Look here, my lads, what sort of a pig do you call this? Hallo! inside there! what are you 'bout there? trying to stow yourself away to steal a passage to Liverpool? Out of that! out of that, I say." But just then the mate came along and ordered this drunken rascal ashore.

The pig-pen being cleaned out, I was set to work picking up some shavings, which lay about the deck; for there had been carpenters at work on board. The mate ordered me to throw these shavings into the long-boat at a particular place between two of the seats. But as I found it hard work to push the shavings through in that place, and as it looked wet there, I thought it would be better for the shavings as well as myself, to thrust them where there was a larger opening and a dry spot. While I was thus employed, the mate observing me, exclaimed with an oath, "Didn't I tell you to put those shavings somewhere else? Do what I tell you, now, Buttons, or mind your eye!"

Stifling my indignation at his rudeness, which by this time I found was my only plan, I replied that that was not so good a place for the shavings as that which I myself had selected, and asked him to tell me *why* he wanted me to put them in the place he designated. Upon this, he flew into a terrible rage, and without explanation reiterated his order like a clap of thunder.

This was my first lesson in the discipline of the sea, and I never forgot it. From that time I learned that sea-officers never gave reasons for any thing they order to be done. It is enough that they command it, so that the motto is, *"Obey orders, though you break owners."*

I now began to feel very faint and sick *again,* and longed for the ship to be leaving the dock; for then I made no doubt we would soon be having something to eat. But as yet, I saw none of the sailors on board, and as for the men at work in the rigging, I found out that they were *"riggers,"* that is, men living ashore, who worked by the day in getting ships ready for sea; and this I found out to my cost, for yielding to the kind blandishment of one of these *riggers, I* had swapped away my jackknife with him for a much poorer one of his own, thinking to secure a sailor friend for the voyage. At last I watched my chance, and while people's backs were turned, I seized a carrot from several bunches lying on deck, and clapping it under the skirts of my shooting-jacket, went forward to eat it; for I had often eaten raw carrots, which taste something like chestnuts. This carrot refreshed me a good deal, though at the expense of a little pain in my stomach. Hardly had I disposed of it, when I heard the chief mate's voice crying out for "Buttons." I ran after him, and received an order to go aloft and "slush down the main-top mast."

This was all Greek to me, and after receiving the order, I stood staring about me, wondering what it was that was to be done. But the mate had turned on his heel, and made no explanations. At length I followed after him, and asked what I must do.

"Didn't I tell you to slush down the main-top mast?" he shouted.

"You did," said I, "but I don't know what that means."

"Green as grass! a regular cabbage-head!" he exclaimed to himself. "A fine time I'll have with such a greenhorn aboard. Look you, youngster. Look up to that long pole there—d'ye see it? that piece of a tree there, you timber-head—well—take this bucket here, and go up the rigging—that rope-ladder there—do you understand?—and dab this slush all over the mast, and look out for your head if one drop falls on deck. Be off now, Buttons."

The eventful hour had arrived; for the first time in my life I was to ascend a ship's mast. Had I been well and hearty, perhaps I should have felt a little shaky at the thought; but as I was then, weak and faint, the bare thought appalled me.

But there was no hanging back; it would look like cowardice, and I could not bring myself to confess that I was suffering for want of food; so rallying again, I took up the bucket.

It was a heavy bucket, with strong iron hoops, and might have held perhaps two gallons. But it was only half full now of a sort of thick lobbered gravy, which I afterward learned was boiled out of the salt beef used by the sailors. Upon getting into the rigging, I found it was no easy job to carry this heavy bucket up with me. The rope handle of it was so slippery with grease, that although I twisted it several times about my wrist, it would be still twirling round and round, and slipping off. Spite of this, however, I managed to mount as far as the "top," the clumsy bucket half the time straddling and swinging about between my legs, and in momentary danger of capsizing. Arrived at the "top," I came to a dead halt, and looked up. How to surmount that overhanging impediment completely posed me for the time. But at last, with much straining, I contrived to place my bucket in the "top;" and then, trusting to Providence, swung myself up after it. The rest of the road was comparatively easy; though whenever I incautiously looked down toward the deck, my head spun round so from weakness, that I was obliged to shut my eyes to recover myself. I do not remember much more. I only recollect my safe return to the deck.

In a short time the bustle of the ship increased; the trunks of cabin passengers arrived, and the chests and boxes of the steerage passengers, besides baskets of wine and fruit for the captain.

At last we cast loose, and swinging out into the stream, came to anchor, and hoisted the signal for sailing. Every thing, it seemed, was on board but the crew; who in a few hours after, came off, one by one, in Whitehall boats, their chests in the bow, and themselves lying back in the stem like lords; and showing very plainly the complacency they felt in keeping the whole ship waiting for their lordships.

"Ay, ay," muttered the chief mate, as they rolled out of then-boats and swaggered on deck, "it's your turn now, but it will be mine before long. Yaw about while you may, my hearties, I'll do the yawing after the anchor's up."

Several of the sailors were very drunk, and one of them was lifted on board insensible by his landlord, who carried him down below and dumped him into a bunk. And two other sailors, as soon as they made their appearance, immediately went below to sleep off the fumes of their drink.

At last, all the crew being on board, word was passed to go to dinner fore and aft, an order that made my heart jump with delight, for now my long fast would be broken. But though the sailors, surfeited with eating and drinking ashore, did not then touch the salt beef and potatoes which the black cook handed down into the forecastle; and though this left the whole allowance to me; to my surprise, I found that I could eat little or nothing; for now I only felt deadly faint, but not hungry.

CHAPTER VII
HE GETS TO SEA AND FEELS VERY BAD

Every thing at last being in readiness, the pilot came on board, and all hands were called to up anchor. While I worked at my bar, I could not help observing how haggard the men looked, and how much they suffered from this violent exercise, after the terrific dissipation in which they had been indulging ashore. But I soon learnt that sailors breathe nothing about such things, but strive their best to appear all alive and hearty, though it comes very hard for many of them.

The anchor being secured, a steam tug-boat with a strong name, the Hercules, took hold of us; and away we went past the long line of shipping, and wharves, and warehouses; and rounded the green south point of the island where the Battery is, and passed Governor's Island, and pointed right out for the Narrows.

My heart was like lead, and I felt bad enough, Heaven knows; but then, there was plenty of work to be done, which kept my thoughts from becoming too much for me.

And I tried to think all the time, that I was going to England, and that, before many months, I should have actually been there and home again, telling my adventures to my brothers and sisters; and with what delight they would listen, and how they would look up to me then, and reverence my sayings; and how that even my elder brother would be forced to treat me with great consideration, as having crossed the Atlantic Ocean, which he had never done, and there was no probability he ever would.

With such thoughts as these I endeavored to shake off my heavy-heartedness; but it would not do at all; for this was only the first day of the voyage, and many weeks, nay, several whole months must elapse before the voyage was ended; and who could tell what might happen to me; for when I looked up at the high, giddy masts, and thought how often I must be going up and down them, I thought sure enough that some luckless day or other, I would certainly fall overboard and be drowned. And then, I thought of lying down at the bottom of the sea, stark alone, with the great waves rolling over me, and no one in the wide world knowing that I was there. And I thought how much better and sweeter it must be, to be buried under the pleasant hedge that bounded the sunny south side of our village grave-yard, where every Sunday I had used to walk after church in the afternoon; and I almost wished I was there now; yes, dead and buried in that churchyard. All the time my eyes were filled with tears, and I kept holding my breath, to choke down the sobs, for indeed I could not help feeling as I did, and no doubt any boy in the world would have felt just as I did then.

As the steamer carried us further and further down the bay, and we passed ships lying at anchor, with men gazing at us and waving their hats; and small boats with ladies in them waving their handkerchiefs; and passed the green shore of Staten Island, and caught sight of so many beautiful cottages all overrun with vines, and planted on the beautiful fresh mossy hill-sides; oh! then I would have given any thing if instead of sailing *out of* the bay, we were only coming *into* it; if we had crossed the ocean and returned, gone over and come back; and my heart leaped up in me like something alive when I thought of really entering that bay at the end of the voyage. But that was so far distant, that it seemed it could never be. No, never, never more would I see New York again.

And what shocked me more than any thing else, was to hear some of the sailors, while they were at work coiling away the hawsers, talking about the boarding-houses they were going to, when they came back; and how that some friends of theirs had promised to be on the wharf when the ship returned, to take them and their chests right up to Franklin-square where they lived; and how that they would have a good dinner ready, and plenty of cigars and spirits out on the balcony. I say this kind of talking shocked me, for they did not seem to consider, as I did, that before any thing like that could happen, we must cross the great Atlantic Ocean, cross over from America to Europe and back again, many thousand miles of foaming ocean.

At that time I did not know what to make of these sailors; but this much I thought, that when they were boys, they could never have gone to the Sunday School; for they swore so, it made my ears tingle, and used words that I never could hear without a dreadful loathing.

And are these the men, I thought to myself, that I must live with so long? these the men I am to eat with, and sleep with all the time? And besides, I now began to see, that they were not going to be very kind to me; but I will tell all about that when the proper time comes.

Now you must not think, that because all these things were passing through my mind, that I had nothing to do but sit still and think; no, no, I was hard at work: for as long as the steamer had hold of us, we were very busy coiling away ropes and cables, and putting the decks in order; which were littered all over with odds and ends of things that had to be put away.

At last we got as far as the Narrows, which every body knows is the entrance to New York Harbor from sea; and it may well be called the Narrows, for when you go in or out, it seems like going in or out of a doorway; and when you go out of these Narrows on a long voyage like this of mine, it seems like going out into the broad highway, where not a soul is to be seen. For far away and away, stretches the great Atlantic Ocean; and all you can see beyond it where the sky comes down to the water. It looks lonely and desolate enough, and I could hardly believe, as I gazed around me, that there could be any land beyond, or any place like Europe or England or Liverpool in the great wide world. It seemed too strange, and wonderful, and altogether incredible, that there could really be cities and towns and villages and green fields and hedges and farm-yards and orchards, away over that wide blank of sea, and away beyond the place where the sky came down to the water. And to think of steering right out among those waves, and leaving the bright land behind, and the dark night coming on, too, seemed wild and foolhardy; and I looked with a sort of fear at the sailors standing by me, who could be so thoughtless at such a time. But then I remembered, how many times my own father had said he had crossed the ocean; and I had never dreamed of such a thing as doubting him; for I always thought him a marvelous being, infinitely purer and greater than I was, who could not by any possibility do wrong, or say an untruth. Yet now, how could I credit it, that he, my own father, whom I so well remembered; had ever sailed out of these Narrows, and sailed right through the sky and water line, and gone to England, and France, Liverpool, and Marseilles. It was too wonderful to believe.

Now, on the right hand side of the Narrows as you go out, the land is quite high; and on the top of a fine cliff is a great castle or fort, all in ruins, and with the trees growing round it. It was built by Governor Tompkins in the time of the last war with England, but was never used, I believe, and so they left it to decay. I had visited the place once when we lived in New York, as long ago almost as I could remember, with my father, and an uncle of mine, an old sea-captain, with white hair, who used to sail to a place called Archangel in Russia, and who used to tell me that he was with Captain Langsdorff, when Captain Langsdorff crossed over by land from the sea of Okotsk in Asia to St. Petersburgh, drawn by large dogs in a sled. I mention this of my uncle, because he was the very first sea-captain I had ever seen, and his white hair and fine handsome florid face made so strong an impression upon me, that I have never forgotten him, though I only saw him during this one visit of his to New York, for he was lost in the White Sea some years after.

But I meant to speak about the fort. It was a beautiful place, as I remembered it, and very wonderful and romantic, too, as it appeared to me, when I went there with my uncle. On the side away from the water was a green grove of trees, very thick and shady; and through this grove, in a sort of twilight you came to an arch in the wall of the fort, dark as night; and going in, you groped about in long vaults, twisting and turning on every side, till at last you caught a peep of green grass and sunlight, and all at once came out in an open space in the middle of the castle. And there you would see cows quietly grazing, or ruminating under the shade of young trees, and perhaps a calf frisking about, and trying to catch its own tail; and sheep clambering among the mossy ruins, and cropping the little tufts of grass sprouting out of the sides of the embrasures for cannon. And once I saw a black goat with a long beard, and crumpled horns, standing with his forefeet lifted high up on the topmost parapet, and looking to sea, as if he were watching for a ship that was bringing over his cousin. I can see him even now, and though I have changed since then, the black goat looks just the same as ever; and so I suppose he would, if I live to be as old as Methusaleh, and have as great a memory as he must have had. Yes, the fort was a beautiful, quiet, charming spot. I should like to build a little cottage in the middle of it, and live there all my life. It was noon-day when I was there, in the month of June, and there was little wind to stir the trees, and every thing looked as if it was waiting for something, and the sky overhead was blue as my mother's eye, and I was so glad and happy then. But I must not think of those delightful days, before my father became a bankrupt, and died, and we removed from the city; for when I think of those days, something rises up in my throat and almost strangles me.

Now, as we sailed through the Narrows, I caught sight of that beautiful fort on the cliff, and could not help contrasting my situation now, with what it was when with my father and uncle I went there so long ago. Then I never thought of working for my living, and never knew that there were hard hearts in the world; and knew so little of money, that when I bought a stick of candy, and laid down a sixpence, I thought the confectioner returned five cents, only that I might have money to buy something else, and not because the pennies were my change, and therefore mine by good rights. How different my idea of money now!

Then I was a schoolboy, and thought of going to college in time; and had vague thoughts of becoming a great orator like Patrick Henry, whose speeches I used to speak on the stage; but now, I was a poor friendless boy, far away from my home, and voluntarily in the way of becoming a miserable sailor for life. And what made it more bitter to me, was to think of how well off were my cousins, who were happy and rich, and lived at home with my uncles and aunts, with no thought of going to sea for a living. I tried to think that it was all a dream, that I was not where I was, not on board of a ship, but that I was at home again in the city, with my father alive, and my mother bright and happy as she used to be. But it would not do. I was indeed where I was, and here was the ship, and there was the fort. So, after casting a last look at some boys who were standing on the parapet, gazing off to sea, I turned away heavily, and resolved not to look at the land any more.

About sunset we got fairly "outside," and well may it so be called; for I felt thrust out of the world. Then the breeze began to blow, and the sails were loosed, and hoisted; and after a while, the steamboat left us, and for the first time I felt the ship roll, a strange feeling enough, as if it were a great barrel in the water. Shortly after, I observed a swift little schooner running across our bows, and re-crossing again and again; and while I was wondering what she could be, she suddenly lowered her sails, and two men took hold of a little boat on her deck, and launched it overboard as if it had been a chip. Then I noticed that our pilot, a red-faced man in a rough blue coat, who to my astonishment had all this time been giving orders instead of the captain, began to button up his coat to the throat, like a prudent person about leaving a house at night in a lonely square, to go home; and he left the giving orders to the chief mate, and stood apart talking with the captain, and put his hand into his pocket, and gave him some newspapers.

And in a few minutes, when we had stopped our headway, and allowed the little boat to come alongside, he shook hands with the captain and officers and bade them good-by, without saying a syllable of farewell to me and the sailors; and so he went laughing over the side, and got into the boat, and they pulled him off to the schooner, and then the schooner made sail and glided under our stern, her men standing up and waving their hats, and cheering; and that was the last we saw of America.

CHAPTER VIII
HE IS PUT INTO THE LARBOARD WATCH; GETS SEA-SICK; AND RELATES SOME OTHER OF HIS EXPERIENCES

It was now getting dark, when all at once the sailors were ordered on the quarter-deck, and of course I went along with them.

What is to come now, thought I; but I soon found out. It seemed we were going to be divided into watches. The chief mate began by selecting a stout good-looking sailor for his watch; and then the second mate's turn came to choose, and he also chose a stout good-looking sailor. But it was not me;— no; and *I* noticed, as they went on choosing, one after the other in regular rotation, that both of the mates never so much as looked at me, but kept going round among the rest, peering into their faces, for it was dusk, and telling them not to hide themselves away so in their jackets. But the sailors, especially the stout good-looking ones, seemed to make a point of lounging as much out of the way as possible, and slouching their hats over their eyes; and although it may only be a fancy of mine, *I* certainly thought that they affected a sort of lordly indifference as to whose watch they were going to be in; and did not think it worth while to look any way anxious about the matter. And the very men who, a few minutes before, had showed the most alacrity and promptitude in jumping into the rigging and running aloft at the word of command, now lounged against the bulwarks and most lazily; as if they were quite sure, that by this time the officers must know who the best men were, and they valued themselves well enough to be willing to put the officers to the trouble of searching them out; for if they were worth having, they were worth seeking.

At last they were all chosen but me; and it was the chief mate's next turn to choose; though there could be little choosing in my case, since *I* was a thirteener, and must, whether or no, go over to the next column, like the odd figure you carry along when you do a sum in addition.

"Well, Buttons," said the chief mate, "I thought I'd got rid of you. And as it is, Mr. Rigs," he added, speaking to the second mate, "I guess you had better take him into your watch;—there, I'll let you have him, and then you'll be one stronger than me."

"No, I thank you," said Mr. Rigs.

"You had better," said the chief mate—"see, he's not a bad looking chap—he's a little green, to be sure, but you were so once yourself, you know, Rigs."

"No, I thank you," said the second mate again. "Take him yourself—he's yours by good rights—I don't want him." And so they put me in the chief mate's division, that is the larboard watch.

While this scene was going on, I felt shabby enough; there I stood, just like a silly sheep, over whom two butchers are bargaining. Nothing that had yet happened so forcibly reminded me of where I was, and what I had come to. I was very glad when they sent us forward again.

As we were going forward, the second mate called one of the sailors by name:-"You, Bill?" and Bill answered, "Sir?" just as if the second mate was a born gentleman. It surprised me not a little, to see a man in such a shabby, shaggy old jacket addressed so respectfully; but I had been quite as much surprised when I heard the chief mate call him *Mr.* Rigs during the scene on the quarter-deck; as if this *Mr. Rigs* was a great merchant living in a marble house in Lafayette Place. But I was not very long in finding out, that at sea all officers are *Misters*, and would take it for an insult if any seaman presumed to omit calling them so. And it is also one of their rights and privileges to be called *sir* when addressed—Yes, *sir*; No, *sir*; Ay, *ay*, *sir*; and they are as particular about being sirred as so many knights and baronets; though their titles are not hereditary, as is the case with the Sir Johns and Sir Joshuas in England. But so far as the second mate is concerned, his tides are the only dignities he enjoys; for, upon the whole, he leads a puppyish life indeed. He is not deemed company at any time for the captain, though the chief mate occasionally is, at least deck-company, though not in the cabin; and besides this, the second mate has to breakfast, lunch, dine, and sup off the leavings of the cabin table, and even the steward, who is accountable to nobody but the captain, sometimes treats him cavalierly; and he has to run aloft when topsails are reefed; and put his hand a good way down into the tar-bucket; and keep the key of the boatswain's locker, and fetch and carry balls of marline and seizing-stuff for the sailors when at work in the rigging; besides doing many other things, which a true-born baronet of any spirit would rather die and give up his title than stand.

Having been divided into watches we were sent to supper; but I could not eat any thing except a little biscuit, though I should have liked to have some good tea; but as I had no pot to get it in, and was rather nervous about asking the rough sailors to let me drink out of theirs; I was obliged to go without a sip. I thought of going to the black cook and begging a tin cup; but he looked so cross and ugly then, that the sight of him almost frightened the idea out of me.

When supper was over, for they never talk about going to *tea* aboard of a ship, the watch to which I belonged was called on deck; and we were told it was for us to stand the first night watch, that is, from eight o'clock till midnight.

I now began to feel unsettled and ill at ease about the stomach, as if matters were all topsy-turvy there; and felt strange and giddy about the head; and so I made no doubt that this was the beginning of that dreadful thing, the sea-sickness. Feeling worse and worse, I told one of the sailors how it was with me, and begged him to make my excuses very civilly to the chief mate, for I thought I would go below and spend the night in my bunk. But he only laughed at me, and said something about my mother not being aware of my being out; which enraged me not a little, that a man whom I had heard swear so terribly, should dare to take such a holy name into his mouth. It seemed a sort of blasphemy, and it seemed like dragging out the best and most cherished secrets of my soul, for at that time the name of mother was the center of all my heart's finest feelings, which ere that, I had learned to keep secret, deep down in my being.

But I did not outwardly resent the sailor's words, for that would have only made the matter worse.

Now this man was a Greenlander by birth, with a very white skin where the sun had not burnt it, and handsome blue eyes placed wide apart in his head, and a broad good-humored face, and plenty of curly flaxen hair. He was not very tall, but exceedingly stout-built, though active; and his back was as broad as a shield, and it was a great way between his shoulders. He seemed to be a sort of lady's sailor, for in his broken English he was always talking about the nice ladies of his acquaintance in Stockholm and Copenhagen and a place he called the Hook, which at first I fancied must be the place where lived the hook-nosed men that caught fowling-pieces and every other article that came along. He was dressed very tastefully, too, as if he knew he was a good-looking fellow. He had on a new blue woolen Havre frock, with a new silk handkerchief round his neck, passed through one of the vertebral bones of a shark, highly polished and carved. His trowsers were of clear white duck, and he sported a handsome pair of pumps, and a tarpaulin hat bright as a looking-glass, with a long black ribbon streaming behind, and getting entangled every now and then in the rigging; and he had gold anchors in his ears, and a silver ring on one of his fingers, which was very much worn and bent from pulling ropes and other work on board ship. I thought he might better have left his jewelry at home.

It was a long time before I could believe that this man was really from Greenland, though he looked strange enough to me, then, to have come from the moon; and he was full of stories about that distant country; how they passed the winters there; and how bitter cold it was; and how he used to go to bed and sleep twelve hours, and get up again and run about, and go to bed again, and get up again—there was no telling how many times, and all in one night; for in the winter time in his country, he said, the nights were so many weeks long, that a Greenland baby was sometimes three months old, before it could properly be said to be a day old.

I had seen mention made of such things before, in books of voyages; but that was only reading about them, just as you read the Arabian Nights, which no one ever believes; for somehow, when I read about these wonderful countries, I never used really to believe what I read, but only thought it very strange, and a good deal too strange to be altogether true; though I never thought the men who wrote the book meant to tell lies. But I don't know exactly how to explain what I mean; but this much I will say, that I never believed in Greenland till I saw this Greenlander. And at first, hearing him talk about Greenland, only made me still more incredulous. For what business had a man from Greenland to be in my company? Why was he not at home among the icebergs, and how could he stand a warm summer's sun, and not be melted away? Besides, instead of icicles, there were ear-rings hanging from his ears; and he did not wear bear-skins, and keep his hands in a huge muff; things, which I could not help connecting with Greenland and all Greenlanders.

But I was telling about my being sea-sick and wanting to retire for the night. This Greenlander seeing I was ill, volunteered to turn doctor and cure me; so going down into the forecastle, he came back with a brown jug, like a molasses jug, and a little tin cannikin, and as soon as the brown jug got near my nose, I needed no telling what was in it, for it smelt like a still-house, and sure enough proved to be full of Jamaica spirits.

"Now, Buttons," said he, "one little dose of this will be better for you than a whole night's sleep; there, take that now, and then eat seven or eight biscuits, and you'll feel as strong as the mainmast."

But I felt very little like doing as I was bid, for I had some scruples about drinking spirits; and to tell the plain truth, for I am not ashamed of it, I was a member of a society in the village where my mother lived, called the Juvenile Total Abstinence Association, of which my friend, Tom Legare, was president, secretary, and treasurer, and kept the funds in a little purse that his cousin knit for him. There was three and sixpence on hand, I believe, the last time he brought in his accounts, on a May day, when we had a meeting in a grove on the river-bank. Tom was a very honest treasurer, and never spent the Society's money for peanuts; and besides all, was a fine, generous boy, whom I much loved. But I must not talk about Tom now.

When the Greenlander came to me with his jug of medicine, I thanked him as well as I could; for just then I was leaning with my mouth over the side, feeling ready to die; but I managed to tell him I was under a solemn obligation never to drink spirits upon any consideration whatever; though, as I had a sort of presentiment that the spirits would now, for once in my life, do me good, I began to feel sorry, that when I signed the pledge of abstinence, I had not taken care to insert a little clause, allowing me to drink spirits in case of sea-sickness. And I would advise temperance people to attend to this matter in future; and then if they come to go to sea, there will be no need of breaking their pledges, which I am truly sorry to say was the case with me. And a hard thing it was, too, thus to break a vow before unbroken; especially as the Jamaica tasted any thing but agreeable, and indeed burnt my mouth so, that I did not relish my meals for some time after. Even when I had become quite well and strong again, I wondered how the sailors could really like such stuff; but many of them had a jug of it, besides the Greenlander, which they brought along to sea with them, *to taper off with*, as they called it. But this tapering off did not last very long, for the Jamaica was all gone on the second day, and the jugs were tossed overboard. I wonder where they are now?

But to tell the truth, I found, in spite of its sharp taste, the spirits I drank was just the thing I needed; but I suppose, if I could have had a cup of nice hot coffee, it would have done quite as well, and perhaps much better. But that was not to be had at that time of night, or, indeed, at any other time; for the thing they called *coffee*, which was given to us every morning at breakfast, was the most curious tasting drink I ever drank, and tasted as little like coffee, as it did like lemonade; though, to be sure, it was generally as cold as lemonade, and I used to think the cook had an icehouse, and dropt ice into his coffee. But what was more curious still, was the different quality and taste of it on different mornings. Sometimes it tasted fishy, as if it was a decoction of Dutch herrings; and then it would taste very salty, as if some *old horse*, or sea-beef, had been boiled in it; and then again it would taste a sort of cheesy, as if the captain had sent his cheese-parings forward to make our coffee of; and yet another time it would have such a very bad flavor, that I was almost ready to think some old stocking-heels had been boiled in it. What under heaven it was made of, that it had so many different bad flavors, always remained a mystery; for when at work at his vocation, our old cook used to keep himself close shut-up in his caboose, a little cook-house, and never told any of his secrets.

Though a very serious character, as I shall hereafter show, he was for all that, and perhaps for that identical reason, a very suspicious looking sort of a cook, that I don't believe would ever succeed in getting the cooking at Delmonico's in New York. It was well for him that he was a black cook, for I have no doubt his color kept us from seeing his dirty face! I never saw him wash but once, and that was at one of his own soup pots one dark night when he thought no one saw him. What induced him to be washing his face then, I never could find out; but I suppose he must have suddenly waked up, after dreaming about some real estate on his cheeks. As for his coffee, notwithstanding the disagreeableness of its flavor, I always used to have a strange curiosity every morning, to see what new taste it was going to have; and though, sure enough, I never missed making a new discovery, and adding another taste to my palate, I never found that there was any change in the badness of the beverage, which always seemed the same in that respect as before.

It may well be believed, then, that now when I was seasick, a cup of such coffee as our old cook made would have done me no good, if indeed it would not have come near making an end of me. And bad as it was, and since it was not to be had at that time of night, as I said before, I think I was excusable in taking something else in place of it, as I did; and under the circumstances, it would be unhandsome of them, if my fellow-members of the Temperance Society should reproach me for breaking my bond, which I would not have done except in case of necessity. But the evil effect of breaking one's bond upon any occasion whatever, was witnessed in the present case; for it insidiously opened the way to subsequent breaches of it, which though very slight, yet carried no apology with them.

CHAPTER IX
THE SAILORS BECOMING A LITTLE SOCIAL, REDBURN CONVERSES WITH THEM

The latter part of this first long watch that we stood was very pleasant, so far as the weather was concerned. From being rather cloudy, it became a soft moonlight; and the stars peeped out, plain enough to count one by one; and there was a fine steady breeze; and it was not very cold; and we were going through the water almost as smooth as a sled sliding down hill. And what was still better, the wind held so steady, that there was little running aloft, little pulling ropes, and scarcely any thing disagreeable of that kind.

The chief mate kept walking up and down the quarter-deck, with a lighted long-nine cigar in his mouth by way of a torch; and spoke but few words to us the whole watch. He must have had a good deal of thinking to attend to, which in truth is the case with most seamen the first night out of port, especially when they have thrown away their money in foolish dissipation, and got very sick into the bargain. For when ashore, many of these sea-officers are as wild and reckless in their way, as the sailors they command.

While I stood watching the red cigar-end promenading up and down, the mate suddenly stopped and gave an order, and the men sprang to obey it. It was not much, only something about hoisting one of the sails a little higher up on the mast. The men took hold of the rope, and began pulling upon it; the foremost man of all setting up a song with no words to it, only a strange musical rise and fall of notes. In the dark night, and far out upon the lonely sea, it sounded wild enough, and made me feel as I had sometimes felt, when in a twilight room a cousin of mine, with black eyes, used to play some old German airs on the piano. I almost looked round for goblins, and felt just a little bit afraid. But I soon got used to this singing; for the sailors never touched a rope without it. Sometimes, when no one happened to strike up, and the pulling, whatever it might be, did not seem to be getting forward very well, the mate would always say, "Come, men, can't any of you sing? Sing now, and raise the dead." And then some one of them would begin, and if every man's arms were as much relieved as mine by the song, and he could pull as much better as I did, with such a cheering accompaniment, I am sure the song was well worth the breath expended on it. It is a great thing in a sailor to know how to sing well, for he gets a great name by it from the officers, and a good deal of popularity among his shipmates. Some sea-captains, before shipping a man, always ask him whether he can sing out at a rope.

During the greater part of the watch, the sailors sat on the windlass and told long stories of their adventures by sea and land, and talked about Gibraltar, and Canton, and Valparaiso, and Bombay, just as you and I would about Peck Slip and the Bowery. Every man of them almost was a volume of Voyages and Travels round the World. And what most struck me was that like books of voyages they often contradicted each other, and would fall into long and violent disputes about who was keeping the Foul Anchor tavern in Portsmouth at such a time; or whether the King of Canton lived or did not live in Persia; or whether the bar-maid of a particular house in Hamburg had black eyes or blue eyes; with many other mooted points of that sort.

At last one of them went below and brought up a box of cigars from his chest, for some sailors always provide little delicacies of that kind, to break off the first shock of the salt water after laying idle ashore; and also by way of *tapering off,* as I mentioned a little while ago. But I wondered that they never carried any pies and tarts to sea with them, instead of spirits and cigars.

Ned, for that was the man's name, split open the box with a blow of his fist, and then handed it round along the windlass, just like a waiter at a party, every one helping himself. But I was a member of an Anti-Smoking Society that had been organized in our village by the Principal of the Sunday School there, in conjunction with the Temperance Association. So I did not smoke any then, though I did afterward upon the voyage, I am sorry to say. Notwithstanding I declined; with a good deal of unnecessary swearing, Ned assured me that the cigars were real genuine Havannas; for he had been in Havanna, he said, and had them made there under his own eye. According to his account, he was very particular about his cigars and other things, and never made any importations, for they were unsafe; but always made a voyage himself direct to the place where any foreign thing was to be had that he wanted. He went to Havre for his woolen shirts, to Panama for his hats, to China for his silk handkerchiefs, and direct to Calcutta for his cheroots; and as a great joker in the watch used to say, no doubt he would at last have occasion to go to Russia for his halter; the wit of which saying was presumed to be in the fact, that the Russian hemp is the best; though that is not wit which needs explaining.

By dint of the spirits which, besides stimulating my fainting strength, united with the cool air of the sea to give me an appetite for our hard biscuit; and also by dint of walking briskly up and down the deck before the windlass, I had now recovered in good part from my sickness, and finding the sailors all very pleasant and sociable, at least among themselves, and seated smoking together like old cronies, and nothing on earth to do but sit the watch out, I began to think that they were a pretty good set of fellows after all, barring their swearing and another ugly way of talking they had; and I thought I had misconceived their true characters; for at the outset I had deemed them such a parcel of wicked hard-hearted rascals that it would be a severe affliction to associate with them.

Yes, I now began to look on them with a sort of incipient love; but more with an eye of pity and compassion, as men of naturally gentle and kind dispositions, whom only hardships, and neglect, and ill-usage had made outcasts from good society; and not as villains who loved wickedness for the sake of it, and would persist in wickedness, even in Paradise, if they ever got there. And I called to mind a sermon I had once heard in a church in behalf of sailors, when the preacher called them strayed lambs from the fold, and compared them to poor lost children, babes in the wood, orphans without fathers or mothers.

And I remembered reading in a magazine, called the Sailors' Magazine, with a sea-blue cover, and a ship painted on the back, about pious seamen who never swore, and paid over all their wages to the poor heathen in India; and how that when they were too old to go to sea, these pious old sailors found a delightful home for life in the Hospital, where they had nothing to do, but prepare themselves for their latter end. And I wondered whether there were any such good sailors among my ship-mates; and observing that one of them laid on deck apart from the rest, I thought to be sure he must be one of them: so I did not disturb his devotions: but I was afterward shocked at discovering that he was only fast asleep, with one of the brown jugs by his side.

I forgot to mention by the way, that every once in a while, the men went into one corner, where the chief mate could not see them, to take a "swig at the halyards," as they called it; and this swigging at the halyards it was, that enabled them "to taper off" handsomely, and no doubt it was this, too, that had something to do with making them so pleasant and sociable that night, for they were seldom so pleasant and sociable afterward, and never treated me so kindly as they did then. Yet this might have been owing to my being something of a stranger to them, then; and our being just out of port. But that very night they turned about, and taught me a bitter lesson; but all in good time.

I have said, that seeing how agreeable they were getting, and how friendly their manner was, I began to feel a sort of compassion for them, grounded on their sad conditions as amiable outcasts; and feeling so warm an interest in them, and being full of pity, and being truly desirous of benefiting them to the best of my poor powers, for I knew they were but poor indeed, I made bold to ask one of them, whether he was ever in the habit of going to church, when he was ashore, or dropping in at the Floating Chapel I had seen lying off the dock in the East River at New York; and whether he would think it too much of a liberty, if I asked him, if he had any good books in his chest. He stared a little at first, but marking what good language I used, seeing my civil bearing toward him, he seemed for a moment to be filled with a certain involuntary respect for me, and answered, that he had been to church once, some ten or twelve years before, in London, and on a week-day had helped to move the Floating Chapel round the Battery, from the North River; and that was the only time he had seen it. For his books, he said he did not know what I meant by good books; but if I wanted the Newgate Calendar, and Pirate's Own, he could lend them to me.

When I heard this poor sailor talk in this manner, showing so plainly his ignorance and absence of proper views of religion, I pitied him more and more, and contrasting my own situation with his, I was grateful that I was different from him; and I thought how pleasant it was, to feel wiser and better than he could feel; though I was willing to confess to myself, that it was not altogether my own good endeavors, so much as my education, which I had received from others, that had made me the upright and sensible boy I at that time thought myself to be. And it was now, that I began to feel a good degree of complacency and satisfaction in surveying my own character; for, before this, I had previously associated with persons of a very discreet life, so that there was little opportunity to magnify myself, by comparing myself with my neighbors.

Thinking that my superiority to him in a moral way might sit uneasily upon this sailor, I thought it would soften the matter down by giving him a chance to show his own superiority to me, in a minor thing; for I was far from being vain and conceited.

Having observed that at certain intervals a little bell was rung on the quarter-deck by the man at the wheel; and that as soon as it was heard, some one of the sailors forward struck a large bell which hung on the forecastle; and having observed that how many times soever the man astern rang his bell, the man forward struck his—tit for tat,—I inquired of this Floating Chapel sailor, what all this ringing meant; and whether, as the big bell hung right over the scuttle that went down to the place where the watch below were sleeping, such a ringing every little while would not tend to disturb them and beget unpleasant dreams; and in asking these questions I was particular to address him in a civil and condescending way, so as to show him very plainly that I did not deem myself one whit better than he was, that is, taking all things together, and not going into particulars. But to my great surprise and mortification, he in the rudest land of manner laughed aloud in my face, and called me a "Jimmy Dux," though that was not my real name, and he must have known it; and also the "son of a farmer," though as I have previously related, my father was a great merchant and French importer in Broad-street in New York. And then he began to laugh and joke about me, with the other sailors, till they all got round me, and if I had not felt so terribly angry, I should certainly have felt very much like a fool. But my being so angry prevented me from feeling foolish, which is very lucky for people in a passion.

CHAPTER X
HE IS VERY MUCH FRIGHTENED; THE SAILORS ABUSE HIM; AND HE BECOMES MISERABLE AND FORLORN

While the scene last described was going on, we were all startled by a horrid groaning noise down in the forecastle; and all at once some one came rushing up the scuttle in his shirt, clutching something in his hand, and trembling and shrieking in the most frightful manner, so that I thought one of the sailors must be murdered below.

But it all passed in a moment; and while we stood aghast at the sight, and almost before we knew what it was, the shrieking man jumped over the bows into the sea, and we saw him no more. Then there was a great uproar; the sailors came running up on deck; and the chief mate ran forward, and learning what had happened, began to yell out his orders about the sails and yards; and we all went to pulling and hauling the ropes, till at last the ship lay almost still on the water. Then they loosed a boat, which kept pulling round the ship for more than an hour, but they never caught sight of the man. It seemed that he was one of the sailors who had been brought aboard dead drunk, and tumbled into his bunk by his landlord; and there he had lain till now. He must have suddenly waked up, I suppose, raging mad with the delirium tremens, as the chief mate called it, and finding himself in a strange silent place, and knowing not how he had got there, he rushed on deck, and so, in a fit of frenzy, put an end to himself.

This event, happening at the dead of night, had a wonderfully solemn and almost awful effect upon me. I would have given the whole world, and the sun and moon, and all the stars in heaven, if they had been mine, had I been safe back at Mr. Jones', or still better, in my home on the Hudson River. I thought it an ill-omened voyage, and railed at the folly which had sent me to sea, sore against the advice of my best friends, that is to say, my mother and sisters.

Alas! poor Wellingborough, thought I, you will never see your home any more. And in this melancholy mood I went below, when the watch had expired, which happened soon after. But to my terror, I found that the suicide had been occupying the very bunk which I had appropriated to myself, and there was no other place for me to sleep in. The thought of lying down there now, seemed too horrible to me, and what made it worse, was the way in which the sailors spoke of my being frightened. And they took this opportunity to tell me what a hard and wicked life I had entered upon, and how that such things happened frequently at sea, and they were used to it. But I did not believe this; for when the suicide came rushing and shrieking up the scuttle, they looked as frightened as I did; and besides that, and what makes their being frightened still plainer, is the fact, that if they had had any presence of mind, they could have prevented his plunging overboard, since he brushed right by them. However, they lay in their bunks smoking, and kept talking on some time in this strain, and advising me as soon as ever I got home to pin my ears back, so as not to hold the wind, and sail straight away into the interior of the country, and never stop until deep in the bush, far off from the least running brook, never mind how shallow, and out of sight of even the smallest puddle of rainwater.

 This kind of talking brought the tears into my eyes, for it was so true and real, and the sailors who spoke it seemed so false-hearted and insincere; but for all that, in spite of the sickness at my heart, it made me mad, and stung me to the quick, that they should speak of me as a poor trembling coward, who could never be brought to endure the hardships of a sailor's life; for I felt myself trembling, and knew that I was but a coward then, well enough, without their telling me of it. And they did not say I was cowardly, because they perceived it in me, but because they merely supposed I must be, judging, no doubt, from their own secret thoughts about themselves; for I felt sure that the suicide frightened them very badly. And at last, being provoked to desperation by their taunts, I told them so to their faces; but I might better have kept silent; for they now all united to abuse me. They asked me what business I, a boy like me, had to go to sea, and take the bread out of the mouth of honest sailors, and fill a good seaman's place; and asked me whether I ever dreamed of becoming a captain, since I was a gentleman with white hands; and if I ever *should* be, they would like nothing better than to ship aboard my vessel and stir up a mutiny. And one of them, whose name was Jackson, of whom I shall have a good deal more to say by-and-by, said, I had better steer clear of him ever after, for if ever I crossed his path, or got into his way, he would be the death of me, and if ever I stumbled about in the rigging near *him*, he would make nothing of pitching me overboard; and that he swore too, with an oath. At first, all this nearly stunned me, it was so unforeseen; and then I could not believe that they meant what they said, or that they could be so cruel and black-hearted. But how could I help seeing, that the men who could thus talk to a poor, friendless boy, on the very first night of his voyage to sea, must be capable of almost any enormity. I loathed, detested, and hated them with all that was left of my bursting heart and soul, and I thought myself the most forlorn and miserable wretch that ever breathed. May I never be a man, thought I, if to be a boy is to be such a wretch. And I wailed and wept, and my heart cracked within me, but all the time I defied them through my teeth, and dared them to do their worst.

At last they ceased talking and fell fast asleep, leaving me awake, seated on a chest with my face bent over my knees between my hands. And there I sat, till at length the dull beating against the ship's bows, and the silence around soothed me down, and I fell asleep as I sat.

CHAPTER XI
HE HELPS WASH THE DECKS, AND THEN GOES TO BREAKFAST

The next thing I knew, was the loud thumping of a handspike on deck as the watch was called again. It was now four o'clock in the morning, and when we got on deck the first signs of day were shining in the east. The men were very sleepy, and sat down on the windlass without speaking, and some of them nodded and nodded, till at last they fell off like little boys in church during a drowsy sermon. At last it was broad day, and an order was given to wash down the decks. A great tub was dragged into the waist, and then one of the men went over into the chains, and slipped in behind a band fastened to the shrouds, and leaning over, began to swing a bucket into the sea by a long rope; and in that way with much expertness and sleight of hand, he managed to fill the tub in a very short time. Then the water began to splash about all over the decks, and I began to think I should surely get my feet wet, and catch my death of cold. So I went to the chief mate, and told him I thought I would just step below, till this miserable wetting was over; for I did not have any water-proof boots, and an aunt of mine had died of consumption. But he only roared out for me to get a broom and go to scrubbing, or he would prove a worse consumption to me than ever got hold of my poor aunt. So I scrubbed away fore and aft, till my back was almost broke, for the brooms had uncommon short handles, and we were told to scrub hard.

At length the scrubbing being over, the mate began heaving buckets of water about, to wash every thing clean, by way of finishing off. He must have thought this fine sport, just as captains of fire engines love to point the tube of their hose; for he kept me running after him with full buckets of water, and sometimes chased a little chip all over the deck, with a continued flood, till at last he sent it flying out of a scupper-hole into the sea; when if he had only given me permission, I could have picked it up in a trice, and dropped it overboard without saying one word, and without wasting so much water. But he said there was plenty of water in the ocean, and to spare; which was true enough, but then I who had to trot after him with the buckets, had no more legs and arms than I wanted for my own use.

I thought this washing down the decks was the most foolish thing in the world, and besides that it was the most uncomfortable. It was worse than my mother's house-cleanings at home, which I used to abominate so.

At eight o'clock the bell was struck, and we went to breakfast. And now some of the worst of my troubles began. For not having had any friend to tell me what I would want at sea, I had not provided myself, as I should have done, with a good many things that a sailor needs; and for my own part, it had never entered my mind, that sailors had no table to sit down to, no cloth, or napkins, or tumblers, and had to provide every thing themselves. But so it was.

The first thing they did was this. Every sailor went to the cook-house with his tin pot, and got it filled with coffee; but of course, having no pot, there was no coffee for me. And after that, a sort of little tub called a "kid," was passed down into the forecastle, filled with something they called "burgoo." This was like mush, made of Indian corn, meal, and water. With the *"kid,"* a little tin cannikin was passed down with molasses. Then the Jackson that I spoke of before, put the kid between his knees, and began to pour in the molasses, just like an old landlord mixing punch for a party. He scooped out a little hole in the middle of the mush, to hold the molasses; so it looked for all the world like a little black pool in the Dismal Swamp of Virginia.

Then they all formed a circle round the kid; and one after the other, with great regularity, dipped their spoons into the mush, and after stirring them round a little in the molasses-pool, they swallowed down their mouthfuls, and smacked their lips over it, as if it tasted very good; which I have no doubt it did; but not having any spoon, I wasn't sure.

I sat some time watching these proceedings, and wondering how polite they were to each other; for, though there were a great many spoons to only one dish, they never got entangled. At last, seeing that the mush was getting thinner and thinner, and that it was getting low water, or rather low molasses in the little pool, I ran on deck, and after searching about, returned with a bit of stick; and thinking I had as good a right as any one else to the mush and molasses, I worked my way into the circle, intending to make one of the party. So I shoved in my stick, and after twirling it about, was just managing to carry a little *burgoo* toward my mouth, which had been for some time standing ready open to receive it, when one of the sailors perceiving what I was about, knocked the stick out of my hands, and asked me where I learned my manners; Was that the way gentlemen eat in my country? Did they eat their victuals with splinters of wood, and couldn't that wealthy gentleman my father afford to buy his gentlemanly son a spoon?

All the rest joined in, and pronounced me an ill-bred, coarse, and unmannerly youngster, who, if permitted to go on with such behavior as that, would corrupt the whole crew, and make them no better than swine.

As I felt conscious that a stick was indeed a thing very unsuitable to eat with, I did not say much to this, though it vexed me enough; but remembering that I had seen one of the steerage passengers with a pan and spoon in his hand eating his breakfast on the fore hatch, I now ran on deck again, and to my great joy succeeded in borrowing his spoon, for he had got through his meal, and down I came again, though at the eleventh hour, and offered myself once more as a candidate.

But alas! there was little more of the Dismal Swamp left, and when I reached over to the opposite end of the kid, I received a rap on the knuckles from a spoon, and was told that I must help myself from my own side, for that was the rule. But *my* side was scraped clean, so I got no *burgoo* that morning.

But I made it up by eating some salt beef and biscuit, which I found to be the invariable accompaniment of every meal; the sailors sitting cross-legged on their chests in a circle, and breaking the hard biscuit, very sociably, over each other's heads, which was very convenient indeed, but gave me the headache, at least for the first four or five days till I got used to it; and then I did not care much about it, only it kept my hair full of crumbs; and I had forgot to bring a fine comb and brush, so I used to shake my hair out to windward over the bulwarks every evening.

CHAPTER XII
HE GIVES SOME ACCOUNT OF ONE OF HIS SHIPMATES CALLED JACKSON

While we sat eating our beef and biscuit, two of the men got into a dispute, about who had been sea-faring the longest; when Jackson, who had mixed the *burgoo,* called upon them in a loud voice to cease their clamor, for he would decide the matter for them. Of this sailor, I shall have something more to say, as I get on with my narrative; so, I will here try to describe him a little.

Did you ever see a man, with his hair shaved off, and just recovered from the yellow fever? Well, just such a looking man was this sailor. He was as yellow as gamboge, had no more whisker on his cheek, than I have on my elbows. His hair had fallen out, and left him very bald, except in the nape of his neck, and just behind the ears, where it was stuck over with short little tufts, and looked like a worn-out shoe-brush. His nose had broken down in the middle, and he squinted with one eye, and did not look very straight out of the other. He dressed a good deal like a Bowery boy; for he despised the ordinary sailor-rig; wearing a pair of great over-all blue trowsers, fastened with suspenders, and three red woolen shirts, one over the other; for he was subject to the rheumatism, and was not in good health, he said; and he had a large white wool hat, with a broad rolling brim. He was a native of New York city, and had a good deal to say about *highlanders,* and *rowdies,* whom he denounced as only good for the gallows; but I thought he looked a good deal like a *highlander* himself.

His name, as I have said, was Jackson; and he told us, he was a near relation of General Jackson of New Orleans, and swore terribly, if any one ventured to question what he asserted on that head. In fact he was a great bully, and being the best seaman on board, and very overbearing every way, all the men were afraid of him, and durst not contradict him, or cross his path in any thing. And what made this more wonderful was, that he was the weakest man, bodily, of the whole crew; and I have no doubt that young and small as I was then, compared to what I am now, I could have thrown him down. But he had such an overawing way with him; such a deal of brass and impudence, such an unflinching face, and withal was such a hideous looking mortal, that Satan himself would have run from him. And besides all this, it was quite plain, that he was by nature a marvelously clever, cunning man, though without education; and understood human nature to a kink, and well knew whom he had to deal with; and then, one glance of his squinting eye, was as good as a knock-down, for it was the most deep, subtle, infernal looking eye, that I ever saw lodged in a human head. I believe, that by good rights it must have belonged to a wolf, or starved tiger; at any rate, I would defy any oculist, to turn out a glass eye, half so cold, and snaky, and deadly. It was a horrible thing; and I would give much to forget that I have ever seen it; for it haunts me to this day.

It was impossible to tell how old this Jackson was; for he had no beard, and no wrinkles, except small crowsfeet about the eyes. He might have seen thirty, or perhaps fifty years. But according to his own account, he had been to sea ever since he was eight years old, when he first went as a cabin-boy in an Indiaman, and ran away at Calcutta. And according to his own account, too, he had passed through every kind of dissipation and abandonment in the worst parts of the world. He had served in Portuguese slavers on the coast of Africa; and with a diabolical relish used to tell of the *middle-passage,* where the slaves were stowed, heel and point, like logs, and the suffocated and dead were unmanacled, and weeded out from the living every morning, before washing down the decks; how he had been in a slaving schooner, which being chased by an English cruiser off Cape Verde, received three shots in her hull, which raked through and through a whole file of slaves, that were chained.

He would tell of lying in Batavia during a fever, when his ship lost a man every few days, and how they went reeling ashore with the body, and got still more intoxicated by way of precaution against the plague. He would talk of finding a cobra-di-capello, or hooded snake, under his pillow in India, when he slept ashore there. He would talk of sailors being poisoned at Canton with drugged *"shampoo,"* for the sake of their money; and of the Malay ruffians, who stopped ships in the straits of Caspar, and always saved the captain for the last, so as to make him point out where the most valuable goods were stored.

His whole talk was of this land; full of piracies, plagues and poisonings. And often he narrated many passages in his own individual career, which were almost incredible, from the consideration that few men could have plunged into such infamous vices, and clung to them so long, without paying the death-penalty.

But in truth, he carried about with him the traces of these things, and the mark of a fearful end nigh at hand; like that of King Antiochus of Syria, who died a worse death, history says, than if he had been stung out of the world by wasps and hornets.

Nothing was left of this Jackson but the foul lees and dregs of a man; he was thin as a shadow; nothing but skin and bones; and sometimes used to complain, that it hurt him to sit on the hard chests. And I sometimes fancied, it was the consciousness of his miserable, broken-down condition, and the prospect of soon dying like a dog, in consequence of his sins, that made this poor wretch always eye me with such malevolence as he did. For I was young and handsome, at least my mother so thought me, and as soon as I became a little used to the sea, and shook off my low spirits somewhat, I began to have my old color in my cheeks, and, spite of misfortune, to appear well and hearty; whereas *he* was being consumed by an incurable malady, that was eating up his vitals, and was more fit for a hospital than a ship.

As I am sometimes by nature inclined to indulge in unauthorized surmisings about the thoughts going on with regard to me, in the people I meet; especially if I have reason to think they dislike me; I will not put it down for a certainty that what I suspected concerning this Jackson relative to his thoughts of me, was really the truth. But only state my honest opinion, and how it struck me at the time; and even now, I think I was not wrong. And indeed, unless it was so, how could I account to myself, for the shudder that would run through me, when I caught this man gazing at me, as I often did; for he was apt to be dumb at times, and would sit with his eyes fixed, and his teeth set, like a man in the moody madness.

I well remember the first time I saw him, and how I was startled at his eye, which was even then fixed upon me. He was standing at the ship's helm, being the first man that got there, when a steersman was called for by the pilot; for this Jackson was always on the alert for easy duties, and used to plead his delicate health as the reason for assuming them, as he did; though I used to think, that for a man in poor health, he was very swift on the legs; at least when a good place was to be jumped to; though that might only have been a sort of spasmodic exertion under strong inducements, which every one knows the greatest invalids will sometimes show.

And though the sailors were always very bitter against any thing like *sogering*, as they called it; that is, any thing that savored of a desire to get rid of downright hard work; yet, I observed that, though this Jackson was a notorious old *soger* the whole voyage (I mean, in all things not perilous to do, from which he was far from hanging back), and in truth was a great veteran that way, and one who must have passed unhurt through many campaigns;

yet, they never presumed to call him to account in any way; or to let him so much as think, what they thought of his conduct. But I often heard them call him many hard names behind his back; and sometimes, too, when, perhaps, they had just been tenderly inquiring after his health before his face. They all stood in mortal fear of him; and cringed and fawned about him like so many spaniels; and used to rub his back, after he was undressed and lying in his bunk; and used to run up on deck to the cook-house, to warm some cold coffee for him; and used to fill his pipe, and give him chews of tobacco, and mend his jackets and trowsers; and used to watch, and tend, and nurse him every way. And all the time, he would sit scowling on them, and found fault with what they did; and I noticed, that those who did the most for him, and cringed the most before him, were the very ones he most abused; while two or three who held more aloof, he treated with a little consideration.

It is not for me to say, what it was that made a whole ship's company submit so to the whims of one poor miserable man like Jackson. I only know that so it was; but I have no doubt, that if he had had a blue eye in his head, or had had a different face from what he did have, they would not have stood in such awe of him. And it astonished me, to see that one of the seamen, a remarkably robust and good-humored young man from Belfast in Ireland, was a person of no mark or influence among the crew; but on the contrary was hooted at, and trampled upon, and made a butt and laughing-stock; and more than all, was continually being abused and snubbed by Jackson, who seemed to hate him cordially, because of his great strength and fine person, and particularly because of his red cheeks.

But then, this Belfast man, although he had shipped for an *able-seaman*, was not much of a sailor; and that always lowers a man in the eyes of a ship's company; I mean, when he ships for an *able-seaman*, but is not able to do the duty of one. For sailors are of three classes—*able-seaman, ordinary-seaman*, and *boys*; and they receive different wages according to their rank. Generally, a ship's company of twelve men will only have five or six able seamen, who if they prove to understand their duty every way (and that is no small matter either, as I shall hereafter show, perhaps), are looked up to, and thought much of by the ordinary-seamen and boys, who reverence their very pea-jackets, and lay up their sayings in their hearts.

But you must not think from this, that persons called *boys* aboard merchant-ships are all youngsters, though to be sure, I myself was called a *boy*, and a boy I was. No. In merchant-ships, a *boy* means a green-hand, a landsman on his first voyage. And never mind if he is old enough to be a grandfather, he is still called a *boy;* and boys' work is put upon him.

But I am straying off from what I was going to say about Jackson's putting an end to the dispute between the two sailors in the forecastle after breakfast. After they had been disputing some time about who had been to sea the longest, Jackson told them to stop talking; and then bade one of them open his mouth; for, said he, I can tell a sailor's age just like a horse's—by his teeth. So the man laughed, and opened his mouth; and Jackson made him step out under the scuttle, where the light came down from deck; and then made him throw his head back, while he looked into it, and probed a little with his jackknife, like a baboon peering into a junk-bottle. I trembled for the poor fellow, just as if I had seen him under the hands of a crazy barber, making signs to cut his throat, and he all the while sitting stock still, with the lather on, to be shaved. For I watched Jackson's eye and saw it snapping, and a sort of going in and out, very quick, as if it were something like a forked tongue; and somehow, I felt as if he were longing to kill the man; but at last he grew more composed, and after concluding his examination, said, that the first man was the oldest sailor, for the ends of his teeth were the evenest and most worn down; which, he said, arose from eating so much hard sea-biscuit; and this was the reason he could tell a sailor's age like a horse's.

At this, every body made merry, and looked at each other, as much as to *say—come, boys, let's laugh;* and they did laugh; and declared it was a rare joke.

This was always the way with them. They made a point of shouting out, whenever Jackson said any thing with a grin; that being the sign to them that he himself thought it funny; though I heard many good jokes from others pass off without a smile; and once Jackson himself (for, to tell the truth, he sometimes had a comical way with him, that is, when his back did not ache) told a truly funny story, but with a grave face; when, not knowing how he meant it, whether for a laugh or otherwise, they all sat still, waiting what to do, and looking perplexed enough; till at last Jackson roared out upon them for a parcel of fools and idiots; and told them to their beards, how it was; that he had purposely put on his grave face, to see whether they would not look grave, too; even when he was telling something that ought to split their sides. And with that, he flouted, and jeered at them, and laughed them all to scorn; and broke out in such a rage, that his lips began to glue together at the corners with a fine white foam.

He seemed to be full of hatred and gall against every thing and every body in the world; as if all the world was one person, and had done him some dreadful harm, that was rankling and festering in his heart. Sometimes I thought he was really crazy; and often felt so frightened at him, that I thought of going to the captain about it, and telling him Jackson ought to be confined, lest he should do some terrible thing at last. But upon second thoughts, I always gave it up; for the captain would only have called me a fool, and sent me forward again.

But you must not think that all the sailors were alike in abasing themselves before this man. No: there were three or four who used to stand up sometimes against him; and when he was absent at the wheel, would plot against him among the other sailors, and tell them what a shame and ignominy it was, that such a poor miserable wretch should be such a tyrant over much better men than himself. And they begged and conjured them as men, to put up with it no longer, but the very next time, that Jackson presumed to play the dictator, that they should all withstand him, and let him know his place. Two or three times nearly all hands agreed to it, with the exception of those who used to slink off during such discussions; and swore that they would not any more submit to being ruled by Jackson. But when the time came to make good their oaths, they were mum again, and let every thing go on the old way; so that those who had put them up to it, had to bear all the brunt of Jackson's wrath by themselves. And though these last would stick up a little at first, and even mutter something about a fight to Jackson; yet in the end, finding themselves unbefriended by the rest, they would gradually become silent, and leave the field to the tyrant, who would then fly out worse than ever, and dare them to do their worst, and jeer at them for white-livered poltroons, who did not have a mouthful of heart in them. At such times, there were no bounds to his contempt; and indeed, all the time he seemed to have even more contempt than hatred, for every body and every thing.

As for me, I was but a boy; and at any time aboard ship, a boy is expected to keep quiet, do what he is bid, never presume to interfere, and seldom to talk, unless spoken to. For merchant sailors have a great idea of their dignity, and superiority to *greenhorns* and *landsmen*, who know nothing about a ship; and they seem to think, that an *able seaman* is a great man; at least a much greater man than a little boy. And the able seamen in the Highlander had such grand notions about their seamanship, that I almost thought that able seamen received diplomas, like those given at colleges; and were made a sort *A.M.S*, or *Masters of Arts*.

But though I kept thus quiet, and had very little to say, and well knew that my best plan was to get along peaceably with every body, and indeed endure a good deal before showing fight, yet I could not avoid Jackson's evil eye, nor escape his bitter enmity. And his being my foe, set many of the rest against me; or at least they were afraid to speak out for me before Jackson; so that at last I found myself a sort of Ishmael in the ship, without a single friend or companion; and I began to feel a hatred growing up in me against the whole crew—so much so, that I prayed against it, that it might not master my heart completely, and so make a fiend of me, something like Jackson.

CHAPTER XIII
HE HAS A FINE DAY AT SEA, BEGINS TO LIKE IT; BUT CHANGES HIS MIND

The second day out of port, the decks being washed down and breakfast over, the watch was called, and the mate set us to work.

It was a very bright day. The sky and water were both of the same deep hue; and the air felt warm and sunny; so that we threw off our jackets. I could hardly believe that I was sailing in the same ship I had been in during the night, when every thing had been so lonely and dim; and I could hardly imagine that this was the same ocean, now so beautiful and blue, that during part of the night-watch had rolled along so black and forbidding.

There were little traces of sunny clouds all over the heavens; and little fleeces of foam all over the sea; and the ship made a strange, musical noise under her bows, as she glided along, with her sails all still. It seemed a pity to go to work at such a time; and if we could only have sat in the windlass again; or if they would have let me go out on the bowsprit, and lay down between the *manropes* there, and look over at the fish in the water, and think of home, I should have been almost happy for a time.

I had now completely got over my sea-sickness, and felt very well; at least in my body, though my heart was far from feeling right; so that I could now look around me, and make observations.

And truly, though we were at sea, there was much to behold and wonder at; to me, who was on my first voyage. What most amazed me was the sight of the great ocean itself, for we were out of sight of land. All round us, on both sides of the ship, ahead and astern, nothing was to be seen but water—water—water; not a single glimpse of green shore, not the smallest island, or speck of moss any where. Never did I realize till now what the ocean was: how grand and majestic, how solitary, and boundless, and beautiful and blue; for that day it gave no tokens of squalls or hurricanes, such as I had heard my father tell of; nor could I imagine, how any thing that seemed so playful and placid, could be lashed into rage, and troubled into rolling avalanches of foam, and great cascades of waves, such as I saw in the end.

As I looked at it so mild and sunny, I could not help calling to mind my little brother's face, when he was sleeping an infant in the cradle. It had just such a happy, careless, innocent look; and every happy little wave seemed gamboling about like a thoughtless little kid in a pasture; and seemed to look up in your face as it passed, as if it wanted to be patted and caressed. They seemed all live things with hearts in them, that could feel; and I almost felt grieved, as we sailed in among them, scattering them under our broad bows in sun-flakes, and riding over them like a great elephant among lambs. But what seemed perhaps the most strange to me of all, was a certain wonderful rising and falling of the sea; I do not mean the waves themselves, but a sort of wide heaving and swelling and sinking all over the ocean. It was something I can not very well describe; but I know very well what it was, and how it affected me. It made me almost dizzy to look at it; and yet I could not keep my eyes off it, it seemed so passing strange and wonderful.

I felt as if in a dream all the time; and when I could shut the ship out, almost thought I was in some new, fairy world, and expected to hear myself called to, out of the clear blue air, or from the depths of the deep blue sea. But I did not have much leisure to indulge in such thoughts; for the men were now getting some *stun'-sails* ready to hoist aloft, as the wind was getting fairer and fairer for us; and these stun'-sails are light canvas which are spread at such times, away out beyond the ends of the yards, where they overhang the wide water, like the wings of a great bird.

For my own part, I could do but little to help the rest, not knowing the name of any thing, or the proper way to go about aught. Besides, I felt very dreamy, as I said before; and did not exactly know where, or what I was; every thing was so strange and new.

While the stun'-sails were lying all tumbled upon the deck, and the sailors were fastening them to the booms, getting them ready to hoist, the mate ordered me to do a great many simple things, none of which could I comprehend, owing to the queer words he used; and then, seeing me stand quite perplexed and confounded, he would roar out at me, and call me all manner of names, and the sailors would laugh and wink to each other, but durst not go farther than that, for fear of the mate, who in his own presence would not let any body laugh at me but himself.

However, I tried to wake up as much as I could, and keep from dreaming with my eyes open; and being, at bottom, a smart, apt lad, at last I managed to learn a thing or two, so that I did not appear so much like a fool as at first.

People who have never gone to sea for the first time as sailors, can not imagine how puzzling and confounding it is. It must be like going into a barbarous country, where they speak a strange dialect, and dress in strange clothes, and live in strange houses. For sailors have their own names, even for things that are familiar ashore; and if you call a thing by its shore name, you are laughed at for an ignoramus and a landlubber. This first day I speak of, the mate having ordered me to draw some water, I asked him where I was to get the pail; when I thought I had committed some dreadful crime; for he flew into a great passion, and said they never had any *pails* at sea, and then I learned that they were always called *buckets*. And once I was talking about sticking a little wooden peg into a bucket to stop a leak, when he flew out again, and said there were no *pegs* at sea, only *plugs*. And just so it was with every thing else.

But besides all this, there is such an infinite number of totally new names of new things to learn, that at first it seemed impossible for me to master them all. If you have ever seen a ship, you must have remarked what a thicket of ropes there are; and how they all seemed mixed and entangled together like a great skein of yarn. Now the very smallest of these ropes has its own proper name, and many of them are very lengthy, like the names of young royal princes, such as the *starboard-main-top-gallant-bow-line,* or the *larboard-fore-top-sail-clue-line.*

I think it would not be a bad plan to have a grand new naming of a ship's ropes, as I have read, they once had a simplifying of the classes of plants in Botany. It is really wonderful how many names there are in the world. There is no counting the names, that surgeons and anatomists give to the various parts of the human body; which, indeed, is something like a ship; its bones being the stiff standing-rigging, and the sinews the small running ropes, that manage all the motions.

I wonder whether mankind could not get along without all these names, which keep increasing every day, and hour, and moment; till at last the very air will be full of them; and even in a great plain, men will be breathing each other's breath, owing to the vast multitude of words they use, that consume all the air, just as lamp-burners do gas. But people seem to have a great love for names; for to know a great many names, seems to look like knowing a good many things; though I should not be surprised, if there were a great many more names than things in the world. But I must quit this rambling, and return to my story.

At last we hoisted the stun'-sails up to the top-sail yards, and as soon as the vessel felt them, she gave a sort of bound like a horse, and the breeze blowing more and more, she went plunging along, shaking off the foam from her bows, like foam from a bridle-bit. Every mast and timber seemed to have a pulse in it that was beating with life and joy; and I felt a wild exulting in my own heart, and felt as if I would be glad to bound along so round the world.

Then was I first conscious of a wonderful thing in me, that responded to all the wild commotion of the outer world; and went reeling on and on with the planets in their orbits, and was lost in one delirious throb at the center of the All. A wild bubbling and bursting was at my heart, as if a hidden spring had just gushed out there; and my blood ran tingling along my frame, like mountain brooks in spring freshets.

Yes! yes! give me this glorious ocean life, this salt-sea life, this briny, foamy life, when the sea neighs and snorts, and you breathe the very breath that the great whales respire! Let me roll around the globe, let me rock upon the sea; let me race and pant out my life, with an eternal breeze astern, and an endless sea before!

But how soon these raptures abated, when after a brief idle interval, we were again set to work, and I had a vile commission to clean out the chicken coops, and make up the beds of the pigs in the long-boat.

Miserable dog's life is this of the sea! commanded like a slave, and set to work like an ass! vulgar and brutal men lording it over me, as if I were an African in Alabama. Yes, yes, blow on, ye breezes, and make a speedy end to this abominable voyage!

CHAPTER XIV
HE CONTEMPLATES MAKING A SOCIAL CALL ON THE CAPTAIN IN HIS CABIN

What reminded me most forcibly of my ignominious condition, was the widely altered manner of the captain toward me.

I had thought him a fine, funny gentleman, full of mirth and good humor, and good will to seamen, and one who could not fail to appreciate the difference between me and the rude sailors among whom I was thrown. Indeed, I had made no doubt that he would in some special manner take me under his protection, and prove a kind friend and benefactor to me; as I had heard that some sea-captains are fathers to their crew; and so they are; but such fathers as Solomon's precepts tend to make—severe and chastising fathers, fathers whose sense of duty overcomes the sense of love, and who every day, in some sort, play the part of Brutus, who ordered his son away to execution, as I have read in our old family Plutarch.

Yes, I thought that Captain Riga, for Riga was his name, would be attentive and considerate to me, and strive to cheer me up, and comfort me in my lonesomeness. I did not even deem it at all impossible that he would invite me down into the cabin of a pleasant night, to ask me questions concerning my parents, and prospects in life; besides obtaining from me some anecdotes touching my great-uncle, the illustrious senator; or give me a slate and pencil, and teach me problems in navigation; or perhaps engage me at a game of chess. I even thought he might invite me to dinner on a sunny Sunday, and help me plentifully to the nice cabin fare, as knowing how distasteful the salt beef and pork, and hard biscuit of the forecastle must at first be to a boy like me, who had always lived ashore, and at home.

And I could not help regarding him with peculiar emotions, almost of tenderness and love, as the last visible link in the chain of associations which bound me to my home. For, while yet in port, I had seen him and Mr. Jones, my brother's friend, standing together and conversing; so that from the captain to my brother there was but one intermediate step; and my brother and mother and sisters were one.

And this reminds me how often I used to pass by the places on deck, where I remembered Mr. Jones had stood when we first visited the ship lying at the wharf; and how I tried to convince myself that it was indeed true, that he had stood there, though now the ship was so far away on the wide Atlantic Ocean, and he perhaps was walking down Wall-street, or sitting reading the newspaper in his counting room, while poor I was so differently employed.

When two or three days had passed without the captain's speaking to me in any way, or sending word into the forecastle that he wished me to drop into the cabin to pay my respects, I began to think whether I should not make the first advances, and whether indeed he did not expect it of me, since I was but a boy, and he a man; and perhaps that might have been the reason why he had not spoken to me yet, deeming it more proper and respectful for me to address him first. I thought he might be offended, too, especially if he were a proud man, with tender feelings. So one evening, a little before sundown, in the second dog-watch, when there was no more work to be done, I concluded to call and see him.

After drawing a bucket of water, and having a good washing, to get off some of the chicken-coop stains, I went down into the forecastle to dress myself as neatly as I could. I put on a white shirt in place of my red one, and got into a pair of cloth trowsers instead of my duck ones, and put on my new pumps, and then carefully brushing my shooting-jacket, I put that on over all, so that upon the whole, I made quite a genteel figure, at least for a forecastle, though I would not have looked so well in a drawing-room.

When the sailors saw me thus employed, they did not know what to make of it, and wanted to know whether I was dressing to go ashore; I told them no, for we were then out of sight of mind; but that I was going to pay my respects to the captain. Upon which they all laughed and shouted, as if I were a simpleton; though there seemed nothing so very simple in going to make an evening call upon a friend. When some of them tried to dissuade me, saying I was green and raw; but Jackson, who sat looking on, cried out, with a hideous grin, "Let him go, let him go, men—he's a nice boy. Let him go; the captain has some nuts and raisins for him." And so he was going on, when one of his violent fits of coughing seized him, and he almost choked.

As I was about leaving the forecastle, I happened to look at my hands, and seeing them stained all over of a deep yellow, for that morning the mate had set me to tarring some strips of canvas for the rigging I thought it would never do to present myself before a gentleman that way; so for want of lads, I slipped on a pair of woolen mittens, which my mother had knit for me to carry to sea. As I was putting them on, Jackson asked me whether he shouldn't call a carriage; and another bade me not forget to present his best respects to the skipper. I left them all tittering, and coming on deck was passing the cook-house, when the old cook called after me, saying I had forgot my cane.

But I did not heed their impudence, and was walking straight toward the cabin-door on the quarter-deck, when the chief mate met me. I touched my hat, and was passing him, when, after staring at me till I thought his eyes would burst out, he all at once caught me by the collar, and with a voice of thunder, wanted to know what I meant by playing such tricks aboard a ship that he was mate of? I told him to let go of me, or I would complain to my friend the captain, whom I intended to visit that evening. Upon this he gave me such a whirl round, that I thought the Gulf Stream was in my head; and then shoved me forward, roaring out I know not what. Meanwhile the sailors were all standing round the windlass looking aft, mightily tickled.

Seeing I could not effect my object that night, I thought it best to defer it for the present; and returning among the sailors, Jackson asked me how I had found the captain, and whether the next time I went, I would not take a friend along and introduce him.

The upshot of this business was, that before I went to sleep that night, I felt well satisfied that it was not customary for sailors to call on the captain in the cabin; and I began to have an inkling of the fact, that I had acted like a fool; but it all arose from my ignorance of sea usages.

And here I may as well state, that I never saw the inside of the cabin during the whole interval that elapsed from our sailing till our return to New York; though I often used to get a peep at it through a little pane of glass, set in the house on deck, just before the helm, where a watch was kept hanging for the helmsman to strike the half hours by, with his little bell in the binnacle, where the compass was. And it used to be the great amusement of the sailors to look in through the pane of glass, when they stood at the wheel, and watch the proceedings in the cabin; especially when the steward was setting the table for dinner, or the captain was lounging over a decanter of wine on a little mahogany stand, or playing the game called *solitaire*, at cards, of an evening; for at times he was all alone with his dignity; though, as will ere long be shown, he generally had one pleasant companion, whose society he did not dislike.

The day following my attempt to drop in at the cabin, I happened to be making fast a rope on the quarter-deck, when the captain suddenly made his appearance, promenading up and down, and smoking a cigar. He looked very good-humored and amiable, and it being just after his dinner, I thought that this, to be sure, was just the chance I wanted.

I waited a little while, thinking he would speak to me himself; but as he did not, I went up to him, and began by saying it was a very pleasant day, and hoped he was very well. I never saw a man fly into such a rage; I thought he was going to knock me down; but after standing speechless awhile, he all at once plucked his cap from his head and threw it at me. I don't know what impelled me, but I ran to the lee-scuppers where it fell, picked it up, and gave it to him with a bow; when the mate came running up, and thrust me forward again; and after he had got me as far as the windlass, he wanted to know whether I was crazy or not; for if I was, he would put me in irons right off, and have done with it.

But I assured him I was in my right mind, and knew perfectly well that I had been treated in the most rude and un-gentlemanly manner both by him and Captain Riga. Upon this, he rapped out a great oath, and told me if I ever repeated what I had done that evening, or ever again presumed so much as to lift my hat to the captain, he would tie me into the rigging, and keep me there until I learned better manners. "You are very green," said he, "but I'll ripen you." Indeed this chief mate seemed to have the keeping of the dignity of the captain; who, in some sort, seemed too dignified personally to protect his own dignity.

I thought this strange enough, to be reprimanded, and charged with rudeness for an act of common civility. However, seeing how matters stood, I resolved to let the captain alone for the future, particularly as he had shown himself so deficient in the ordinary breeding of a gentleman. And I could hardly credit it, that this was the same man who had been so very civil, and polite, and witty, when Mr. Jones and I called upon him in port.

But this astonishment of mine was much increased, when some days after, a storm came upon us, and the captain rushed out of the cabin in his nightcap, and nothing else but his shirt on; and leaping up on the poop, began to jump up and down, and curse and swear, and call the men aloft all manner of hard names, just like a common loafer in the street.

Besides all this, too, I noticed that while we were at sea, he wore nothing but old shabby clothes, very different from the glossy suit I had seen him in at our first interview, and after that on the steps of the City Hotel, where he always boarded when in New York. Now, he wore nothing but old-fashioned snuff-colored coats, with high collars and short waists; and faded, short-legged pantaloons, very tight about the knees; and vests, that did not conceal his waistbands, owing to their being so short, just like a little boy's. And his hats were all caved in, and battered, as if they had been knocked about in a cellar; and his boots were sadly patched. Indeed, I began to think that he was but a shabby fellow after all; particularly as his whiskers lost their gloss, and he went days together without shaving; and his hair, by a sort of miracle, began to grow of a pepper and salt color, which might have been owing, though, to his discontinuing the use of some kind of dye while at sea. I put him down as a sort of impostor; and while ashore, a gentleman on false pretenses; for no gentleman would have treated another gentleman as he did me.

Yes, Captain Riga, thought I, you are no gentleman, and you know it!

CHAPTER XV
THE MELANCHOLY STATE OF HIS WARDROBE

And now that I have been speaking of the captain's old clothes, I may as well speak of mine.

It was very early in the month of June that we sailed; and I had greatly rejoiced that it was that time of the year; for it would be warm and pleasant upon the ocean, I thought; and my voyage would be like a summer excursion to the sea shore, for the benefit of the salt water, and a change of scene and society.

So I had not given myself much concern about what I should wear; and deemed it wholly unnecessary to provide myself with a great outfit of pilot-cloth jackets, and browsers, and Guernsey frocks, and oil-skin suits, and sea-boots, and many other things, which old seamen carry in their chests. But one reason was, that I did not have the money to buy them with, even if I had wanted to. So in addition to the clothes I had brought from home, I had only bought a red shirt, a tarpaulin hat, and a belt and knife, as I have previously related, which gave me a sea outfit, something like the Texan rangers', whose uniform, they say, consists of a shirt collar and a pair of spurs.

But I was not many days at sea, when I found that my shore clothing, or *"long togs,"* as the sailors call them, were but ill adapted to the life I now led. When I went aloft, at my yard-arm gymnastics, my pantaloons were all the time ripping and splitting in every direction, particularly about the seat, owing to their not being cut sailor-fashion, with low waistbands, and to wear without suspenders. So that I was often placed in most unpleasant predicaments, straddling the rigging, sometimes in plain sight of the cabin, with my table linen exposed in the most inelegant and ungentlemanly manner possible.

And worse than all, my best pair of pantaloons, and the pair I most prided myself upon, was a very conspicuous and remarkable looking pair.

I had had them made to order by our village tailor, a little fat man, very thin in the legs, and who used to say he imported the latest fashions direct from Paris; though all the fashion plates in his shop were very dirty with fly-marks.

Well, this tailor made the pantaloons I speak of, and while he had them in hand, I used to call and see him two or three times a day to try them on, and hurry him forward; for he was an old man with large round spectacles, and could not see very well, and had no one to help him but a sick wife, with five grandchildren to take care of; and besides that, he was such a great snuff-taker, that it interfered with his business; for he took several pinches for every stitch, and would sit snuffing and blowing his nose over my pantaloons, till I used to get disgusted with him. Now, this old tailor had shown me the pattern, after which he intended to make my pantaloons; but I improved upon it, and bade him have a slit on the outside of each leg, at the foot, to button up with a row of six brass bell buttons; for a grown-up cousin of mine, who was a great sportsman, used to wear a beautiful pair of pantaloons, made precisely in that way.

And these were the very pair I now had at sea; the sailors made a great deal of fun of them, and were all the time calling on each other to "twig" them; and they would ask me to lend them a button or two, by way of a joke; and then they would ask me if I was not a soldier. Showing very plainly that they had no idea that my pantaloons were a very genteel pair, made in the height of the sporting fashion, and copied from my cousin's, who was a young man of fortune and drove a tilbury.

When my pantaloons ripped and tore, as I have said, I did my best to mend and patch them; but not being much of a sempstress, the more I patched the more they parted; because I put my patches on, without heeding the joints of the legs, which only irritated my poor pants the more, and put them out of temper.

Nor must I forget my boots, which were almost new when I left home. They had been my Sunday boots, and fitted me to a charm. I never had had a pair of boots that I liked better; I used to turn my toes out when I walked in them, unless it was night time, when no one could see me, and I had something else to think of; and I used to keep looking at them during church; so that I lost a good deal of the sermon. In a word, they were a beautiful pair of boots. But all this only unfitted them the more for sea-service; as I soon discovered. They had very high heels, which were all the time tripping me in the rigging, and several times came near pitching me overboard; and the salt water made them shrink in such a manner, that they pinched me terribly about the instep; and I was obliged to gash them cruelly, which went to my very heart. The legs were quite long, coming a good way up toward my knees, and the edges were mounted with red morocco. The sailors used to call them my *"gaff-topsail-boots."* And sometimes they used to call me "Boots," and sometimes "Buttons," on account of the ornaments on my pantaloons and shooting-jacket.

At last, I took their advice, and *"razeed"* them, as they phrased it. That is, I amputated the legs, and shaved off the heels to the bare soles; which, however, did not much improve them, for it made my feet feel flat as flounders, and besides, brought me down in the world, and made me slip and slide about the decks, as I used to at home, when I wore straps on the ice.

As for my tarpaulin hat, it was a very cheap one; and therefore proved a real sham and shave; it leaked like an old shingle roof; and in a rain storm, kept my hair wet and disagreeable. Besides, from lying down on deck in it, during the night watches, it got bruised and battered, and lost all its beauty; so that it was unprofitable every way.

But I had almost forgotten my shooting-jacket, which was made of moleskin. Every day, it grew smaller and smaller, particularly after a rain, until at last I thought it would completely exhale, and leave nothing but the bare seams, by way of a skeleton, on my back. It became unspeakably unpleasant, when we got into rather cold weather, crossing the Banks of Newfoundland, when the only way I had to keep warm during the night, was to pull on my waistcoat and my roundabout, and then clap the shooting-jacket over all. This made it pinch me under the arms, and it vexed, irritated, and tormented me every way; and used to incommode my arms seriously when I was pulling the ropes; so much so, that the mate asked me once if I had the cramp.

I may as well here glance at some trials and tribulations of a similar kind. I had no mattress, or bed-clothes, of any sort; for the thought of them had never entered my mind before going to sea; so that I was obliged to sleep on the bare boards of my bunk; and when the ship pitched violently, and almost stood upon end, I must have looked like an Indian baby tied to a plank, and hung up against a tree like a crucifix.

I have already mentioned my total want of table-tools; never dreaming, that, in this respect, going to sea as a sailor was something like going to a boarding-school, where you must furnish your own spoon and knife, fork, and napkin. But at length, I was so happy as to barter with a steerage passenger a silk handkerchief of mine for a half-gallon iron pot, with hooks to it, to hang on a grate; and this pot I used to present at the cook-house for my allowance of coffee and tea. It gave me a good deal of trouble, though, to keep it clean, being much disposed to rust; and the hooks sometimes scratched my face when I was drinking; and it was unusually large and heavy; so that my breakfasts were deprived of all ease and satisfaction, and became a toil and a labor to me. And I was forced to use the same pot for my bean-soup, three times a week, which imparted to it a bad flavor for coffee.

I can not tell how I really suffered in many ways for my improvidence and heedlessness, in going to sea so ill provided with every thing calculated to make my situation at all comfortable, or even tolerable. In time, my wretched "long togs" began to drop off my back, and I looked like a Sam Patch, shambling round the deck in my rags and the wreck of my gaff-topsail-boots. I often thought what my friends at home would have said, if they could but get one peep at me. But I hugged myself in my miserable shooting-jacket, when I considered that that degradation and shame never could overtake me; yet, I thought it a galling mockery, when I remembered that my sisters had promised to tell all inquiring friends, that Wellingborough had gone *"abroad"* just as if I was visiting Europe on a tour with my tutor, as poor simple Mr. Jones had hinted to the captain.

Still, in spite of the melancholy which sometimes overtook me, there were several little incidents that made me forget myself in the contemplation of the strange and to me most wonderful sights of the sea.

And perhaps nothing struck into me such a feeling of wild romance, as a view of the first vessel we spoke. It was of a clear sunny afternoon, and she came bearing down upon us, a most beautiful sight, with all her sails spread wide. She came very near, and passed under our stern; and as she leaned over to the breeze, showed her decks fore and aft; and I saw the strange sailors grouped upon the forecastle, and the cook looking out of his cook-house with a ladle in his hand, and the captain in a green jacket sitting on the taffrail with a speaking-trumpet.

And here, had this vessel come out of the infinite blue ocean, with all these human beings on board, and the smoke tranquilly mounting up into the sea-air from the cook's funnel as if it were a chimney in a city; and every thing looking so cool, and calm, and of-course, in the midst of what to me, at least, seemed a superlative marvel.

Hoisted at her mizzen-peak was a red flag, with a turreted white castle in the middle, which looked foreign enough, and made me stare all the harder.

Our captain, who had put on another hat and coat, and was lounging in an elegant attitude on the poop, now put his high polished brass trumpet to his mouth, and said in a very rude voice for conversation, *"Where from?"*

To which the other captain rejoined with some outlandish Dutch gibberish, of which we could only make out, that the ship belonged to Hamburg, as her flag denoted.

Hamburg!

Bless my soul! and here I am on the great Atlantic Ocean, actually beholding a ship from Holland! It was passing strange. In my intervals of leisure from other duties, I followed the strange ship till she was quite a little speck in the distance.

I could not but be struck with the manner of the two sea-captains during their brief interview. Seated at their ease on their respective "poops" toward the stern of their ships, while the sailors were obeying their behests; they touched hats to each other, exchanged compliments, and drove on, with all the indifference of two Arab horsemen accosting each other on an airing in the Desert. To them, I suppose, the great Atlantic Ocean was a puddle.

CHAPTER XVI
AT DEAD OF NIGHT HE IS SENT UP TO LOOSE THE MAIN-SKYSAIL

I must now run back a little, and tell of my first going aloft at middle watch, when the sea was quite calm, and the breeze was mild.

The order was given to loose the *main-skysail*, which is the fifth and highest sail from deck. It was a very small sail, and from the forecastle looked no bigger than a cambric pocket-handkerchief. But I have heard that some ships carry still smaller sails, above the skysail; called *moon-sails*, and *skyscrapers*, and *cloud-rakers*. But I shall not believe in them till I see them; a *skysail* seems high enough in all conscience; and the idea of any thing higher than that, seems preposterous. Besides, it looks almost like tempting heaven, to brush the very firmament so, and almost put the eyes of the stars out; when a flaw of wind, too, might very soon take the conceit out of these cloud-defying *cloud-rakers*.

Now, when the order was passed to loose the skysail, an old Dutch sailor came up to me, and said, "Buttons, my boy, it's high time you be doing something; and it's boy's business, Buttons, to loose de royals, and not old men's business, like me. Now, d'ye see dat leelle fellow way up dare? *dare*, just behind dem stars dare: well, tumble up, now, Buttons, I zay, and looze him; way you go, Buttons."

All the rest joining in, and seeming unanimous in the opinion, that it was high time for me to be stirring myself, and doing *boy's business*, as they called it, I made no more ado, but jumped into the rigging. Up I went, not daring to look down, but keeping my eyes glued, as it were, to the shrouds, as I ascended.

It was a long road up those stairs, and I began to pant and breathe hard, before I was half way. But I kept at it till I got to the *Jacob's Ladder;* and they may well call it so, for it took me almost into the clouds; and at last, to my own amazement, I found myself hanging on the skysail-yard, holding on might and main to the mast; and curling my feet round the rigging, as if they were another pair of hands.

For a few moments I stood awe-stricken and mute. I could not see far out upon the ocean, owing to the darkness of the night; and from my lofty perch, the sea looked like a great, black gulf, hemmed in, all round, by beetling black cliffs. I seemed all alone; treading the midnight clouds; and every second, expected to find myself falling—falling—falling, as I have felt when the nightmare has been on me.

I could but just perceive the ship below me, like a long narrow plank in the water; and it did not seem to belong at all to the yard, over which I was hanging. A gull, or some sort of sea-fowl, was flying round the truck over my head, within a few yards of my face; and it almost frightened me to hear it; it seemed so much like a spirit, at such a lofty and solitary height.

Though there was a pretty smooth sea, and little wind; yet, at this extreme elevation, the ship's motion was very great; so that when the ship rolled one way, I felt something as a fly must feel, walking the ceiling; and when it rolled the other way, I felt as if I was hanging along a slanting pine-tree.

But presently I heard a distant, hoarse noise from below; and though I could not make out any thing intelligible, I knew it was the mate hurrying me. So in a nervous, trembling desperation, I went to casting off the *gaskets*, or lines tying up the sail; and when all was ready, sung out as I had been told, to *"hoist away!"* And hoist they did, and me too along with the yard and sail; for I had no time to get off, they were so unexpectedly quick about it. It seemed like magic; there I was, going up higher and higher; the yard rising under me, as if it were alive, and no soul in sight. Without knowing it at the time, I was in a good deal of danger, but it was so dark that I could not see well enough to feel afraid—at least on that account; though I felt frightened enough in a promiscuous way. I only held on hard, and made good the saying of old sailors, that the last person to fall overboard from the rigging is a landsman, because he grips the ropes so fiercely; whereas old tars are less careful, and sometimes pay the penalty.

After this feat, I got down rapidly on deck, and received something like a compliment from Max the Dutchman.

This man was perhaps the best natured man among the crew; at any rate, he treated me better than the rest did; and for that reason he deserves some mention.

Max was an old bachelor of a sailor, very precise about his wardrobe, and prided himself greatly upon his seamanship, and entertained some straight-laced, old-fashioned notions about the duties of boys at sea. His hair, whiskers, and cheeks were of a fiery red; and as he wore a red shirt, he was altogether the most combustible looking man I ever saw.

Nor did his appearance belie him; for his temper was very inflammable; and at a word, he would explode in a shower of hard words and imprecations. It was Max that several times set on foot those conspiracies against Jackson, which I have spoken of before; but he ended by paying him a grumbling homage, full of resentful reservations.

Max sometimes manifested some little interest in my welfare; and often discoursed concerning the sorry figure I would cut in my tatters when we got to Liverpool, and the discredit it would bring on the American Merchant Service; for like all European seamen in American ships, Max prided himself not a little upon his naturalization as a Yankee, and if he could, would have been very glad to have passed himself off for a born native.

But notwithstanding his grief at the prospect of my reflecting discredit upon his adopted country, he never offered to better my wardrobe, by loaning me any thing from his own well-stored chest. Like many other well-wishers, he contented him with sympathy. Max also betrayed some anxiety to know whether I knew how to dance; lest, when the ship's company went ashore, I should disgrace them by exposing my awkwardness in some of the sailor saloons. But I relieved his anxiety on that head.

He was a great scold, and fault-finder, and often took me to task about my short-comings; but herein, he was not alone; for every one had a finger, or a thumb, and sometimes both hands, in my unfortunate pie.

CHAPTER XVII
THE COOK AND STEWARD

It was on a Sunday we made the Banks of Newfoundland; a drizzling, foggy, clammy Sunday. You could hardly see the water, owing to the mist and vapor upon it; and every thing was so flat and calm, I almost thought we must have somehow got back to New York, and were lying at the foot of Wall-street again in a rainy twilight. The decks were dripping with wet, so that in the dense fog, it seemed as if we were standing on the roof of a house in a shower.

It was a most miserable Sunday; and several of the sailors had twinges of the rheumatism, and pulled on their monkey-jackets. As for Jackson, he was all the time rubbing his back and snarling like a dog.

I tried to recall all my pleasant, sunny Sundays ashore; and tried to imagine what they were doing at home; and whether our old family friend, Mr. Bridenstoke, would drop in, with his silver-mounted tasseled cane, between churches, as he used to; and whether he would inquire about myself.

But it would not do. I could hardly realize that it was Sunday at all. Every thing went on pretty much the same as before. There was no church to go to; no place to take a walk in; no friend to call upon. I began to think it must be a sort of second Saturday; a foggy Saturday, when school-boys stay at home reading Robinson Crusoe.

The only man who seemed to be taking his ease that day, was our black cook; who according to the invariable custom at sea, always went by the name of *the doctor*.

And *doctors*, cooks certainly are, the very best medicos in the world; for what pestilent pills and potions of the Faculty are half so serviceable to man, and health-and-strength-giving, as roasted lamb and green peas, say, in spring; and roast beef and cranberry sauce in winter? Will a dose of calomel and jalap do you as much good? Will a bolus build up a fainting man? Is there any satisfaction in dining off a powder? But these doctors of the frying-pan sometimes loll men off by a surfeit; or give them the headache, at least. Well, what then? No matter. For if with their most goodly and ten times jolly medicines, they now and then fill our nights with tribulations, and abridge our days, what of the social homicides perpetrated by the Faculty? And when you die by a pill-doctor's hands, it is never with a sweet relish in your mouth, as though you died by a frying-pan-doctor; but your last breath villainously savors of ipecac and rhubarb. Then, what charges they make for the abominable lunches they serve out so stingily! One of their bills for boluses would keep you in good dinners a twelve-month.

Now, our doctor was a serious old fellow, much given to metaphysics, and used to talk about original sin. All that Sunday morning, he sat over his boiling pots, reading out of a book which was very much soiled and covered with grease spots: for he kept it stuck into a little leather strap, nailed to the keg where he kept the fat skimmed off the water in which the salt beef was cooked. I could hardly believe my eyes when I found this book was the Bible.

I loved to peep in upon him, when he was thus absorbed; for his smoky studio or study was a strange-looking place enough; not more than five feet square, and about as many high; a mere box to hold the stove, the pipe of which stuck out of the roof.

Within, it was hung round with pots and pans; and on one side was a little looking-glass, where he used to shave; and on a small shelf were his shaving tools, and a comb and brush. Fronting the stove, and very close to it, was a sort of narrow shelf, where he used to sit with his legs spread out very wide, to keep them from scorching; and there, with his book in one hand, and a pewter spoon in the other, he sat all that Sunday morning, stirring up his pots, and studying away at the same time; seldom taking his eye off the page. Reading must have been very hard work for him; for he muttered to himself quite loud as he read; and big drops of sweat would stand upon his brow, and roll off, till they hissed on the hot stove before him. But on the day I speak of, it was no wonder that he got perplexed, for he was reading a mysterious passage in the Book of Chronicles. Being aware that I knew how to read, he called me as I was passing his premises, and read the passage over, demanding an explanation. I told him it was a mystery that no one could explain; not even a parson. But this did not satisfy him, and I left him poring over it still.

He must have been a member of one of those negro churches, which are to be found in New York. For when we lay at the wharf, I remembered that a committee of three reverend looking old darkies, who, besides their natural canonicals, wore quaker-cut black coats, and broad-brimmed black hats, and white neck-cloths; these colored gentlemen called upon him, and remained conversing with him at his cookhouse door for more than an hour;

and before they went away they stepped inside, and the sliding doors were closed; and then we heard some one reading aloud and preaching; and after that a psalm was sung and a benediction given; when the door opened again, and the congregation came out in a great perspiration; owing, I suppose, to the chapel being so small, and there being only one seat besides the stove.

But notwithstanding his religious studies and meditations, this old fellow used to use some bad language occasionally; particularly of cold, wet stormy mornings, when he had to get up before daylight and make his fire; with the sea breaking over the bows, and now and then dashing into his stove.

So, under the circumstances, you could not blame him much, if he did rip a little, for it would have tried old Job's temper, to be set to work making a fire in the water.

Without being at all neat about his premises, this old cook was very particular about them; he had a warm love and affection for his cook-house. In fair weather, he spread the skirt of an old jacket before the door, by way of a mat; and screwed a small ring-bolt into the door for a knocker; and wrote his name, "Mr. Thompson," over it, with a bit of red chalk.

The men said he lived round the corner of *Forecastle-square,* opposite the *Liberty Pole;* because his cook-house was right behind the foremast, and very near the quarters occupied by themselves.

Sailors have a great fancy for naming things that way on shipboard. When a man is hung at sea, which is always done from one of the lower yard-arms, they say he *"takes a walk up Ladder-lane, and down Hemp-street."*

Mr. Thompson was a great crony of the steward's, who, being a handsome, dandy mulatto, that had once been a barber in West-Broadway, went by the name of Lavender. I have mentioned the gorgeous turban he wore when Mr. Jones and I visited the captain in the cabin. He never wore that turban at sea, though; but sported an uncommon head of frizzled hair, just like the large, round brush, used for washing windows, called a *Pope's Head.*

He kept it well perfumed with Cologne water, of which he had a large supply, the relics of his West-Broadway stock in trade. His clothes, being mostly cast-off suits of the captain of a London liner, whom he had sailed with upon many previous voyages, were all in the height of the exploded fashions, and of every kind of color and cut. He had claret-colored suits, and snuff-colored suits, and red velvet vests, and buff and brimstone pantaloons, and several full suits of black, which, with his dark-colored face, made him look quite clerical; like a serious young colored gentleman of Barbados, about to take orders.

He wore an uncommon large pursy ring on his forefinger, with something he called a real diamond in it; though it was very dim, and looked more like a glass eye than any thing else. He was very proud of his ring, and was always calling your attention to something, and pointing at it with his ornamented finger.

He was a sentimental sort of a darky, and read the *"Three Spaniards,"* and *"Charlotte Temple,"* and carried a lock of frizzled hair in his vest pocket, which he frequently volunteered to show to people, with his handkerchief to his eyes. Every fine evening, about sunset, these two, the cook and steward, used to sit on the little shelf in the cook-house, leaning up against each other like the Siamese twins, to keep from falling off, for the shelf was very short; and there they would stay till after dark, smoking their pipes, and gossiping about the events that had happened during the day in the cabin.

And sometimes Mr. Thompson would take down his Bible, and read a chapter for the edification of Lavender, whom he knew to be a sad profligate and gay deceiver ashore; addicted to every youthful indiscretion. He would read over to him the story of Joseph and Potiphar's wife; and hold Joseph up to him as a young man of excellent principles, whom he ought to imitate, and not be guilty of his indiscretion any more. And Lavender would look serious, and say that he knew it was all true—he was a wicked youth, he knew it—he had broken a good many hearts, and many eyes were weeping for him even then, both in New York, and Liverpool, and London, and Havre. But how could he help it? He hadn't made his handsome face, and fine head of hair, and graceful figure. It was not *he,* but the others, that were to blame; for his bewitching person turned all heads and subdued all hearts, wherever he went. And then he would look very serious and penitent, and go up to the little glass, and pass his hands through his hair, and see how his whiskers were coming on.

CHAPTER XVIII
HE ENDEAVORS TO IMPROVE HIS MIND; AND TELLS OF ONE BLUNT AND HIS DREAM BOOK

On the Sunday afternoon I spoke of, it was my watch below, and I thought I would spend it profitably, in improving my mind.

My bunk was an upper one; and right over the head of it was a *bull's-eye*, or circular piece of thick ground glass, inserted into the deck to give light. It was a dull, dubious light, though; and I often found myself looking up anxiously to see whether the bull's-eye had not suddenly been put out; for whenever any one trod on it, in walking the deck, it was momentarily quenched; and what was still worse, sometimes a coil of rope would be thrown down on it, and stay there till I dressed myself and went up to remove it—a kind of interruption to my studies which annoyed me very much, when diligently occupied in reading.

However, I was glad of any light at all, down in that gloomy hole, where we burrowed like rabbits in a warren; and it was the happiest time I had, when all my messmates were asleep, and I could lie on my back, during a forenoon watch below, and read in comparative quiet and seclusion.

I had already read two books loaned to me by Max, to whose share they had fallen, in dividing the effects of the sailor who had jumped overboard. One was an account of Shipwrecks and Disasters at Sea, and the other was a large black volume, with *Delirium Tremens* in great gilt letters on the back. This proved to be a popular treatise on the subject of that disease; and I remembered seeing several copies in the sailor book-stalls about Fulton Market, and along South-street, in New York.

But this Sunday I got out a book, from which I expected to reap great profit and sound instruction. It had been presented to me by Mr. Jones, who had quite a library, and took down this book from a top shelf, where it lay very dusty. When he gave it to me, he said, that although I was going to sea, I must not forget the importance of a good education; and that there was hardly any situation in life, however humble and depressed, or dark and gloomy, but one might find leisure in it to store his mind, and build himself up in the exact sciences. And he added, that though it *did* look rather unfavorable for my future prospects, to be going to sea as a common sailor so early in life; yet, it would no doubt turn out for my benefit in the end; and, at any rate, if I would only take good care of myself, would give me a sound constitution, if nothing more; and *that* was not to be undervalued, for how many very rich men would give all their bonds and mortgages for my boyish robustness.

He added, that I need not expect any light, trivial work, that was merely entertaining, and nothing more; but here I would find entertainment and edification beautifully and harmoniously combined; and though, at first, I might possibly find it dull, yet, if I perused the book thoroughly, it would soon discover hidden charms and unforeseen attractions; besides teaching me, perhaps, the true way to retrieve the poverty of my family, and again make them all well-to-do in the world.

Saying this, he handed it to me, and I blew the dust off, and looked at the back: *"Smith's Wealth of Nations."* This not satisfying me, I glanced at the title page, and found it was an *"Enquiry into the Nature and Causes"* of the alleged wealth of nations. But happening to look further down, I caught sight of *"Aberdeen,"* where the book was printed; and thinking that any thing from Scotland, a foreign country, must prove some way or other pleasing to me, I thanked Mr. Jones very kindly, and promised to peruse the volume carefully.

So, now, lying in my bunk, I began the book methodically, at page number one, resolved not to permit a few flying glimpses into it, taken previously, to prevent me from making regular approaches to the gist and body of the book, where I fancied lay something like the philosopher's stone, a secret talisman, which would transmute even pitch and tar to silver and gold.

Pleasant, though vague visions of future opulence floated before me, as I commenced the first chapter, entitled *"Of the causes of improvement in the productive power of labor."* Dry as crackers and cheese, to be sure; and the chapter itself was not much better. But this was only getting initiated; and if I read on, the grand secret would be opened to me. So I read on and on, about *"wages and profits of labor,"* without getting any profits myself for my pains in perusing it.

Dryer and dryer; the very leaves smelt of saw-dust; till at last I drank some water, and went at it again. But soon I had to give it up for lost work; and thought that the old backgammon board, we had at home, lettered on the back, *"The History of Rome"* was quite as full of matter, and a great deal more entertaining. I wondered whether Mr. Jones had ever read the volume himself; and could not help remembering, that he had to get on a chair when he reached it down from its dusty shelf; *that* certainly looked suspicious.

The best reading was on the fly leaves; and, on turning them over, I lighted upon some half effaced pencil-marks to the following effect: "*Jonathan Jones, from his particular friend Daniel Dods,* 1798." So it must have originally belonged to Mr. Jones' father; and I wondered whether *he* had ever read it; or, indeed, whether any body had ever read it, even the author himself; but then authors, they say, never read their own books; writing them, being enough in all conscience.

At length I fell asleep, with the volume in my hand; and never slept so sound before; after that, I used to wrap my jacket round it, and use it for a pillow; for which purpose it answered very well; only I sometimes waked up feeling dull and stupid; but of course the book could not have been the cause of that.

And now I am talking of books, I must tell of Jack Blunt the sailor, and his Dream Book.

Jackson, who seemed to know every thing about all parts of the world, used to tell Jack in reproach, that he was an *Irish Cockney*. By which I understood, that he was an Irishman born, but had graduated in London, somewhere about Radcliffe Highway; but he had no sort of brogue that I could hear.

He was a curious looking fellow, about twenty-five years old, as I should judge; but to look at his back, you would have taken him for a little old man. His arms and legs were very large, round, short, and stumpy; so that when he had on his great monkey-jacket, and sou'west cap flapping in his face, and his sea boots drawn up to his knees, he looked like a fat porpoise, standing on end. He had a round face, too, like a walrus; and with about the same expression, half human and half indescribable. He was, upon the whole, a good-natured fellow, and a little given to looking at sea-life romantically; singing songs about susceptible mermaids who fell in love with handsome young oyster boys and gallant fishermen. And he had a sad story about a man-of-war's-man who broke his heart at Portsmouth during the late war, and threw away his life recklessly at one of the quarter-deck cannonades, in the battle between the Guerriere and Constitution; and another incomprehensible story about a sort of fairy sea-queen, who used to be dunning a sea-captain all the time for his autograph to boil in some eel soup, for a spell against the scurvy.

He believed in all kinds of witch-work and magic; and had some wild Irish words he used to mutter over during a calm for a fair wind.

And he frequently related his interviews in Liverpool with a fortune-teller, an old negro woman by the name of De Squak, whose house was much frequented by sailors; and how she had two black cats, with remarkably green eyes, and nightcaps on their heads, solemnly seated on a claw-footed table near the old goblin; when she felt his pulse, to tell what was going to befall him.

This Blunt had a large head of hair, very thick and bushy; but from some cause or other, it was rapidly turning gray; and in its transition state made him look as if he wore a shako of badger skin.

The phenomenon of gray hairs on a young head, had perplexed and confounded this Blunt to such a degree that he at last came to the conclusion it must be the result of the black art, wrought upon him by an enemy; and that enemy, he opined, was an old sailor landlord in Marseilles, whom he had once seriously offended, by knocking him down in a fray.

So while in New York, finding his hair growing grayer and grayer, and all his friends, the ladies and others, laughing at him, and calling him an old man with one foot in the grave, he slipt out one night to an apothecary's, stated his case, and wanted to know what could be done for him.

The apothecary immediately gave him a pint bottle of something he called *"Trafalgar Oil* for restoring the hair," *price one dollar;* and told him that after he had used that bottle, and it did not have the desired effect, he must try bottle No. 2, called *"Balm of Paradise, or the Elixir of the Battle of Copenhagen."* These high-sounding naval names delighted Blunt, and he had no doubt there must be virtue in them.

I saw both bottles; and on one of them was an engraving, representing a young man, presumed to be gray-headed, standing in his night-dress in the middle of his chamber, and with closed eyes applying the Elixir to his head, with both hands; while on the bed adjacent stood a large bottle, conspicuously labeled, *"Balm of Paradise."* It seemed from the text, that this gray-headed young man was so smitten with his hair-oil, and was so thoroughly persuaded of its virtues, that he had got out of bed, even in his sleep; groped into his closet, seized the precious bottle, applied its contents, and then to bed again, getting up in the morning without knowing any thing about it. Which, indeed, was a most mysterious occurrence; and it was still more mysterious, how the engraver came to know an event, of which the actor himself was ignorant, and where there were no bystanders.

Three times in the twenty-four hours, Blunt, while at sea, regularly rubbed in his liniments; but though the first bottle was soon exhausted by his copious applications, and the second half gone, he still stuck to it, that by the time we got to Liverpool, his exertions would be crowned with success. And he was not a little delighted, that this gradual change would be operating while we were at sea; so as not to expose him to the invidious observations of people ashore; on the same principle that dandies go into the country when they purpose raising whiskers. He would often ask his shipmates, whether they noticed any change yet; and if so, how much of a change? And to tell the truth, there was a very great change indeed; for the constant soaking of his hair with oil, operating in conjunction with the neglect of his toilet, and want of a brush and comb, had matted his locks together like a wild horse's mane, and imparted to it a blackish and extremely glossy hue. Besides his collection of hair-oils, Blunt had also provided himself with several boxes of pills, which he had purchased from a sailor doctor in New York, who by placards stuck on the posts along the wharves, advertised to remain standing at the northeast corner of Catharine Market, every Monday and Friday, between the hours of ten and twelve in the morning, to receive calls from patients, distribute medicines, and give advice gratis.

Whether Blunt thought he had the dyspepsia or not, I can not say; but at breakfast, he always took three pills with his coffee; something as they do in Iowa, when the bilious fever prevails; where, at the boarding-houses, they put a vial of blue pills into the castor, along with the pepper and mustard, and next door to another vial of toothpicks. But they are very ill-bred and unpolished in the western country.

Several times, too, Blunt treated himself to a flowing bumper of *horse salts* (Glauber salts); for like many other seamen, he never went to sea without a good supply of that luxury. He would frequently, also, take this medicine in a wet jacket, and then go on deck into a rain storm. But this is nothing to other sailors, who at sea will doctor themselves with calomel off Cape Horn, and still remain on duty. And in this connection, some really frightful stories might be told; but I forbear.

For a landsman to take salts as this Blunt did, it would perhaps be the death of him; but at sea the salt air and the salt water prevent you from catching cold so readily as on land; and for my own part, on board this very ship, being so illy-provided with clothes, I frequently turned into my bunk soaking wet, and turned out again piping hot, and smoking like a roasted sirloin; and yet was never the worse for it; for then, I bore a charmed life of youth and health, and was dagger-proof to bodily ill.

But it is time to tell of the Dream Book. Snugly hidden in one corner of his chest, Blunt had an extraordinary looking pamphlet, with a red cover, marked all over with astrological signs and ciphers, and purporting to be a full and complete treatise on the art of Divination; so that the most simple sailor could teach it to himself.

It also purported to be the selfsame system, by aid of which Napoleon Bonaparte had risen in the world from being a corporal to an emperor. Hence it was entitled the *Bonaparte Dream Book;* for the magic of it lay in the interpretation of dreams, and their application to the foreseeing of future events; so that all preparatory measures might be taken beforehand; which would be exceedingly convenient, and satisfactory every way, if true. The problems were to be cast by means of figures, in some perplexed and difficult way, which, however, was facilitated by a set of tables in the end of the pamphlet, something like the Logarithm Tables at the end of Bowditch's Navigator.

Now, Blunt revered, adored, and worshiped this *Bonaparte Dream Book* of his; and was fully persuaded that between those red covers, and in his own dreams, lay all the secrets of futurity. Every morning before taking his pills, and applying his hair-oils, he would steal out of his bunk before the rest of the watch were awake; take out his pamphlet, and a bit of chalk; and then straddling his chest, begin scratching his oily head to remember his fugitive dreams; marking down strokes on his chest-lid, as if he were casting up his daily accounts.

Though often perplexed and lost in mazes concerning the cabalistic figures in the book, and the chapter of directions to beginners; for he could with difficulty read at all; yet, in the end, if not interrupted, he somehow managed to arrive at a conclusion satisfactory to him. So that, as he generally wore a good-humored expression, no doubt he must have thought, that all his future affairs were working together for the best.

But one night he started us all up in a fright, by springing from his bunk, his eyes ready to start out of his head, and crying, in a husky voice—"Boys! boys! get the benches ready! Quick, quick!"

"What benches?" growled Max—"What's the matter?"

"Benches! benches!" screamed Blunt, without heeding him, "cut down the forests, bear a hand, boys; the Day of Judgment's coming!"

But the next moment, he got quietly into his bunk, and laid still, muttering to himself, he had only been rambling in his sleep.

I did not know exactly what he had meant by his *benches;* till, shortly after, I overheard two of the sailors debating, whether mankind would stand or sit at the Last Day.

CHAPTER XIX
A NARROW ESCAPE

This Dream Book of Blunt's reminds me of a narrow escape we had, early one morning.

It was the larboard watch's turn to remain below from midnight till four o'clock; and having turned in and slept, Blunt suddenly turned out again about three o'clock, with a wonderful dream in his head; which he was desirous of at once having interpreted.

So he goes to his chest, gets out his tools, and falls to ciphering on the lid. When, all at once, a terrible cry was heard, that routed him and all the rest of us up, and sent the whole ship's company flying on deck in the dark. We did not know what it was; but somehow, among sailors at sea, they seem to know when real danger of any land is at hand, even in their sleep.

When we got on deck, we saw the mate standing on the bowsprit, and crying out *Luff! Luff!* to some one in the dark water before the ship. In that direction, we could just see a light, and then, the great black hull of a strange vessel, that was coming down on us obliquely; and so near, that we heard the flap of her topsails as they shook in the wind, the trampling of feet on the deck, and the same cry of *Luff! Luff!* that our own mate, was raising.

In a minute more, I caught my breath, as I heard a snap and a crash, like the fall of a tree, and suddenly, one of our flying-jib guys jerked out the bolt near the cat-head; and presently, we heard our jib-boom thumping against our bows.

Meantime, the strange ship, scraping by us thus, shot off into the darkness, and we saw her no more. But she, also, must have been injured; for when it grew light, we found pieces of strange rigging mixed with ours. We repaired the damage, and replaced the broken spar with another jib-boom we had; for all ships carry spare spars against emergencies.

The cause of this accident, which came near being the death of all on board, was nothing but the drowsiness of the look-out men on the forecastles of both ships. The sailor who had the look-out on our vessel was terribly reprimanded by the mate.

No doubt, many ships that are never heard of after leaving port, meet their fate in this way; and it may be, that sometimes two vessels coming together, jib-boom-and-jib-boom, with a sudden shock in the middle watch of the night, mutually destroy each other; and like fighting elks, sink down into the ocean, with their antlers locked in death.

While I was at Liverpool, a fine ship that lay near us in the docks, having got her cargo on board, went to sea, bound for India, with a good breeze; and all her crew felt sure of a prosperous voyage. But in about seven days after, she came back, a most distressing object to behold. All her starboard side was torn and splintered; her starboard anchor was gone; and a great part of the starboard bulwarks; while every one of the lower yard-arms had been broken, in the same direction; so that she now carried small and unsightly *jury-yards*.

When I looked at this vessel, with the whole of one side thus shattered, but the other still in fine trim; and when I remembered her gay and gallant appearance, when she left the same harbor into which she now entered so forlorn; I could not help thinking of a young man I had known at home, who had left his cottage one morning in high spirits, and was brought back at noon with his right side paralyzed from head to foot.

It seems that this vessel had been run against by a strange ship, crowding all sail before a fresh breeze; and the stranger had rushed past her starboard side, reducing her to the sad state in which she now was.

Sailors can not be too wakeful and cautious, when keeping their night look-outs; though, as I well know, they too often suffer themselves to become negligent, and nod. And this is not so wonderful, after all; for though every seaman has heard of those accidents at sea; and many of them, perhaps, have been in ships that have suffered from them; yet, when you find yourself sailing along on the ocean at night, without having seen a sail for weeks and weeks, it is hard for you to realize that any are near. Then, if they *are* near, it seems almost incredible that on the broad, boundless sea, which washes Greenland at one end of the world, and the Falkland Islands at the other, that any one vessel upon such a vast highway, should come into close contact with another. But the likelihood of great calamities occurring, seldom obtrudes upon the minds of ignorant men, such as sailors generally are; for the things which wise people know, anticipate, and guard against, the ignorant can only become acquainted with, by meeting them face to face. And even when experience has taught them, the lesson only serves for that day; inasmuch as the foolish in prosperity are infidels to the possibility of adversity; they see the sun in heaven, and believe it to be far too bright ever to set. And even, as suddenly as the bravest and fleetest ships, while careering in pride of canvas over the sea, have been struck, as by lightning, and quenched out of sight; even so, do some lordly men, with all their plans and prospects gallantly trimmed to the fair, rushing breeze of life, and with no thought of death and disaster, suddenly encounter a shock unforeseen, and go down, foundering, into death.

CHAPTER XX
IN A FOG HE IS SET TO WORK AS A BELL-TOLLER, AND BEHOLDS A HERD OF OCEAN-ELEPHANTS

What is this that we sail through? What palpable obscure? What smoke and reek, as if the whole steaming world were revolving on its axis, as a spit?

It is a Newfoundland Fog; and we are yet crossing the Grand Banks, wrapt in a mist, that no London in the Novemberest November ever equaled. The chronometer pronounced it noon; but do you call this midnight or midday? So dense is the fog, that though we have a fair wind, we shorten sail for fear of accidents; and not only that, but here am I, poor Wellingborough, mounted aloft on a sort of belfry, the top of the *"Sampson-Post,"* a lofty tower of timber, so called; and tolling the ship's bell, as if for a funeral.

This is intended to proclaim our approach, and warn all strangers from our track.

Dreary sound! toll, toll, toll, through the dismal mist and fog.

The bell is green with verdigris, and damp with dew; and the little cord attached to the clapper, by which I toll it, now and then slides through my fingers, slippery with wet. Here I am, in my slouched black hat, like the *"bull that could pull,"* announcing the decease of the lamented Cock-Robin.

A better device than the bell, however, was once pitched upon by an ingenious sea-captain, of whom I have heard. He had a litter of young porkers on board; and while sailing through the fog, he stationed men at both ends of the pen with long poles, wherewith they incessantly stirred up and irritated the porkers, who split the air with their squeals; and no doubt saved the ship, as the geese saved the Capitol.

The most strange and unheard-of noises came out of the fog at times: a vast sound of sighing and sobbing. What could it be? This would be followed by a spout, and a gush, and a cascading commotion, as if some fountain had suddenly jetted out of the ocean.

Seated on my Sampson-Post, I stared more and more, and suspended my duty as a sexton. But presently some one cried out—*"There she blows! whales! whales close alongside!"*

A whale! Think of it! whales close to *me*, Wellingborough;— would my own brother believe it? I dropt the clapper as if it were red-hot, and rushed to the side; and there, dimly floating, lay four or five long, black snaky-looking shapes, only a few inches out of the water.

Can these be whales? Monstrous whales, such as I had heard of? I thought they would look like mountains on the sea; hills and valleys of flesh! regular krakens, that made it high tide, and inundated continents, when they descended to feed!

It was a bitter disappointment, from which I was long in recovering. I lost all respect for whales; and began to be a little dubious about the story of Jonah; for how could Jonah reside in such an insignificant tenement; how could he have had elbow-room there? But perhaps, thought I, the whale which according to Rabbinical traditions was a female one, might have expanded to receive him like an anaconda, when it swallows an elk and leaves the antlers sticking out of its mouth.

Nevertheless, from that day, whales greatly fell in my estimation.

But it is always thus. If you read of St. Peter's, they say, and then go and visit it, ten to one, you account it a dwarf compared to your high-raised ideal. And, doubtless, Jonah himself must have been disappointed when he looked up to the domed midriff surmounting the whale's belly, and surveyed the ribbed pillars around him. A pretty large belly, to be sure, thought he, but not so big as it might have been.

On the next day, the fog lifted; and by noon, we found ourselves sailing through fleets of fishermen at anchor. They were very small craft; and when I beheld them, I perceived the force of that sailor saying, intended to illustrate restricted quarters, or being *on the limits. It is like a fisherman's walk*, say they, *three steps and overboard.*

Lying right in the track of the multitudinous ships crossing the ocean between England and America, these little vessels are sometimes run down, and obliterated from the face of the waters; the cry of the sailors ceasing with the last whirl of the whirlpool that closes over their craft. Their sad fate is frequently the result of their own remissness in keeping a good look-out by day, and not having their lamps trimmed, like the wise virgins, by night.

As I shall not make mention of the Grand Banks on our homeward-bound passage, I may as well here relate, that on our return, we approached them in the night; and by way of making sure of our whereabouts, the deep-sea-lead was heaved. The line attached is generally upward of three hundred fathoms in length; and the lead itself, weighing some forty or fifty pounds, has a hole in the lower end, in which, previous to sounding, some tallow is thrust, that it may bring up the soil at the bottom, for the captain to inspect. This is called "arming" the lead.

We "hove" our deep-sea-line by night, and the operation was very interesting, at least to me. In the first place, the vessel's heading was stopt; then, coiled away in a tub, like a whale-rope, the line was placed toward the after part of the quarter-deck; and one of the sailors carried the lead outside of the ship, away along to the end of the jib-boom, and at the word of command, far ahead and overboard it went, with a plunge; scraping by the side, till it came to the stern, when the line ran out of the tub like light.

When we came to haul *it* up, I was astonished at the force necessary to perform the work. The whole watch pulled at the line, which was rove through a block in the mizzen-rigging, as if we were hauling up a fat porpoise. When the lead came in sight, I was all eagerness to examine the tallow, and get a peep at a specimen of the bottom of the sea; but the sailors did not seem to be much interested by it, calling me a fool for wanting to preserve a few grains of the sand.

I had almost forgotten to make mention of the Gulf Stream, in which we found ourselves previous to crossing the Banks. The fact of our being in it was proved by the captain in person, who superintended the drawing of a bucket of salt water, in which he dipped his thermometer. In the absence of the Gulf-weed, this is the general test; for the temperature of this current is eight degrees higher than that of the ocean, and the temperature of the ocean is twenty degrees higher than that of the Grand Banks. And it is to this remarkable difference of temperature, for which there can be no equilibrium, that many seamen impute the fogs on the coast of Nova Scotia and Newfoundland; but why there should always be such ugly weather in the Gulf, is something that I do not know has ever been accounted for.

It is curious to dip one's finger in a bucket full of the Gulf Stream, and find it so warm; as if the Gulf of Mexico, from whence this current comes, were a great caldron or boiler, on purpose to keep warm the North Atlantic, which is traversed by it for a distance of two thousand miles, as some large halls in winter are by hot air tubes. Its mean breadth being about two hundred leagues, it comprises an area larger than that of the whole Mediterranean, and may be deemed a sort of Mississippi of hot water flowing through the ocean; off the coast of Florida, running at the rate of one mile and a half an hour.

CHAPTER XXI
A WHALEMAN AND A MAN-OF-WAR'S-MAN

The sight of the whales mentioned in the preceding chapter was the bringing out of Larry, one of our crew, who hitherto had been quite silent and reserved, as if from some conscious inferiority, though he had shipped as an *ordinary seaman*, and, for aught I could see, performed his duty very well.

When the men fell into a dispute concerning what kind of whales they were which we saw, Larry stood by attentively, and after garnering in their ignorance, all at once broke out, and astonished every body by his intimate acquaintance with the monsters.

"They ar'n't sperm whales," said Larry, "their spouts ar'n't bushy enough; they ar'n't Sulphur-bottoms, or they wouldn't stay up so long; they ar'n't Hump-backs, for they ar'n't got any humps; they ar'n't Fin-backs, for you won't catch a Finback so near a ship; they ar'n't Greenland whales, for we ar'n't off the coast of Greenland; and they ar'n't right whales, for it wouldn't be right to say so. I tell ye, men, them's Crinkum-crankum whales."

"And what are them?" said a sailor.

"Why, them is whales that can't be cotched."

Now, as it turned out that this Larry had been bred to the sea in a whaler, and had sailed out of Nantucket many times; no one but Jackson ventured to dispute his opinion; and even Jackson did not press him very hard. And ever after, Larry's judgment was relied upon concerning all strange fish that happened to float by us during the voyage; for whalemen are far more familiar with the wonders of the deep than any other class of seaman.

This was Larry's first voyage in the merchant service, and that was the reason why, hitherto, he had been so reserved; since he well knew that merchant seamen generally affect a certain superiority to *"blubber-boilers,"* as they contemptuously style those who hunt the leviathan. But Larry turned out to be such an inoffensive fellow, and so well understood his business aboard ship, and was so ready to jump to an order, that he was exempted from the taunts which he might otherwise have encountered.

He was a somewhat singular man, who wore his hat slanting forward over the bridge of his nose, with his eyes cast down, and seemed always examining your boots, when speaking to you. I loved to hear him talk about the wild places in the Indian Ocean, and on the coast of Madagascar, where he had frequently touched during his whaling voyages. And this familiarity with the life of nature led by the people in that remote part of the world, had furnished Larry with a sentimental distaste for civilized society. When opportunity offered, he never omitted extolling the delights of the free and easy Indian Ocean.

"Why," said Larry, talking through his nose, as usual, "in *Madagasky* there, they don't wear any togs at all, nothing but a bowline round the midships; they don't have no dinners, but keeps a dinin' all day off fat pigs and dogs; they don't go to bed any where, but keeps a noddin' all the time; and they gets drunk, too, from some first rate arrack they make from cocoa-nuts; and smokes plenty of 'baccy, too, I tell ye. Fine country, that! Blast Ameriky, I say!"

To tell the truth, this Larry dealt in some illiberal insinuations against civilization.

"And what's the use of bein' *snivelized!*" said he to me one night during our watch on deck; "snivelized chaps only learns the way to take on 'bout life, and snivel. You don't see any Methodist chaps feelin' dreadful about their souls; you don't see any darned beggars and pesky constables in *Madagasky*, I tell ye; and none o' them kings there gets their big toes pinched by the gout. Blast Ameriky, I say."

Indeed, this Larry was rather cutting in his innuendoes.

"Are *you* now, Buttons, any better off for bein' snivelized?" coming close up to me and eying the wreck of my gaff-topsail-boots very steadfastly. "No; you ar'n't a bit—but you're a good deal *worse* for it, Buttons. I tell ye, ye wouldn't have been to sea here, leadin' this dog's life, if you hadn't been snivelized—that's the cause why, now. Snivelization has been the ruin on ye; and it's spiled me complete; I might have been a great man in Madagasky; it's too darned bad! Blast Ameriky, I say." And in bitter grief at the social blight upon his whole past, present, and future, Larry turned away, pulling his hat still lower down over the bridge of his nose.

In strong contrast to Larry, was a young man-of-war's man we had, who went by the name of *"Gun-Deck,"* from his always talking of sailor life in the navy. He was a little fellow with a small face and a prodigious mop of brown hair; who always dressed in man-of-war style, with a wide, braided collar to his frock, and Turkish trowsers. But he particularly prided himself upon his feet, which were quite small; and when we washed down decks of a morning, never mind how chilly it might be, he always took off his boots, and went paddling about like a duck, turning out his pretty toes to show his charming feet.

He had served in the armed steamers during the Seminole War in Florida, and had a good deal to say about sailing up the rivers there, through the everglades, and popping off Indians on the banks. I remember his telling a story about a party being discovered at quite a distance from them; but one of the savages was made very conspicuous by a pewter plate, which he wore round his neck, and which glittered in the sun. This plate proved his death; for, according to *Gun-Deck*, he himself shot it through the middle, and the ball entered the wearer's heart. It was a rat-killing war, he said.

Gun-Deck had touched at Cadiz: had been to Gibraltar; and ashore at Marseilles. He had sunned himself in the Bay of Naples: eaten figs and oranges in Messina; and cheerfully lost one of his hearts at Malta, among the ladies there. And about all these things, he talked like a romantic man-of-war's man, who had seen the civilized world, and loved it; found it good, and a comfortable place to live in. So he and Larry never could agree in their respective views of civilization, and of savagery, of the Mediterranean and *Madagasky*.

CHAPTER XXII
THE HIGHLANDER PASSES A WRECK

We were still on the Banks, when a terrific storm came down upon us, the like of which I had never before beheld, or imagined. The rain poured down in sheets and cascades; the scupper holes could hardly carry it off the decks; and in bracing the yards we waded about almost up to our knees; every thing floating about, like chips in a dock.

This violent rain was the precursor of a hard squall, for which we duly prepared, taking in our canvas to double-reefed-top-sails.

The tornado came rushing along at last, like a troop of wild horses before the flaming rush of a burning prairie. But after bowing and cringing to it awhile, the good Highlander was put off before it; and with her nose in the water, went wallowing on, ploughing milk-white waves, and leaving a streak of illuminated foam in her wake.

It was an awful scene. It made me catch my breath as I gazed. I could hardly stand on my feet, so violent was the motion of the ship. But while I reeled to and fro, the sailors only laughed at me; and bade me look out that the ship did not fall overboard; and advised me to get a handspike, and hold it down hard in the weather-scuppers, to steady her wild motions. But I was now getting a little too wise for this foolish kind of talk; though all through the voyage, they never gave it over.

This storm past, we had fair weather until we got into the Irish Sea.

The morning following the storm, when the sea and sky had become blue again, the man aloft sung out that there was a wreck on the lee-beam. We bore away for it, all hands looking eagerly toward it, and the captain in the mizzen-top with his spy-glass. Presently, we slowly passed alongside of it.

It was a dismantled, water-logged schooner, a most dismal sight, that must have been drifting about for several long weeks. The bulwarks were pretty much gone; and here and there the bare *stanchions*, or posts, were left standing, splitting in two the waves which broke clear over the deck, lying almost even with the sea. The foremast was snapt off less than four feet from its base; and the shattered and splintered remnant looked like the stump of a pine tree thrown over in the woods. Every time she rolled in the trough of the sea, her open main-hatchway yawned into view; but was as quickly filled, and submerged again, with a rushing, gurgling sound, as the water ran into it with the lee-roll.

At the head of the stump of the mainmast, about ten feet above the deck, something like a sleeve seemed nailed; it was supposed to be the relic of a jacket, which must have been fastened there by the crew for a signal, and been frayed out and blown away by the wind.

Lashed, and leaning over sideways against the taffrail, were three dark, green, grassy objects, that slowly swayed with every roll, but otherwise were motionless. I saw the captain's, glass directed toward them, and heard him say at last, "They must have been dead a long time." These were sailors, who long ago had lashed themselves to the taffrail for safety; but must have famished.

Full of the awful interest of the scene, I surely thought the captain would lower a boat to bury the bodies, and find out something about the schooner. But we did not stop at all; passing on our course, without so much as learning the schooner's name, though every one supposed her to be a New Brunswick lumberman.

On the part of the sailors, no surprise was shown that our captain did not send off a boat to the wreck; but the steerage passengers were indignant at what they called his barbarity. For me, I could not but feel amazed and shocked at his indifference; but my subsequent sea experiences have shown me, that such conduct as this is very common, though not, of course, when human life can be saved.

So away we sailed, and left her; drifting, drifting on; a garden spot for barnacles, and a playhouse for the sharks.

"Look there," said Jackson, hanging over the rail and coughing—"look there; that's a sailor's coffin. Ha! ha! Buttons," turning round to me—"how do you like that, Buttons? Wouldn't you like to take a sail with them 'ere dead men? Wouldn't it be nice?" And then he tried to laugh, but only coughed again. "Don't laugh at dem poor fellows," said Max, looking grave; "do' you see dar bodies, dar souls are farder off dan de Cape of Dood Hope."

"Dood Hope, Dood Hope," shrieked Jackson, with a horrid grin, mimicking the Dutchman, "dare is no dood hope for dem, old boy; dey are drowned and d .... d, as you and I will be, Red Max, one of dese dark nights."

"No, no," said Blunt, "all sailors are saved; they have plenty of squalls here below, but fair weather aloft."

"And did you get that out of your silly Dream Book, you Greek?" howled Jackson through a cough. "Don't talk of heaven to me—it's a lie—I know it—and they are all fools that believe in it. Do you think, you Greek, that there's any heaven for *you?* Will they let *you* in there, with that tarry hand, and that oily head of hair? Avast! when some shark gulps you down his hatchway one of these days, you'll find, that by dying, you'll only go from one gale of wind to another; mind that, you Irish cockney! Yes, you'll be bolted down like one of your own pills: and I should like to see the whole ship swallowed down in the Norway maelstrom, like a box on 'em. That would be a dose of salts for ye!" And so saying, he went off, holding his hands to his chest, and coughing, as if his last hour was come.

Every day this Jackson seemed to grow worse and worse, both in body and mind. He seldom spoke, but to contradict, deride, or curse; and all the time, though his face grew thinner and thinner, his eyes seemed to kindle more and more, as if he were going to die out at last, and leave them burning like tapers before a corpse.

Though he had never attended churches, and knew nothing about Christianity; no more than a Malay pirate; and though he could not read a word, yet he was spontaneously an atheist and an infidel; and during the long night watches, would enter into arguments, to prove that there was nothing to be believed; nothing to be loved, and nothing worth living for; but every thing to be hated, in the wide world. He was a horrid desperado; and like a wild Indian, whom he resembled in his tawny skin and high cheek bones, he seemed to run amuck at heaven and earth. He was a Cain afloat; branded on his yellow brow with some inscrutable curse; and going about corrupting and searing every heart that beat near him.

But there seemed even more woe than wickedness about the man; and his wickedness seemed to spring from his woe; and for all his hideousness, there was that in his eye at times, that was ineffably pitiable and touching; and though there were moments when I almost hated this Jackson, yet I have pitied no man as I have pitied him.

CHAPTER XXIII
AN UNACCOUNTABLE CABIN-PASSENGER, AND A MYSTERIOUS YOUNG LADY

As yet, I have said nothing special about the passengers we carried out. But before making what little mention I shall of them, you must know that the Highlander was not a Liverpool liner, or packet-ship, plying in connection with a sisterhood of packets, at stated intervals, between the two ports. No: she was only what is called a *regular trader* to Liverpool; sailing upon no fixed days, and acting very much as she pleased, being bound by no obligations of any kind: though in all her voyages, ever having New York or Liverpool for her destination. Merchant vessels which are neither liners nor regular traders, among sailors come under the general head of *transient ships*; which implies that they are here to-day, and somewhere else to-morrow, like Mullins's dog.

But I had no reason to regret that the Highlander was not a liner; for aboard of those liners, from all I could gather from those who had sailed in them, the crew have terrible hard work, owing to their carrying such a press of sail, in order to make as rapid passages as possible, and sustain the ship's reputation for speed. Hence it is, that although they are the very best of sea-going craft, and built in the best possible manner, and with the very best materials, yet, a few years of scudding before the wind, as they do, seriously impairs their constitutions— like robust young men, who live too fast in their teens—and they are soon sold out for a song; generally to the people of Nantucket, New Bedford, and Sag Harbor, who repair and fit them out for the whaling business.

Thus, the ship that once carried over gay parties of ladies and gentlemen, as tourists, to Liverpool or London, now carries a crew of harpooners round Cape Horn into the Pacific. And the mahogany and bird's-eye maple cabin, which once held rosewood card-tables and brilliant coffee-urns, and in which many a bottle of champagne, and many a bright eye sparkled, *now* accommodates a bluff Quaker captain from Martha's Vineyard; who, perhaps, while lying with his ship in the Bay of Islands, in New Zealand, entertains a party of naked chiefs and savages at dinner, in place of the packet-captain doing the honors to the literati, theatrical stars, foreign princes, and gentlemen of leisure and fortune, who generally talked gossip, politics, and nonsense across the table, in transatlantic trips. The broad quarter-deck, too, where these gentry promenaded, is now often choked up by the enormous head of the sperm-whale, and vast masses of unctuous blubber; and every where reeks with oil during the prosecution of the fishery. Sic *transit gloria mundi!* Thus departs the pride and glory of packet-ships! *It is* like a broken down importer of French silks embarking in the soap-boning business.

So, not being a liner, the Highlander of course did not have very ample accommodations for cabin passengers. I believe there were not more than five or six state-rooms, with two or three berths in each. At any rate, on this particular voyage she only carried out one regular cabin-passenger; that is, a person previously unacquainted with the captain, who paid his fare down, and came on board soberly, and in a business-like manner with his baggage.

He was an extremely little man, that solitary cabin-passenger—the passenger who came on board in a business-like manner with his baggage; never spoke to any one, and the captain seldom spoke to him.

Perhaps he was a deputy from the Deaf and Dumb Institution in New York, going over to London to address the public in pantomime at Exeter Hall concerning the signs of the times.

He was always in a brown study; sometimes sitting on the quarter-deck with arms folded, and head hanging upon his chest. Then he would rise, and gaze out to windward, as if he had suddenly discovered a friend. But looking disappointed, would retire slowly into his state-room, where you could see him through the little window, in an irregular sitting position, with the back part of him inserted into his berth, and his head, arms, and legs hanging out, buried in profound meditation, with his fore-finger aside of his nose. He never was seen reading; never took a hand at cards; never smoked; never drank wine; never conversed; and never staid to the dessert at dinner-time.

He seemed the true microcosm, or little world to himself: standing in no need of levying contributions upon the surrounding universe. Conjecture was lost in speculating as to who he was, and what was his business. The sailors, who are always curious with regard to such matters, and criticise cabin-passengers more than cabin-passengers are perhaps aware at the time, completely exhausted themselves in suppositions, some of which are characteristically curious.

One of the crew said he was a mysterious bearer of secret dispatches to the English court; others opined that he was a traveling surgeon and bonesetter, but for what reason they thought so, I never could learn; and others declared that he must either be an unprincipled bigamist, flying from his last wife and several small children; or a scoundrelly forger, bank-robber, or general burglar, who was returning to his beloved country with his ill-gotten booty. One observing sailor was of opinion that he was an English murderer, overwhelmed with speechless remorse, and returning home to make a full confession and be hanged.

But it was a little singular, that among all their sage and sometimes confident opinions, not one charitable one was made; no! they were all sadly to the prejudice of his moral and religious character. But this is the way all the world over. Miserable man! could you have had an inkling of what they thought of you, I know not what you would have done.

However, not knowing any thing about these surmisings and suspicions, this mysterious cabin-passenger went on his way, calm, cool, and collected; never troubled any body, and nobody troubled him. Sometimes, of a moonlight night he glided about the deck, like the ghost of a hospital attendant; flitting from mast to mast; now hovering round the skylight, now vibrating in the vicinity of the binnacle. Blunt, the Dream Book tar, swore he was a magician; and took an extra dose of salts, by way of precaution against his spells.

When we were but a few days from port, a comical adventure befell this cabin-passenger. There is an old custom, still in vogue among some merchant sailors, of tying fast in the rigging any lubberly landsman of a passenger who may be detected taking excursions aloft, however moderate the flight of the awkward fowl. This is called *"making a spread eagle"* of the man; and before he is liberated, a promise is exacted, that before arriving in port, he shall furnish the ship's company with money enough for a treat all round.

Now this being one of the perquisites of sailors, they are always on the keen look-out for an opportunity of levying such contributions upon incautious strangers; though they never attempt it in presence of the captain; as for the mates, they purposely avert their eyes, and are earnestly engaged about something else, whenever they get an inkling of this proceeding going on. But, with only one poor fellow of a cabin-passenger on board of the Highlander, and *he* such a quiet, unobtrusive, unadventurous wight, there seemed little chance for levying contributions.

One remarkably pleasant morning, however, what should be seen, half way up the mizzen rigging, but the figure of our cabin-passenger, holding on with might and main by all four limbs, and with his head fearfully turned round, gazing off to the horizon. He looked as if he had the nightmare;

and in some sudden and unaccountable fit of insanity, he must have been impelled to the taking up of that perilous position.

"Good heavens!" said the mate, who was a bit of a wag, "you will surely fall, sir! Steward, spread a mattress on deck, under the gentleman!"

But no sooner was our Greenland sailor's attention called to the sight, than snatching up some rope-yarn, he ran softly up behind the passenger, and without speaking a word, began binding him hand and foot. The stranger was more dumb than ever with amazement; at last violently remonstrated; but in vain; for as his fearfulness of falling made him keep his hands glued to the ropes, and so prevented him from any effectual resistance, he was soon made a handsome *spread-eagle* of, to the great satisfaction of the crew.

It was now discovered for the first, that this singular passenger stammered and stuttered very badly, which, perhaps, was the cause of his reservedness.

"Wha-wha-what i-i-is this f-f-for?"

"Spread-eagle, sir," said the Greenlander, thinking that those few words would at once make the matter plain.

"Wha-wha-what that me-me-mean?"

"Treats all round, sir," said the Greenlander, wondering at the other's obtusity, who, however, had never so much as heard of the thing before.

At last, upon his reluctant acquiescence in the demands of the sailor, and handing him two half-crown pieces, the unfortunate passenger was suffered to descend.

The last I ever saw of this man was his getting into a cab at Prince's Dock Gates in Liverpool, and driving off alone to parts unknown. He had nothing but a valise with him, and an umbrella; but his pockets looked stuffed out; perhaps he used them for carpet-bags.

I must now give some account of another and still more mysterious, though very different, sort of an occupant of the cabin, of whom I have previously hinted. What say you to a charming young girl?—just the girl to sing the Dashing White Sergeant; a martial, military-looking girl; her father must have been a general. Her hair was auburn; her eyes were blue; her cheeks were white and red; and Captain Riga was her most devoted.

To the curious questions of the sailors concerning who she was, the steward used to answer, that she was the daughter of one of the Liverpool dock-masters, who, for the benefit of her health and the improvement of her mind, had sent her out to America in the Highlander, under the captain's charge, who was his particular friend; and that now the young lady was returning home from her tour.

And truly the captain proved an attentive father to her, and often promenaded with her hanging on his arm, past the forlorn bearer of secret dispatches, who would look up now and then out of his reveries, and cast a furtive glance of wonder, as if he thought the captain was audacious.

Considering his beautiful ward, I thought the captain behaved ungallantly, to say the least, in availing himself of the opportunity of her charming society, to wear out his remaining old clothes; for no gentleman ever pretends to save his best coat when a lady is in the case; indeed, he generally thirsts for a chance to abase it, by converting it into a pontoon over a puddle, like Sir Walter Raleigh, that the ladies may not soil the soles of their dainty slippers. But this Captain Riga was no Raleigh, and hardly any sort of a true gentleman whatever, as I have formerly declared. Yet, perhaps, he might have worn his old clothes in this instance, for the express purpose of proving, by his disdain for the toilet, that he was nothing but the young lady's guardian; for many guardians do not care one fig how shabby they look.

But for all this, the passage out was one long paternal sort of a shabby flirtation between this hoydenish nymph and the ill-dressed captain. And surely, if her good mother, were she living, could have seen this young lady, she would have given her an endless lecture for her conduct, and a copy of Mrs. Ellis's Daughters of England to read and digest. I shall say no more of this anonymous nymph; only, that when we arrived at Liverpool, she issued from her cabin in a richly embroidered silk dress, and lace hat and veil, and a sort of Chinese umbrella or parasol, which one of the sailors declared "spandangalous;" and the captain followed after in his best broadcloth and beaver, with a gold-headed cane; and away they went in a carriage, and that was the last of her; I hope she is well and happy now; but I have some misgivings.

It now remains to speak of the steerage passengers. There were not more than twenty or thirty of them, mostly mechanics, returning home, after a prosperous stay in America, to escort their wives and families back. These were the only occupants of the steerage that I ever knew of; till early one morning, in the gray dawn, when we made Cape Clear, the south point of Ireland, the apparition of a tall Irishman, in a shabby shirt of bed-ticking, emerged from the fore hatchway, and stood leaning on the rail, looking landward with a fixed, reminiscent expression, and diligently scratching its back with both hands. We all started at the sight, for no one had ever seen the apparition before; and when we remembered that it must have been burrowing all the passage down in its bunk, the only probable reason of its so manipulating its back became shockingly obvious.

I had almost forgotten another passenger of ours, a little boy not four feet high, an English lad, who, when we were about forty-eight hours from New York, suddenly appeared on deck, asking for something to eat.

It seems he was the son of a carpenter, a widower, with this only child, who had gone out to America in the Highlander some six months previous, where he fell to drinking, and soon died, leaving the boy a friendless orphan in a foreign land.

For several weeks the boy wandered about the wharves, picking up a precarious livelihood by sucking molasses out of the casks discharged from West India ships, and occasionally regaling himself upon stray oranges and lemons found floating in the docks. He passed his nights sometimes in a stall in the markets, sometimes in an empty hogshead on the piers, sometimes in a doorway, and once in the watchhouse, from which he escaped the next morning, running as he told me, right between the doorkeeper's legs, when he was taking another vagrant to task for repeatedly throwing himself upon the public charities.

At last, while straying along the docks, he chanced to catch sight of the Highlander, and immediately recognized her as the very ship which brought him and his father out from England. He at once resolved to return in her; and, accosting the captain, stated his case, and begged a passage. The captain refused to give it; but, nothing daunted, the heroic little fellow resolved to conceal himself on board previous to the ship's sailing; which he did, stowing himself away in the *between-decks*; and moreover, as he told us, in a narrow space between two large casks of water, from which he now and then thrust out his head for air. And once a steerage passenger rose in the night and poked in and rattled about a stick where he was, thinking him an uncommon large rat, who was after stealing a passage across the Atlantic. There are plenty of passengers of that kind continually plying between Liverpool and New York.

As soon as he divulged the fact of his being on board, which he took care should not happen till he thought the ship must be out of sight of land; the captain had him called aft, and after giving him a thorough shaking, and threatening to toss him overboard as a tit-bit for *John Shark*, he told the mate to send him forward among the sailors, and let him live there. The sailors received him with open arms; but before caressing him much, they gave him a thorough washing in the lee-scuppers, when he turned out to be quite a handsome lad, though thin and pale with the hardships he had suffered.

However, by good nursing and plenty to eat, he soon improved and grew fat; and before many days was as fine a looking little fellow, as you might pick out of Queen Victoria's nursery. The sailors took the warmest interest in him. One made him a little hat with a long ribbon; another a little jacket; a third a comical little pair of man-of-war's-man's trowsers; so that in the end, he looked like a juvenile boatswain's mate. Then the cook furnished him with a little tin pot and pan; and the steward made him a present of a pewter tea-spoon; and a steerage passenger gave him a jack knife. And thus provided, he used to sit at meal times half way up on the forecastle ladder, making a great racket with his pot and pan, and merry as a cricket. He was an uncommonly fine, cheerful, clever, arch little fellow, only six years old, and it was a thousand pities that he should be abandoned, as he was. Who can say, whether he is fated to be a convict in New South Wales, or a member of Parliament for Liverpool? When we got to that port, by the way, a purse was made up for him; the captain, officers, and the mysterious cabin passenger contributing their best wishes, and the sailors and poor steerage passengers something like fifteen dollars in cash and tobacco. But I had almost forgot to add that the daughter of the dock-master gave him a fine lace pocket-handkerchief and a card-case to remember her by; very valuable, but somewhat inappropriate presents. Thus supplied, the little hero went ashore by himself; and I lost sight of him in the vast crowds thronging the docks of Liverpool.

I must here mention, as some relief to the impression which Jackson's character must have made upon the reader, that in several ways he at first befriended this boy; but the boy always shrunk from him; till, at last, stung by his conduct, Jackson spoke to him no more; and seemed to hate him, harmless as he was, along with all the rest of the world.

As for the Lancashire lad, he was a stupid sort of fellow, as I have before hinted. So, little interest was taken in him, that he was permitted to go ashore at last, without a good-by from any person but one.

CHAPTER XXIV
HE BEGINS TO HOP ABOUT IN THE RIGGING LIKE A SAINT JAGO'S MONKEY

But we have not got to Liverpool yet; though, as there is little more to be said concerning the passage out, the Highlander may as well make sail and get there as soon as possible. The brief interval will perhaps be profitably employed in relating what progress I made in learning the duties of a sailor.

After my heroic feat in loosing the main-skysail, the mate entertained good hopes of my becoming a rare mariner. In the fullness of his heart, he ordered me to turn over the superintendence of the chicken-coop to the Lancashire boy; which I did, very willingly. After that, I took care to show the utmost alacrity in running aloft, which by this time became mere fun for me; and nothing delighted me more than to sit on one of the topsail-yards, for hours together, helping Max or the Greenlander as they worked at the rigging.

At sea, the sailors are continually engaged in *"parcelling," "serving,"* and in a thousand ways ornamenting and repairing the numberless shrouds and stays; mending sails, or turning one side of the deck into a rope-walk, where they manufacture a clumsy sort of twine, called *spun-yarn*. This is spun with a winch; and many an hour the Lancashire boy had to play the part of an engine, and contribute the motive power. For material, they use odds and ends of old rigging called *"junk,"* the yarns of which are picked to pieces, and then twisted into new combinations, something as most books are manufactured. This "junk" is bought at the junk shops along the wharves; outlandish looking dens, generally subterranean, full of old iron, old shrouds, spars, rusty blocks, and superannuated tackles; and kept by villainous looking old men, in tarred trowsers, and with yellow beards like oakum. They look like wreckers; and the scattered goods they expose for sale, involuntarily remind one of the sea-beach, covered with keels and cordage, swept ashore in a gale.

Yes, I was now as nimble as a monkey in the rigging, and at the cry of *"tumble up there, my hearties, and take in sail," I* was among the first ground-and-lofty tumblers, that sprang aloft at the word.

But the first time we reefed top-sails of a dark night, and I found myself hanging over the yard with eleven others, the ship plunging and rearing like a mad horse, till I felt like being jerked off the spar; then, indeed, I thought of a feather-bed at home, and hung on with tooth and nail; with no chance for snoring. But a few repetitions, soon made me used to it; and before long, I tied my reef-point as quickly and expertly as the best of them; never making what they call a *"granny-knot,"* and slipt down on deck by the bare stays, instead of the shrouds. It is surprising, how soon a boy overcomes his timidity about going aloft. For my own part, my nerves became as steady as the earth's diameter, and I felt as fearless on the royal yard, as Sam Patch on the cliff of Niagara. To my amazement, also, I found, that running up the rigging at sea, especially during a squall, was much easier than while lying in port. For as you always go up on the windward side, and the ship leans over, it makes more of a *stairs* of the rigging; whereas, in harbor, it is almost straight up and down.

Besides, the pitching and rolling only imparts a pleasant sort of vitality to the vessel; so that the difference in being aloft in a ship at sea, and a ship in harbor, is pretty much the same, as riding a real live horse and a wooden one. And even if the live charger should pitch you over his head, *that* would be much more satisfactory, than an inglorious fall from the other.

I took great delight in furling the top-gallant sails and royals in a hard blow; which duty required two hands on the yard.

There was a wild delirium about it; a fine rushing of the blood about the heart; and a glad, thrilling, and throbbing of the whole system, to find yourself tossed up at every pitch into the clouds of a stormy sky, and hovering like a judgment angel between heaven and earth; both hands free, with one foot in the rigging, and one somewhere behind you in the air. The sail would fill out like a balloon, with a report like a small cannon, and then collapse and sink away into a handful. And the feeling of mastering the rebellious canvas, and tying it down like a slave to the spar, and binding it over and over with the *gasket*, had a touch of pride and power in it, such as young King Richard must have felt, when he trampled down the insurgents of Wat Tyler.

As for steering, they never would let me go to the helm, except during a calm, when I and the figure-head on the bow were about equally employed.

By the way, that figure-head was a passenger I forgot to make mention of before.

He was a gallant six-footer of a Highlander *"in full fig,"* with bright tartans, bare knees, barred leggings, and blue bonnet and the most vermilion of cheeks. He was game to his wooden marrow, and stood up to it through thick and thin; one foot a little advanced, and his right arm stretched forward, daring on the waves. In a gale of wind it was glorious to watch him standing at his post like a hero, and plunging up and down the watery Highlands and Lowlands, as the ship went roaming on her way. He was a veteran with many wounds of many sea-fights; and when he got to Liverpool a figure-head-builder there, amputated his left leg, and gave him another wooden one, which I am sorry to say, did not fit him very well, for ever after he looked as if he limped. Then this figure-head-surgeon gave him another nose, and touched up one eye, and repaired a rent in his tartans. After that the painter came and made his toilet all over again; giving him a new suit throughout, with a plaid of a beautiful pattern.

I do not know what has become of Donald now, but I hope he is safe and snug with a handsome pension in the "Sailors'-Snug-Harbor" on Staten Island.

The reason why they gave me such a slender chance of learning to steer was this. I was quite young and raw, and steering a ship is a great art, upon which much depends; especially the making a short passage; for if the helmsman be a clumsy, careless fellow, or ignorant of his duty, he keeps the ship going about in a melancholy state of indecision as to its precise destination; so that on a voyage to Liverpool, it may be pointing one while for Gibraltar, then for Rotterdam, and now for John o' Groat's; all of which is worse than wasted time. Whereas, a true steersman keeps her to her work night and day; and tries to make a bee-line from port to port.

Then, in a sudden squall, inattention, or want of quickness at the helm, might make the ship *"lurch to"*—or *"bring her by the lee."* And what those things are, the cabin passengers would never find out, when they found themselves going down, down, down, and bidding good-by forever to the moon and stars.

And they little think, many of them, fine gentlemen and ladies that they are, what an important personage, and how much to be had in reverence, is the rough fellow in the pea-jacket, whom they see standing at the wheel, now cocking his eye aloft, and then peeping at the compass, or looking out to windward.

Why, that fellow has all your lives and eternities in his hand; and with one small and almost imperceptible motion of a spoke, in a gale of wind, might give a vast deal of work to surrogates and lawyers, in proving last wills and testaments.

Ay, you may well stare at him now. He does not look much like a man who might play into the hands of an heir-at-law, does he? Yet such is the case. Watch him close, therefore; take him down into your state-room occasionally after a stormy watch, and make a friend of him. A glass of cordial will do it. And if you or your heirs are interested with the underwriters, then also have an eye on him. And if you remark, that of the crew, all the men who come to the helm are careless, or inefficient; and if you observe the captain scolding them often, and crying out: *"Luff, you rascal; she's falling off!"* or, *"Keep her steady, you scoundrel, you're boxing the compass!"* then hurry down to your state-room, and if you have not yet made a will, get out your stationery and go at it; and when it is done, seal it up in a bottle, like Columbus' log, and it may possibly drift ashore, when you are drowned in the next gale of wind.

CHAPTER XXV
QUARTER-DECK FURNITURE

Though, for reasons hinted at above, they would not let me steer, I contented myself with learning the compass, a graphic facsimile of which I drew on a blank leaf of the *"Wealth of Nations,"* and studied it every morning, like the multiplication table.

I liked to peep in at the binnacle, and watch the needle; and I wondered how it was that it pointed north, rather than south or west; for I do not know that any reason can be given why it points in the precise direction it does. One would think, too, that, as since the beginning of the world almost, the tide of emigration has been setting west, the needle would point that way; whereas, it is forever pointing its fixed fore-finger toward the Pole, where there are few inducements to attract a sailor, unless it be plenty of ice for mint-juleps.

Our binnacle, by the way, the place that holds a ship's compasses, deserves a word of mention. It was a little house, about the bigness of a common bird-cage, with sliding panel doors, and two drawing-rooms within, and constantly perched upon a stand, right in front of the helm. It had two chimney stacks to carry off the smoke of the lamp that burned in it by night.

It was painted green, and on two sides had Venetian blinds; and on one side two glazed sashes; so that it looked like a cool little summer retreat, a snug bit of an arbor at the end of a shady garden lane. Had I been the captain, I would have planted vines in boxes, and placed them so as to overrun this binnacle; or I would have put canary-birds within; and so made an aviary of it. It is surprising what a different air may be imparted to the meanest thing by the dainty hand of taste. Nor must I omit the helm itself, which was one of a new construction, and a particular favorite of the captain. It was a complex system of cogs and wheels and spindles, all of polished brass, and looked something like a printing-press, or power-loom. The sailors, however, did not like it much, owing to the casualties that happened to their imprudent fingers, by catching in among the cogs and other intricate contrivances. Then, sometimes in a calm, when the sudden swells would lift the ship, the helm would fetch a lurch, and send the helmsman revolving round like Ixion, often seriously hurting him; a sort of breaking on the wheel.

The *harness-cask,* also, a sort of sea side-board, or rather meat-safe, in which a week's allowance of salt pork and beef is kept, deserves being chronicled. It formed part of the standing furniture of the quarter-deck. Of an oval shape, it was banded round with hoops all silver-gilt, with gilded bands secured with gilded screws, and a gilded padlock, richly chased. This formed the captain's smoking-seat, where he would perch himself of an afternoon, a tasseled Chinese cap upon his head, and a fragrant Havanna between his white and canine-looking teeth. He took much solid comfort, Captain Riga.

Then the magnificent *capstan!* The pride and glory of the whole ship's company, the constant care and dandled darling of the cook, whose duty it was to keep it polished like a teapot; and it was an object of distant admiration to the steerage passengers. Like a parlor center-table, it stood full in the middle of the quarter-deck, radiant with brazen stars, and variegated with diamond-shaped veneerings of mahogany and satin wood. This was the captain's lounge, and the chief mate's secretary, in the bar-holes keeping paper and pencil for memorandums.

I might proceed and speak of the *booby-hatch,* used as a sort of settee by the officers, and the *fife-rail* round the mainmast, inclosing a little ark of canvas, painted green, where a small white dog with a blue ribbon round his neck, belonging to the dock-master's daughter, used to take his morning walks, and air himself in this small edition of the New York Bowling-Green.

CHAPTER XXVI
A SAILOR A JACK OF ALL TRADES

As I began to learn my sailor duties, and show activity in running aloft, the men, I observed, treated me with a little more consideration, though not at all relaxing in a certain air of professional superiority. For the mere knowing of the names of the ropes, and familiarizing yourself with their places, so that you can lay hold of them in the darkest night; and the loosing and furling of the canvas, and reefing topsails, and hauling braces; all this, though of course forming an indispensable part of a seaman's vocation, and the business in which he is principally engaged; yet these are things which a beginner of ordinary capacity soon masters, and which are far inferior to many other matters familiar to an *"able seaman."*

What did I know, for instance, about *striking a top-gallant-mast*, and sending it down on deck in a gale of wind? Could I have *turned in a dead-eye*, or in the approved nautical style have *clapt a seizing on the main-stay*? What did I know of *"passing a gammoning," "reiving a Burton," "strapping a shoe-block," "clearing a foul hawse,"* and innumerable other intricacies?

The business of a thorough-bred sailor is a special calling, as much of a regular trade as a carpenter's or locksmith's. Indeed, it requires considerably more adroitness, and far more versatility of talent.

In the English merchant service boys serve a long apprenticeship to the sea, of seven years. Most of them first enter the Newcastle colliers, where they see a great deal of severe coasting service. In an old copy of the Letters of Junius, belonging to my father, I remember reading, that coal to supply the city of London could be dug at Blackheath, and sold for one half the price that the people of London then paid for it; but the Government would not suffer the mines to be opened, as it would destroy the great nursery for British seamen.

A thorough sailor must understand much of other avocations. He must be a bit of an embroiderer, to work fanciful collars of hempen lace about the shrouds; he must be something of a weaver, to weave mats of rope-yarns for lashings to the boats; he must have a touch of millinery, so as to tie graceful bows and knots, such as *Matthew Walker's roses,* and *Turk's heads;* he must be a bit of a musician, in order to sing out at the halyards; he must be a sort of jeweler, to set dead-eyes in the standing rigging; he must be a carpenter, to enable him to make a jurymast out of a yard in case of emergency; he must be a sempstress, to darn and mend the sails; a ropemaker, to twist *marline* and *Spanish foxes;* a blacksmith, to make hooks and thimbles for the blocks: in short, he must be a sort of Jack of all trades, in order to master his own. And this, perhaps, in a greater or less degree, is pretty much the case with all things else; for you know nothing till you know all; which is the reason we never know anything.

A sailor, also, in working at the rigging, uses special tools peculiar to his calling—*fids, serving-mallets, toggles, prickers, marlingspikes, palms, heavers,* and many more. The smaller sort he generally carries with him from ship to ship in a sort of canvas reticule.

The estimation in which a ship's crew hold the knowledge of such accomplishments as these, is expressed in the phrase they apply to one who is a clever practitioner. To distinguish such a mariner from those who merely *"hand, reef, and steer,"* that is, run aloft, furl sails, haul ropes, and stand at the wheel, they say he is *"a sailor-man"* which means that he not only knows how to reef a topsail, but is an artist in the rigging.

Now, alas! I had no chance given me to become initiated in this art and mystery; no further, at least, than by looking on, and watching how that these things might be done as well as others, the reason was, that I had only shipped for this one voyage in the Highlander, a short voyage too; and it was not worth while to teach *me* any thing, the fruit of which instructions could be only reaped by the next ship I might belong to. All they wanted of me was the good-will of my muscles, and the use of my backbone—comparatively small though it was at that time—by way of a lever, for the above-mentioned artists to employ when wanted. Accordingly, when any embroidery was going on in the rigging, I was set to the most inglorious avocations; as in the merchant service it is a religious maxim to keep the hands always employed at something or other, never mind what, during their watch on deck.

Often furnished with a club-hammer, they swung me over the bows in a bowline, to pound the rust off the anchor: a most monotonous, and to me a most uncongenial and irksome business. There was a remarkable fatality attending the various hammers I carried over with me. Somehow they *would* drop out of my hands into the sea. But the supply of reserved hammers seemed unlimited: also the blessings and benedictions I received from the chief mate for my clumsiness.

At other times, they set me to picking oakum, like a convict, which hempen business disagreeably obtruded thoughts of halters and the gallows; or whittling belaying-pins, like a Down-Easter.

However, I endeavored to bear it all like a young philosopher, and whiled away the tedious hours by gazing through a port-hole while my hands were plying, and repeating Lord Byron's Address to the Ocean, which I had often spouted on the stage at the High School at home.

Yes, I got used to all these matters, and took most things coolly, in the spirit of Seneca and the stoics.

All but the *"turning out"* or rising from your berth when the watch was called at night—*that* I never fancied. It was a sort of acquaintance, which the more I cultivated, the more I shrunk from; a thankless, miserable business, truly.

Consider that after walking the deck for four full hours, you go below to sleep: and while thus innocently employed in reposing your wearied limbs, you are started up—it seems but the next instant after closing your lids—and hurried on deck again, into the same disagreeably dark and, perhaps, stormy night, from which you descended into the forecastle.

The previous interval of slumber was almost wholly lost to me; at least the golden opportunity could not be appreciated: for though it is usually deemed a comfortable thing to be asleep, yet at the time no one is conscious that he is so enjoying himself. Therefore I made a little private arrangement with the Lancashire lad, who was in the other watch, just to step below occasionally, and shake me, and whisper in my ear—"Watch below, Buttons; watch below"—which pleasantly reminded me of the delightful fact. Then I would turn over on my side, and take another nap; and in this manner I enjoyed several complete watches in my bunk to the other sailor's one. I recommend the plan to all landsmen contemplating a voyage to sea.

But notwithstanding all these contrivances, the dreadful sequel could not be avoided. Eight bells would at last be struck, and the men on deck, exhilarated by the prospect of changing places with us, would call the watch in a most provoking but mirthful and facetious style.

As thus:—

"Starboard watch, ahoy! eight bells there, below! Tumble up, my lively hearties; steamboat alongside waiting for your trunks: bear a hand, bear a hand with your knee-buckles, my sweet and pleasant fellows! fine shower-bath here on deck. Hurrah, hurrah! your ice-cream is getting cold!"

Whereupon some of the old croakers who were getting into their trowsers would reply with—"Oh, stop your gabble, will you? don't be in such a hurry, now. You feel sweet, don't you?" with other exclamations, some of which were full of fury.

And it was not a little curious to remark, that at the expiration of the ensuing watch, the tables would be turned; and we on deck became the wits and jokers, and those below the grizzly bears and growlers.

CHAPTER XXVII
HE GETS A PEEP AT IRELAND, AND AT LAST ARRIVES AT LIVERPOOL

The Highlander was not a grayhound, not a very fast sailer; and so, the passage, which some of the packet ships make in fifteen or sixteen days, employed us about thirty.

At last, one morning I came on deck, and they told me that Ireland was in sight.

Ireland in sight! A foreign country actually visible! I peered hard, but could see nothing but a bluish, cloud-like spot to the northeast. Was that Ireland? Why, there was nothing remarkable about that; nothing startling. If *that's* the way a foreign country looks, I might as well have staid at home.

Now what, exactly, I had fancied the shore would look like, I can not say; but I had a vague idea that it would be something strange and wonderful. However, there it was; and as the light increased and the ship sailed nearer and nearer, the land began to magnify, and I gazed at it with increasing interest.

Ireland! I thought of Robert Emmet, and that last speech of his before Lord Norbury; I thought of Tommy Moore, and his amatory verses: I thought of Curran, Grattan, Plunket, and O'Connell; I thought of my uncle's ostler, Patrick Flinnigan; and I thought of the shipwreck of the gallant Albion, tost to pieces on the very shore now in sight; and I thought I should very much like to leave the ship and visit Dublin and the Giant's Causeway.

Presently a fishing-boat drew near, and I rushed to get a view of it; but it was a very ordinary looking boat, bobbing up and down, as any other boat would have done; yet, when I considered that the solitary man in it was actually a born native of the land in sight; that in all probability he had never been in America, and knew nothing about my friends at home, I began to think that he looked somewhat strange.

He was a very fluent fellow, and as soon as we were within hailing distance, cried out—"Ah, my fine sailors, from Ameriky, ain't ye, my beautiful sailors?" And concluded by calling upon us to stop and heave a rope. Thinking he might have something important to communicate, the mate accordingly backed the main yard, and a rope being thrown, the stranger kept hauling in upon it, and coiling it down, crying, "pay out! pay out, my honeys; ah! but you're noble fellows!" Till at last the mate asked him why he did not come alongside, adding, "Haven't you enough rope yet?"

"Sure and I have," replied the fisherman, "and it's time for Pat to cut and run!" and so saying, his knife severed the rope, and with a Kilkenny grin, he sprang to his tiller, put his little craft before the wind, and bowled away from us, with some fifteen fathoms of our tow-line.

"And may the Old Boy hurry after you, and hang you in your stolen hemp, you Irish blackguard!" cried the mate, shaking his fist at the receding boat, after recovering from his first fit of amazement.

Here, then, was a beautiful introduction to the eastern hemisphere; fairly robbed before striking soundings. This trick upon experienced travelers certainly beat all I had ever heard about the wooden nutmegs and basswood pumpkin seeds of Connecticut. And I thought if there were any more Hibernians like our friend Pat, the Yankee peddlers might as well give it up.

The next land we saw was Wales. It was high noon, and a long line of purple mountains lay like banks of clouds against the east.

Could this be really Wales?—Wales?—and I thought of the Prince of Wales.

And did a real queen with a diadem reign over that very land I was looking at, with the identical eyes in my own head?—And then I thought of a grandfather of mine, who had fought against the ancestor of this queen at Bunker's Hill.

But, after all, the general effect of these mountains was mortifyingly like the general effect of the Kaatskill Mountains on the Hudson River.

With a light breeze, we sailed on till next day, when we made Holyhead and Anglesea. Then it fell almost calm, and what little wind we had, was ahead; so we kept tacking to and fro, just gliding through the water, and always hovering in sight of a snow-white tower in the distance, which might have been a fort, or a light-house. I lost myself in conjectures as to what sort of people might be tenanting that lonely edifice, and whether they knew any thing about us.

The third day, with a good wind over the taffrail, we arrived so near our destination, that we took a pilot at dusk.

He, and every thing connected with him were very different from our New York pilot. In the first place, the pilot boat that brought him was a plethoric looking sloop-rigged boat, with flat bows, that went wheezing through the water; quite in contrast to the little gull of a schooner, that bade us adieu off Sandy Hook. Aboard of her were ten or twelve other pilots, fellows with shaggy brows, and muffled in shaggy coats, who sat grouped together on deck like a fire-side of bears, wintering in Aroostook. They must have had fine sociable times, though, together; cruising about the Irish Sea in quest of Liverpool-bound vessels; smoking cigars, drinking brandy-and-water, and spinning yarns; till at last, one by one, they are all scattered on board of different ships, and meet again by the side of a blazing sea-coal fire in some Liverpool taproom, and prepare for another yachting.

Now, when this English pilot boarded us, I stared at him as if he had been some wild animal just escaped from the Zoological Gardens; for here was a real live Englishman, just from England. Nevertheless, as he soon fell to ordering us here and there, and swearing vociferously in a language quite familiar to me; I began to think him very common-place, and considerable of a bore after all.

After running till about midnight, we *"hove-to"* near the mouth of the Mersey; and next morning, before day-break, took the first of the flood; and with a fair wind, stood into the river; which, at its mouth, is quite an arm of the sea. Presently, in the misty twilight, we passed immense buoys, and caught sight of distant objects on shore, vague and shadowy shapes, like Ossian's ghosts.

As I stood leaning over the side, and trying to summon up some image of Liverpool, to see how the reality would answer to my conceit; and while the fog, and mist, and gray dawn were investing every thing with a mysterious interest, I was startled by the doleful, dismal sound of a great bell, whose slow intermitting tolling seemed in unison with the solemn roll of the billows. I thought I had never heard so boding a sound; a sound that seemed to speak of judgment and the resurrection, like belfry-mouthed Paul of Tarsus.

It was not in the direction of the shore; but seemed to come out of the vaults of the sea, and out of the mist and fog.

Who was dead, and what could it be?

I soon learned from my shipmates, that this was the famous *Bett-Buoy*, which is precisely what its name implies; and tolls fast or slow, according to the agitation of the waves. In a calm, it is dumb; in a moderate breeze, it tolls gently; but in a gale, it is an alarum like the tocsin, warning all mariners to flee. But it seemed fuller of dirges for the past, than of monitions for the future; and no one can give ear to it, without thinking of the sailors who sleep far beneath it at the bottom of the deep.

As we sailed ahead the river contracted. The day came, and soon, passing two lofty land-marks on the Lancashire shore, we rapidly drew near the town, and at last, came to anchor in the stream.

Looking shoreward, I beheld lofty ranges of dingy warehouses, which seemed very deficient in the elements of the marvelous; and bore a most unexpected resemblance to the ware-houses along South-street in New York. There was nothing strange; nothing extraordinary about them. There they stood; a row of calm and collected ware-houses; very good and substantial edifices, doubtless, and admirably adapted to the ends had in view by the builders; but plain, matter-of-fact ware-houses, nevertheless, and that was all that could be said of them.

To be sure, I did not expect that every house in Liverpool must be a Leaning Tower of Pisa, or a Strasbourg Cathedral; but yet, these edifices I must confess, were a sad and bitter disappointment to me.

But it was different with Larry the whaleman; who to my surprise, looking about him delighted, exclaimed, "Why, this 'ere is a considerable place—I'm *dummed if* it ain't quite a place.—Why, them 'ere houses is considerable houses. It beats the coast of Afriky, all hollow; nothing like this in *Madagasky,* I tell you;—I'm *dummed,* boys if Liverpool ain't a city!"

Upon this occasion, indeed, Larry altogether forgot his hostility to civilization. Having been so long accustomed to associate foreign lands with the savage places of the Indian Ocean, he had been under the impression, that Liverpool must be a town of bamboos, situated in some swamp, and whose inhabitants turned their attention principally to the cultivation of log-wood and curing of flying-fish. For that any great commercial city existed three thousand miles from home, was a thing, of which Larry had never before had a *"realizing sense."* He was accordingly astonished and delighted; and began to feel a sort of consideration for the country which could boast so extensive a town. Instead of holding Queen Victoria on a par with the Queen of Madagascar, as he had been accustomed to do; he ever after alluded to that lady with feeling and respect.

As for the other seamen, the sight of a foreign country seemed to kindle no enthusiasm in them at all: no emotion in the least. They looked around them with great presence of mind, and acted precisely as you or I would, if, after a morning's absence round the corner, we found ourselves returning home. Nearly all of them had made frequent voyages to Liverpool.

Not long after anchoring, several boats came off; and from one of them stept a neatly-dressed and very respectable-looking woman, some thirty years of age, I should think, carrying a bundle. Coming forward among the sailors, she inquired for Max the Dutchman, who immediately was forthcoming, and saluted her by the mellifluous appellation of *Sally*.

Now during the passage, Max in discoursing to me of Liverpool, had often assured me, that that city had the honor of containing a spouse of his; and that in all probability, I would have the pleasure of seeing her. But having heard a good many stories about the bigamies of seamen, and their having wives and sweethearts in every port, the round world over; and having been an eye-witness to a nuptial parting between this very Max and a lady in New York; I put down this relation of his, for what I thought it might reasonably be worth. What was my astonishment, therefore, to see this really decent, civil woman coming with a neat parcel of Max's shore clothes, all washed, plaited, and ironed, and ready to put on at a moment's warning.

They stood apart a few moments giving loose to those transports of pleasure, which always take place, I suppose, between man and wife after long separations.

At last, after many earnest inquiries as to how he had behaved himself in New York; and concerning the state of his wardrobe; and going down into the forecastle, and inspecting it in person, Sally departed; having exchanged her bundle of clean clothes for a bundle of soiled ones, and this was precisely what the New York wife had done for Max, not thirty days previous.

So long as we laid in port, Sally visited the Highlander daily; and approved herself a neat and expeditious getter-up of duck frocks and trowsers, a capital tailoress, and as far as I could see, a very well-behaved, discreet, and reputable woman.

But from all I had seen of her, I should suppose Meg, the New York wife, to have been equally well-behaved, discreet, and reputable; and equally devoted to the keeping in good order Max's wardrobe.

And when we left England at last, Sally bade Max good-by, just as Meg had done; and when we arrived at New York, Meg greeted Max precisely as Sally had greeted him in Liverpool. Indeed, a pair of more amiable wives never belonged to one man; they never quarreled, or had so much as a difference of any kind; the whole broad Atlantic being between them; and Max was equally polite and civil to both. For many years, he had been going Liverpool and New York voyages, plying between wife and wife with great regularity, and sure of receiving a hearty domestic welcome on either side of the ocean.

Thinking this conduct of his, however, altogether wrong and every way immoral, I once ventured to express to him my opinion on the subject. But I never did so again. He turned round on me, very savagely; and after rating me soundly for meddling in concerns not my own, concluded by asking me triumphantly, whether *old King Sol,* as he called the son of David, did not have a whole frigate-full of wives; and that being the case, whether he, a poor sailor, did not have just as good a right to have two? "What was not wrong then, is right now," said Max; "so, mind your eye, Buttons, or I'll crack your pepper-box for you!"

CHAPTER XXVIII
HE GOES TO SUPPER AT THE SIGN OF THE BALTIMORE CLIPPER

In the afternoon our pilot was all alive with his orders; we hove up the anchor, and after a deal of pulling, and hauling, and jamming against other ships, we wedged our way through a lock at high tide; and about dark, succeeded in working up to a berth in *Prince's Dock*. The hawsers and towlines being then coiled away, the crew were told to go ashore, select their boarding-house, and sit down to supper.

Here it must be mentioned, that owing to the strict but necessary regulations of the Liverpool docks, no fires of any kind are allowed on board the vessels within them; and hence, though the sailors are supposed to sleep in the forecastle, yet they must get their meals ashore, or live upon cold potatoes. To a ship, the American merchantmen adopt the former plan; the owners, of course, paying the landlord's bill; which, in a large crew remaining at Liverpool more than six weeks, as we of the Highlander did, forms no inconsiderable item in the expenses of the voyage. Other ships, however—the economical Dutch and Danish, for instance, and sometimes the prudent Scotch—feed their luckless tars in dock, with precisely the same fare which they give them at sea; taking their salt junk ashore to be cooked, which, indeed, is but scurvy sort of treatment, since it is very apt to induce the scurvy. A parsimonious proceeding like this is regarded with immeasurable disdain by the crews of the New York vessels, who, if their captains treated them after that fashion, would soon bolt and run.

It was quite dark, when we all sprang ashore; and, for the first time, I felt dusty particles of the renowned British soil penetrating into my eyes and lungs. As for *stepping* on it, that was out of the question, in the well-paved and flagged condition of the streets; and I did not have an opportunity to do so till some time afterward, when I got out into the country; and then, indeed, I saw England, and snuffed its immortal loam—but not till then.

Jackson led the van; and after stopping at a tavern, took us up this street, and down that, till at last he brought us to a narrow lane, filled with boarding-houses, spirit-vaults, and sailors. Here we stopped before the sign of a Baltimore Clipper, flanked on one side by a gilded bunch of grapes and a bottle, and on the other by the British Unicorn and American Eagle, lying down by each other, like the lion and lamb in the millennium.—A very judicious and tasty device, showing a delicate apprehension of the propriety of conciliating American sailors in an English boarding-house; and yet in no way derogating from the honor and dignity of England, but placing the two nations, indeed, upon a footing of perfect equality.

Near the unicorn was a very small animal, which at first I took for a young unicorn; but it looked more like a yearling lion. It was holding up one paw, as if it had a splinter in it; and on its head was a sort of basket-hilted, low-crowned hat, without a rim. I asked a sailor standing by, what this animal meant, when, looking at me with a grin, he answered, "Why, youngster, don't you know what that means? It's a young jackass, limping off with a kedgeree pot of rice out of the cuddy."

Though it was an English boarding-house, it was kept by a broken-down American mariner, one Danby, a dissolute, idle fellow, who had married a buxom English wife, and now lived upon her industry; for the lady, and not the sailor, proved to be the head of the establishment.

She was a hale, good-looking woman, about forty years old, and among the seamen went by the name of *"Handsome Mary."* But though, from the dissipated character of her spouse, Mary had become the business personage of the house, bought the marketing, overlooked the tables, and conducted all the more important arrangements, yet she was by no means an Amazon to her husband, if she *did* play a masculine part in other matters. No; and the more is the pity, poor Mary seemed too much attached to Danby, to seek to rule him as a termagant. Often she went about her household concerns with the tears in her eyes, when, after a fit of intoxication, this brutal husband of hers had been beating her. The sailors took her part, and many a time volunteered to give him a thorough thrashing before her eyes; but Mary would beg them not to do so, as Danby would, no doubt, be a better boy next time.

But there seemed no likelihood of this, so long as that abominable bar of his stood upon the premises. As you entered the passage, it stared upon you on one side, ready to entrap all guests.

It was a grotesque, old-fashioned, castellated sort of a sentry-box, made of a smoky-colored wood, and with a grating in front, that lifted up like a portcullis. And here would this Danby sit all the day long; and when customers grew thin, would patronize his own ale himself, pouring down mug after mug, as if he took himself for one of his own quarter-casks.

Sometimes an old crony of his, one Bob Still, would come in; and then they would occupy the sentry-box together, and swill their beer in concert. This pot-friend of Danby was portly as a dray-horse, and had a round, sleek, oily head, twinkling eyes, and moist red cheeks. He was a lusty troller of ale-songs; and, with his mug in his hand, would lean his waddling bulk partly out of the sentry-box, singing:

> "No frost, no snow, no wind, I trow,
>   Can hurt me if I wold,
> I am so wrapt, and thoroughly lapt
>   In jolly good ale and old,—
> I stuff my skin so full within,
>   Of jolly good ale and old."

Or this,

> "Four wines and brandies I detest,
> Here's richer juice from barley press'd.
> It is the quintessence of malt,
> And they that drink it want no salt.
> Come, then, quick come, and take this beer,
> And water henceforth you'll forswear."

Alas! Handsome Mary. What avail all thy private tears and remonstrances with the incorrigible Danby, so long as that brewery of a toper, Bob Still, daily eclipses thy threshold with the vast diameter of his paunch, and enthrones himself in the sentry-box, holding divided rule with thy spouse?

The more he drinks, the fatter and rounder waxes Bob; and the songs pour out as the ale pours in, on the well-known principle, that the air in a vessel is displaced and expelled, as the liquid rises higher and higher in it.

But as for Danby, the miserable Yankee grows sour on good cheer, and dries up the thinner for every drop of fat ale he imbibes. It is plain and demonstrable, that much ale is not good for Yankees, and operates differently upon them from what it does upon a Briton: ale must be drank in a fog and a drizzle.

Entering the sign of the Clipper, Jackson ushered us into a small room on one side, and shortly after, Handsome Mary waited upon us with a courtesy, and received the compliments of several old guests among our crew. She then disappeared to provide our supper. While my shipmates were now engaged in tippling, and talking with numerous old acquaintances of theirs in the neighborhood, who thronged about the door, I remained alone in the little room, meditating profoundly upon the fact, that I was now seated upon an English bench, under an English roof, in an English tavern, forming an integral part of the English empire. It was a staggering fact, but none the less true.

I examined the place attentively; it was a long, narrow, little room, with one small arched window with red curtains, looking out upon a smoky, untidy yard, bounded by a dingy brick-wall, the top of which was horrible with pieces of broken old bottles, stuck into mortar.

A dull lamp swung overhead, placed in a wooden ship suspended from the ceiling. The walls were covered with a paper, representing an endless succession of vessels of all nations continually circumnavigating the apartment. By way of a pictorial mainsail to one of these ships, a map was hung against it, representing in faded colors the flags of all nations. From the street came a confused uproar of ballad-singers, bawling women, babies, and drunken sailors.

And this is England?

But where are the old abbeys, and the York Minsters, and the lord mayors, and coronations, and the May-poles, and fox-hunters, and Derby races, and the dukes and duchesses, and the Count d'Orsays, which, from all my reading, I had been in the habit of associating with England? Not the most distant glimpse of them was to be seen.

Alas! Wellingborough, thought I, I fear you stand but a poor chance to see the sights. You are nothing but a poor sailor boy; and the Queen is not going to send a deputation of noblemen to invite you to St. James's.

It was then, I began to see, that my prospects of seeing the world as a sailor were, after all, but very doubtful; for sailors only go *round* the world, without going *into* it; and their reminiscences of travel are only a dim recollection of a chain of tap-rooms surrounding the globe, parallel with the Equator. They but touch the perimeter of the circle; hover about the edges of terra-firma; and only land upon wharves and pier-heads. They would dream as little of traveling inland to see Kenilworth, or Blenheim Castle, as they would of sending a car overland to the Pope, when they touched at Naples.

From these reveries I was soon roused, by a servant girl hurrying from room to room, in shrill tones exclaiming, "Supper, supper ready."

Mounting a rickety staircase, we entered a room on the second floor. Three tall brass candlesticks shed a smoky light upon smoky walls, of what had once been sea-blue, covered with sailor-scrawls of foul anchors, lovers' sonnets, and ocean ditties. On one side, nailed against the wainscot in a row, were the four knaves of cards, each Jack putting his best foot foremost as usual. What these signified I never heard.

But such ample cheer! Such a groaning table! Such a superabundance of solids and substantial! Was it possible that sailors fared thus? — the sailors, who at sea live upon salt beef and biscuit?

First and foremost, was a mighty pewter dish, big as Achilles' shield, sustaining a pyramid of smoking sausages. This stood at one end; midway was a similar dish, heavily laden with farmers' slices of head-cheese; and at the opposite end, a congregation of beef-steaks, piled tier over tier. Scattered at intervals between, were side dishes of boiled potatoes, eggs by the score, bread, and pickles; and on a stand adjoining, was an ample reserve of every thing on the supper table.

We fell to with all our hearts; wrapt ourselves in hot jackets of beef-steaks; curtailed the sausages with great celerity; and sitting down before the head-cheese, soon razed it to its foundations.

Toward the close of the entertainment, I suggested to Peggy, one of the girls who had waited upon us, that a cup of tea would be a nice thing to take; and I would thank her for one. She replied that it was too late for tea; but she would get me a cup of *"swipes"* if I wanted it.

Not knowing what *"swipes"* might be, I thought I would run the risk and try it; but it proved a miserable beverage, with a musty, sour flavor, as if it had been a decoction of spoiled pickles. I never patronized *swipes* again; but gave it a wide berth; though, at dinner afterward, it was furnished to an unlimited extent, and drunk by most of my shipmates, who pronounced it good.

But Bob Still would not have pronounced it so; for this *stripes, as I* learned, was a sort of cheap substitute for beer; or a bastard kind of beer; or the washings and rinsings of old beer-barrels. But I do not remember now what they said it was, precisely. I only know, that *swipes* was my abomination. As for the taste of it, I can only describe it as answering to the name itself; which is certainly significant of something vile. But it is drunk in large quantities by the poor people about Liverpool, which, perhaps, in some degree, accounts for their poverty.

CHAPTER XXIX
REDBURN DEFERENTIALLY DISCOURSES CONCERNING THE PROSPECTS OF SAILORS

The ship remained in Prince's Dock over six weeks; but as I do not mean to present a diary of my stay there, I shall here simply record the general tenor of the life led by our crew during that interval; and will then proceed to note down, at random, my own wanderings about town, and impressions of things as they are recalled to me now, after the lapse of so many years.

But first, I must mention that we saw little of the captain during our stay in the dock. Sometimes, cane in hand, he sauntered down of a pleasant morning from the *Arms Hotel*, I believe it was, where he boarded; and after lounging about the ship, giving orders to his Prime Minister and Grand Vizier, the chief mate, he would saunter back to his drawing-rooms.

From the glimpse of a play-bill, which I detected peeping out of his pocket, I inferred that he patronized the theaters; and from the flush of his cheeks, that he patronized the fine old Port wine, for which Liverpool is famous.

Occasionally, however, he spent his nights on board; and mad, roystering nights they were, such as rare Ben Jonson would have delighted in. For company over the cabin-table, he would have four or five whiskered sea-captains, who kept the steward drawing corks and filling glasses all the time. And once, the whole company were found under the table at four o'clock in the morning, and were put to bed and tucked in by the two mates. Upon this occasion, I agreed with our woolly Doctor of Divinity, the black cook, that they should have been ashamed of themselves; but there is no shame in some sea-captains, who only blush after the third bottle.

During the many visits of Captain Riga to the ship, he always said something courteous to a gentlemanly, friendless custom-house officer, who staid on board of us nearly all the time we lay in the dock.

And weary days they must have been to this friendless custom-house officer; trying to kill time in the cabin with a newspaper; and rapping on the transom with his knuckles. He was kept on board to prevent smuggling; but he used to smuggle himself ashore very often, when, according to law, he should have been at his post on board ship. But no wonder; he seemed to be a man of fine feelings, altogether above his situation; a most inglorious one, indeed; worse than driving geese to water.

And now, to proceed with the crew.

At daylight, all hands were called, and the decks were washed down; then we had an hour to go ashore to breakfast; after which we worked at the rigging, or picked oakum, or were set to some employment or other, never mind how trivial, till twelve o'clock, when we went to dinner. At half-past nine we resumed work; and finally *knocked off* at four o'clock in the afternoon, unless something particular was in hand. And after four o'clock, we could go where we pleased, and were not required to be on board again till next morning at daylight.

As we had nothing to do with the cargo, of course, our duties were light enough; and the chief mate was often put to it to devise some employment for us.

We had no watches to stand, a ship-keeper, hired from shore, relieving us from that; and all the while the men's wages ran on, as at sea. Sundays we had to ourselves.

Thus, it will be seen, that the life led by sailors of American ships in Liverpool, is an exceedingly easy one, and abounding in leisure. They live ashore on the fat of the land; and after a little wholesome exercise in the morning, have the rest of the day to themselves.

Nevertheless, these Liverpool voyages, likewise those to London and Havre, are the least profitable that an improvident seaman can take. Because, in New York he receives his month's advance; in Liverpool, another; both of which, in most cases, quickly disappear; so that by the time his voyage terminates, he generally has but little coming to him; sometimes not a cent. Whereas, upon a long voyage, say to India or China, his wages accumulate; he has more inducements to economize, and far fewer motives to extravagance; and when he is paid off at last, he goes away jingling a quart measure of dollars.

Besides, of all sea-ports in the world, Liverpool, perhaps, most abounds in all the variety of land-sharks, land-rats, and other vermin, which make the hapless mariner their prey. In the shape of landlords, bar-keepers, clothiers, crimps, and boarding-house loungers, the land-sharks devour him, limb by limb; while the land-rats and mice constantly nibble at his purse.

Other perils he runs, also, far worse; from the denizens of notorious Corinthian haunts in the vicinity of the docks, which in depravity are not to be matched by any thing this side of the pit that is bottomless.

And yet, sailors love this Liverpool; and upon long voyages to distant parts of the globe, will be continually dilating upon its charms and attractions, and extolling it above all other seaports in the world. For in Liverpool they find their Paradise—not the well known street of that name—and one of them told me he would be content to lie in Prince's Dock till *he hove up anchor* for the world to come.

Much is said of ameliorating the condition of sailors; but it must ever prove a most difficult endeavor, so long as the antidote is given before the bane is removed.

Consider, that, with the majority of them, the very fact of their being sailors, argues a certain recklessness and sensualism of character, ignorance, and depravity; consider that they are generally friendless and alone in the world; or if they have friends and relatives, they are almost constantly beyond the reach of their good influences; consider that after the rigorous discipline, hardships, dangers, and privations of a voyage, they are set adrift in a foreign port, and exposed to a thousand enticements, which, under the circumstances, would be hard even for virtue itself to withstand, unless virtue went about on crutches; consider that by their very vocation they are shunned by the better classes of people, and cut off from all access to respectable and improving society; consider all this, and the reflecting mind must very soon perceive that the case of sailors, as a class, is not a very promising one.

Indeed, the bad things of their condition come under the head of those chronic evils which can only be ameliorated, it would seem, by ameliorating the moral organization of all civilization.

Though old seventy-fours and old frigates are converted into chapels, and launched into the docks; though the "Boatswain's Mate" and other clever religious tracts in the nautical dialect are distributed among them; though clergymen harangue them from the pier-heads: and chaplains in the navy read sermons to them on the gun-deck; though evangelical boarding-houses are provided for them; though the parsimony of ship-owners has seconded the really sincere and pious efforts of Temperance Societies, to take away from seamen their old rations of grog while at sea:—notwithstanding all these things, and many more, the relative condition of the great bulk of sailors to the rest of mankind, seems to remain pretty much where it was, a century ago.

It is too much the custom, perhaps, to regard as a special advance, that unavoidable, and merely participative progress, which any one class makes in sharing the general movement of the race. Thus, because the sailor, who to-day steers the Hibernia or Unicorn steam-ship across the Atlantic, is a somewhat different man from the exaggerated sailors of Smollett, and the men who fought with Nelson at Copenhagen, and survived to riot themselves away at North Corner in Plymouth;—because the modem tar is not quite so gross as heretofore, and has shaken off some of his shaggy jackets, and docked his Lord Rodney queue:—therefore, in the estimation of some observers, he has begun to see the evils of his condition, and has voluntarily improved. But upon a closer scrutiny, it will be seen that he has but drifted along with that great tide, which, perhaps, has two flows for one ebb; he has made no individual advance of his own.

There are classes of men in the world, who bear the same relation to society at large, that the wheels do to a coach: and are just as indispensable. But however easy and delectable the springs upon which the insiders pleasantly vibrate: however sumptuous the hammer-cloth, and glossy the door-panels; yet, for all this, the wheels must still revolve in dusty, or muddy revolutions. No contrivance, no sagacity can lift *them* out of the mire; for upon something the coach must be bottomed; on something the insiders must roll.

Now, sailors form one of these wheels: they go and come round the globe; they are the true importers, and exporters of spices and silks; of fruits and wines and marbles; they carry missionaries, embassadors, opera-singers, armies, merchants, tourists, and scholars to their destination: they are a bridge of boats across the Atlantic; they are the *primum mobile* of all commerce; and, in short, were they to emigrate in a body to man the navies of the moon, almost every thing would stop here on earth except its revolution on its axis, and the orators in the American Congress.

And yet, what are sailors? What in your heart do you think of that fellow staggering along the dock? Do you not give him a wide berth, shun him, and account him but little above the brutes that perish? Will you throw open your parlors to him; invite him to dinner? or give him a season ticket to your pew in church?—No. You will do no such thing; but at a distance, you will perhaps subscribe a dollar or two for the building of a hospital, to accommodate sailors already broken down; or for the distribution of excellent books among tars who can not read. And the very mode and manner in which such charities are made, bespeak, more than words, the low estimation in which sailors are held. It is useless to gainsay it; they are deemed almost the refuse and offscourings of the earth; and the romantic view of them is principally had through romances.

But can sailors, one of the wheels of this world, be wholly lifted up from the mire? There seems not much chance for it, in the old systems and programmes of the future, however well-intentioned and sincere; for with such systems, the thought of lifting them up seems almost as hopeless as that of growing the grape in Nova Zembla.

But we must not altogether despair for the sailor; nor need those who toil for his good be at bottom disheartened, or Time must prove his friend in the end; and though sometimes he would almost seem as a neglected step-son of heaven, permitted to run on and riot out his days with no hand to restrain him, while others are watched over and tenderly cared for; yet we feel and we know that God is the true Father of all, and that none of his children are without the pale of his care.

CHAPTER XXX
REDBURN GROWS INTOLERABLY FLAT AND STUPID OVER SOME OUTLANDISH OLD GUIDE-BOOKS

Among the odd volumes in my father's library, was a collection of old European and English guide-books, which he had bought on his travels, a great many years ago. In my childhood, I went through many courses of studying them, and never tired of gazing at the numerous quaint embellishments and plates, and staring at the strange title-pages, some of which I thought resembled the mustached faces of foreigners. Among others was a Parisian-looking, faded, pink-covered pamphlet, the rouge here and there effaced upon its now thin and attenuated cheeks, entitled, *"Voyage Descriptif et Philosophique de L'Ancien et du Nouveau Paris: Miroir Fidèle"* also a time-darkened, mossy old book, in marbleized binding, much resembling verd-antique, entitled, *"Itinéraire Instructif de Rome, ou Description Générale des Monumens Antiques et Modernes et des Ouvrages les plus Remarquables de Peinteur, de Sculpture, et de Architecture de cette Célébre Ville;"* on the russet title-page is a vignette representing a barren rock, partly shaded by a scrub-oak (a forlorn bit of landscape), and under the lee of the rock and the shade of the tree, maternally reclines the houseless foster-mother of Romulus and Remus, giving suck to the illustrious twins; a pair of naked little cherubs sprawling on the ground, with locked arms, eagerly engaged at their absorbing occupation; a large cactus-leaf or diaper hangs from a bough, and the wolf looks a good deal like one of the no-horn breed of barn-yard cows; the work is published *"Avec privilege du Souverain Pontife."* There was also a velvet-bound old volume, in brass clasps, entitled, *"The Conductor through Holland"* with a plate of the Stadt House; also a venerable *"Picture of London"* abounding in representations of St. Paul's, the Monument, Temple-Bar, Hyde-Park-Corner, the Horse Guards, the Admiralty, Charing-Cross, and Vauxhall Bridge. Also, a bulky book, in a dusty-looking yellow cover, reminding one of the paneled doors of a mail-coach, and bearing an elaborate title-page, full of printer's flourishes, in emulation of the cracks of a four-in-hand whip, entitled, in part, *"The Great Roads, both direct and cross, throughout England and Wales, from an actual Admeasurement by order of His Majesty's Postmaster-General: This work describes the Cities, Market and Borough and Corporate Towns, and those at which the Assizes are held, and gives the time of the Mails' arrival and departure from each: Describes the Inns in the Metropolis from which the stages go, and the Inns in the country which supply post-horses and carriages: Describes the Noblemen and Gentlemen's Seats situated near the Road, with Maps of the Environs of London, Bath, Brighton, and Margate."* It is dedicated *"To the Right Honorable the Earls of Chesterfield and Leicester, by their Lordships' Most Obliged, Obedient, and Obsequious Servant, John Gary, 1798."* Also a green pamphlet, with a motto from Virgil, and an intricate coat of arms on the cover, looking like a diagram of the Labyrinth of Crete, entitled, "A *Description of York, its Antiquities and Public Buildings, particularly the Cathedral; compiled with great pains from the most authentic records."* Also a small scholastic-looking volume, in a classic vellum binding, and with a frontispiece bringing together at one view the towers and turrets of King's College and the magnificent Cathedral of Ely, though geographically sixteen miles apart, entitled, *"The Cambridge Guide: its Colleges, Halls, Libraries, and Museums, with the Ceremonies of the Town and University, and some account of Ely Cathedral."* Also a pamphlet, with a japanned sort of cover, stamped with a disorderly higgledy-piggledy group of pagoda-looking structures, claiming to be an accurate representation of the *"North or Grand Front of Blenheim,"* and entitled, "A *Description of Blenheim, the Seat of His Grace the Duke of Marlborough; containing a full account of the Paintings, Tapestry, and Furniture: a Picturesque Tour of the Gardens and Parks, and a General Description of the famous China Gallery,* &.; *with an Essay on Landscape Gardening: and embellished with a View of the Palace, and a New and Elegant Plan of the Great Park."* And lastly, and to the purpose, there was a volume called "THE PICTURE OF LIVERPOOL."

It was a curious and remarkable book; and from the many fond associations connected with it, I should like to immortalize it, if I could.

But let me get it down from its shrine, and paint it, if I may, from the life.

As I now linger over the volume, to and fro turning the pages so dear to my boyhood,—the very pages which, years and years ago, my father turned over amid the very scenes that are here described; what a soft, pleasing sadness steals over me, and how I melt into the past and forgotten!

Dear book! I will sell my Shakespeare, and even sacrifice my old quarto Hogarth, before I will part with you. Yes, I will go to the hammer myself, ere I send you to be knocked down in the auctioneer's shambles. I will, my beloved,—old family relic that you are;—till you drop leaf from leaf, and letter from letter, you shall have a snug shelf somewhere, though I have no bench for myself.

In size, it is what the booksellers call an *18mo*; it is bound in green morocco, which from my earliest recollection has been spotted and tarnished with time; the corners are marked with triangular patches of red, like little cocked hats; and some unknown Goth has inflicted an incurable wound upon the back. There is no lettering outside; so that he who lounges past my humble shelves, seldom dreams of opening the anonymous little book in green. There it stands; day after day, week after week, year after year; and no one but myself regards it. But I make up for all neglects, with my own abounding love for it.

But let us open the volume.

What are these scrawls in the fly-leaves? what incorrigible pupil of a writing-master has been here? what crayon sketcher of wild animals and falling air-castles? Ah, no!—these are all part and parcel of the precious book, which go to make up the sum of its treasure to me.

Some of the scrawls are my own; and as poets do with their juvenile sonnets, I might write under this horse, *"Drawn at the age of three years,"* and under this autograph, *"Executed at the age of eight."*

Others are the handiwork of my brothers, and sisters, and cousins; and the hands that sketched some of them are now moldered away.

But what does this anchor here? this ship? and this sea-ditty of Dibdin's? The book must have fallen into the hands of some tarry captain of a forecastle. No: that anchor, ship, and Dibdin's ditty are mine; this hand drew them; and on this very voyage to Liverpool. But not so fast; I did not mean to tell that yet.

Full in the midst of these pencil scrawlings, completely surrounded indeed, stands in indelible, though faded ink, and in my father's handwriting, the following:—

WALTER REDBURN.

Riddough's Royal Hotel,
Liverpool, March 20th, 1808.

Turning over that leaf, I come upon some half-effaced miscellaneous memoranda in pencil, characteristic of a methodical mind, and therefore indubitably my father's, which he must have made at various times during his stay in Liverpool. These are full of a strange, subdued, old, midsummer interest to me: and though, from the numerous effacements, it is much like cross-reading to make them out; yet, I must here copy a few at random:—

	£	s.	d
Guide-Book		3	6
Dinner at the Star and Garter			10
Trip to Preston (distance 31 m.)	2	6	3
Gratuities			4
Hack		4	6
Thompson's Seasons			5
Library			1
Boat on the river			6
Port wine and cigar			4

And on the opposite page, I can just decipher the following:

Dine with Mr. Roscoe on Monday.
Call upon Mr. Morille same day.
Leave card at Colonel Digby's on Tuesday.
Theatre Friday night—Richard III. and new farce.
Present letter at Miss L——'s on Tuesday.
Call on Sampson & Wilt, Friday.
Get my draft on London cashed.
Write home by the Princess.
Letter bag at Sampson and Wilt's.

Turning over the next leaf, I unfold a map, which in the midst of the British Arms, in one corner displays in sturdy text, that this is *"A Plan of the Town of Liverpool."* But there seems little plan in the confined and crooked looking marks for the streets, and the docks irregularly scattered along the bank of the Mersey, which flows along, a peaceful stream of shaded line engraving.

On the northeast corner of the map, lies a level Sahara of yellowish white: a desert, which still bears marks of my zeal in endeavoring to populate it with all manner of uncouth monsters in crayons. The space designated by that spot is now, doubtless, completely built up in Liverpool.

Traced with a pen, I discover a number of dotted lines, radiating in all directions from the foot of Lord-street, where stands marked *"Riddough's Hotel,"* the house my father stopped at.

These marks delineate his various excursions in the town; and I follow the lines on, through street and lane; and across broad squares; and penetrate with them into the narrowest courts.

By these marks, I perceive that my father forgot not his religion in a foreign land; but attended St. John's Church near the Hay-market, and other places of public worship: I see that he visited the News Room in Duke-street, the Lyceum in Bold-street, and the Theater Royal; and that he called to pay his respects to the eminent Mr. Roscoe, the historian, poet, and banker.

Reverentially folding this map, I pass a plate of the Town Hall, and come upon the Title Page, which, in the middle, is ornamented with a piece of landscape, representing a loosely clad lady in sandals, pensively seated upon a bleak rock on the sea shore, supporting her head with one hand, and with the other, exhibiting to the stranger an oval sort of salver, bearing the figure of a strange bird, with this motto elastically stretched for a border— *"Deus nobis haec otia fecit."*

The bird forms part of the city arms, and is an imaginary representation of a now extinct fowl, called the *"Liver,"* said to have inhabited a *"pool,"* which antiquarians assert once covered a good part of the ground where Liverpool now stands; and from that bird, and this pool, Liverpool derives its name.

At a distance from the pensive lady in sandals, is a ship under full sail; and on the beach is the figure of a small man, vainly essaying to roll over a huge bale of goods.

Equally divided at the top and bottom of this design, is the following title complete; but I fear the printer will not be able to give a facsimile:—

The Picture
of Liverpool:
or, Stranger's Guide
and Gentleman's Pocket Companion
FOR THE TOWN.
Embellished
With Engravings
By the Most Accomplished and Eminent Artists.
Liverpool:
Printed in Swift's Court,
And sold by Woodward and Alderson, 56 Castle St. 1803.

A brief and reverential preface, as if the writer were all the time bowing, informs the reader of the flattering reception accorded to previous editions of the work; and quotes *"testimonies of respect which had lately appeared in various quarters —the British Critic, Review, and the seventh volume of the Beauties of England and Wales"*—and concludes by expressing the hope, that this new, revised, and illustrated edition might *"render it less unworthy of the public notice, and less unworthy also of the subject it is intended to illustrate."*

A very nice, dapper, and respectful little preface, the time and place of writing which is solemnly recorded at the end-Hope *Place, 1st Sept.* 1803.

But how much fuller my satisfaction, as I fondly linger over this circumstantial paragraph, if the writer had recorded the precise hour of the day, and by what timepiece; and if he had but mentioned his age, occupation, and name.

But all is now lost; I know not who he was; and this estimable author must needs share the oblivious fate of all literary incognitos.

He must have possessed the grandest and most elevated ideas of true fame, since he scorned to be perpetuated by a solitary initial. Could I find him out now, sleeping neglected in some churchyard, I would buy him a headstone, and record upon it naught but his title-page, deeming that his noblest epitaph.

After the preface, the book opens with an extract from a prologue written by the excellent Dr. Aiken, the brother of Mrs. Barbauld, upon the opening of the Theater Royal, Liverpool, in 1772:—

> *"Where Mersey's stream, long winding o'er the plain,*
> *Pours his full tribute to the circling main,*
> *A band of fishers chose their humble seat;*
> *Contented labor blessed the fair retreat,*
> *Inured to hardship, patient, bold, and rude,*
> *They braved the billows for precarious food:*
> *Their straggling huts were ranged along the shore,*
> *Their nets and little boats their only store."*

Indeed, throughout, the work abounds with quaint poetical quotations, and old-fashioned classical allusions to the Aeneid and Falconer's Shipwreck.

And the anonymous author must have been not only a scholar and a gentleman, but a man of gentle disinterestedness, combined with true city patriotism; for in his *"Survey of the Town"* are nine thickly printed pages of a neglected poem by a neglected Liverpool poet.

By way of apologizing for what might seem an obtrusion upon the public of so long an episode, he courteously and feelingly introduces it by saying, that *"the poem has now for several years been scarce, and is at present but little known; and hence a very small portion of it will no doubt be highly acceptable to the cultivated reader; especially as this noble epic is written with great felicity of expression and the sweetest delicacy of feeling."*

Once, but once only, an uncharitable thought crossed my mind, that the author of the Guide-Book might have been the author of the epic. But that was years ago; and I have never since permitted so uncharitable a reflection to insinuate itself into my mind.

This epic, from the specimen before me, is composed in the old stately style, and rolls along commanding as a coach and four. It sings of Liverpool and the Mersey; its docks, and ships, and warehouses, and bales, and anchors; and after descanting upon the abject times, when *"his noble waves, inglorious, Mersey rolled,"* the poet breaks forth like all Parnassus with:—

> "Now o'er the wondering world her name resounds,
> From northern climes to India's distant bounds—
> Where'er his shores the broad Atlantic waves;
> Where'er the Baltic rolls his wintry waves;
> Where'er the honored flood extends his tide,
> That clasps Sicilia like a favored bride.
> Greenland for her its bulky whale resigns,
> And temperate Gallia rears her generous vines:
> 'Midst warm Iberia citron orchards blow,
> And the ripe fruitage bends the laboring bough;
> In every clime her prosperous fleets are known,
> She makes the wealth of every clime her own."

It also contains a delicately-curtained allusion to Mr. Roscoe:—

> "And here R*s*o*, with genius all his own,
> New tracks explores, and all before unknown?"

Indeed, both the anonymous author of the Guide-Book, and the gifted bard of the Mersey, seem to have nourished the warmest appreciation of the fact, that to their beloved town Roscoe imparted a reputation which gracefully embellished its notoriety as a mere place of commerce. He is called the modern Guicciardini of the modern Florence, and his histories, translations, and Italian Lives, are spoken of with classical admiration.

The first chapter begins in a methodical, business-like way, by informing the impatient reader of the precise latitude and longitude of Liverpool; so that, at the outset, there may be no misunderstanding on that head. It then goes on to give an account of the history and antiquities of the town, beginning with a record in the *Doomsday-Book* of William the Conqueror.

Here, it must be sincerely confessed, however, that notwithstanding his numerous other merits, my favorite author betrays a want of the uttermost antiquarian and penetrating spirit, which would have scorned to stop in its researches at the reign of the Norman monarch, but would have pushed on resolutely through the dark ages, up to Moses, the man of Uz, and Adam; and finally established the fact beyond a doubt, that the soil of Liverpool was created with the creation.

But, perhaps, one of the most curious passages in the chapter of antiquarian research, is the pious author's moralizing reflections upon an interesting fact he records: to wit, that in a.d. 1571, the inhabitants sent a memorial to Queen Elizabeth, praying relief under a subsidy, wherein they style themselves *"her majesty's poor decayed town of Liverpool."*

As I now fix my gaze upon this faded and dilapidated old guide-book, bearing every token of the ravages of near half a century, and read how this piece of antiquity enlarges like a modern upon previous antiquities, I am forcibly reminded that the world is indeed growing old. And when I turn to the second chapter, *"On the increase of the town, and number of inhabitants,"* and then skim over page after page throughout the volume, all filled with allusions to the immense grandeur of a place, which, since then, has more than quadrupled in population, opulence, and splendor, and whose present inhabitants must look back upon the period here spoken of with a swelling feeling of immeasurable superiority and pride, I am filled with a comical sadness at the vanity of all human exaltation. For the cope-stone of to-day is the corner-stone of tomorrow; and as St. Peter's church was built in great part of the ruins of old Rome, so in all our erections, however imposing, we but form quarries and supply ignoble materials for the grander domes of posterity.

And even as this old guide-book boasts of the, to us, insignificant Liverpool of fifty years ago, the New York guidebooks are now vaunting of the magnitude of a town, whose future inhabitants, multitudinous as the pebbles on the beach, and girdled in with high walls and towers, flanking endless avenues of opulence and taste, will regard all our Broadways and Bowerys as but the paltry nucleus to their Nineveh. From far up the Hudson, beyond Harlem River, where the young saplings are now growing, that will overarch their lordly mansions with broad boughs, centuries old; they may send forth explorers to penetrate into the then obscure and smoky alleys of the Fifth Avenue and Fourteenth-street; and going still farther south, may exhume the present Doric Custom-house, and quote it as a proof that their high and mighty metropolis enjoyed a Hellenic antiquity.

As I am extremely loth to omit giving a specimen of the dignified style of this *"Picture of Liverpool,"* so different from the brief, pert, and unclerkly hand-books to Niagara and Buffalo of the present day, I shall now insert the chapter of antiquarian researches; especially as it is entertaining in itself, and affords much valuable, and perhaps rare information, which the reader may need, concerning the famous town, to which I made *my first voyage*. And I think that with regard to a matter, concerning which I myself am wholly ignorant, it is far better to quote my old friend verbatim, than to mince his substantial baron-of-beef of information into a flimsy ragout of my own; and so, pass it off as original. Yes, I will render unto my honored guide-book its due.

But how can the printer's art so dim and mellow down the pages into a soft sunset yellow; and to the reader's eye, shed over the type all the pleasant associations which the original carries to me!

No! by my father's sacred memory, and all sacred privacies of fond family reminiscences, I will not! I will *not* quote thee, old Morocco, before the cold face of the marble-hearted world; for your antiquities would only be skipped and dishonored by shallow-minded readers; and for me, I should be charged with swelling out my volume by plagiarizing from a guide-book-the most vulgar and ignominious of thefts!

CHAPTER XXXI
WITH HIS PROSY OLD GUIDE-BOOK, HE TAKES A PROSY STROLL THROUGH THE TOWN

When I left home, I took the green morocco guide-book along, supposing that from the great number of ships going to Liverpool, I would most probably ship on board of one of them, as the event itself proved.

Great was my boyish delight at the prospect of visiting a place, the infallible clew to all whose intricacies I held in my hand.

On the passage out I studied its pages a good deal. In the first place, I grounded myself thoroughly in the history and antiquities of the town, as set forth in the chapter I intended to quote. Then I mastered the columns of statistics, touching the advance of population; and pored over them, as I used to do over my multiplication-table. For I was determined to make the whole subject my own; and not be content with a mere smattering of the thing, as is too much the custom with most students of guide-books. Then I perused one by one the elaborate descriptions of public edifices, and scrupulously compared the text with the corresponding engraving, to see whether they corroborated each other. For be it known that, including the map, there were no less than seventeen plates in the work. And by often examining them, I had so impressed every column and cornice in my mind, that I had no doubt of recognizing the originals in a moment.

In short, when I considered that my own father had used this very guide-book, and that thereby it had been thoroughly tested, and its fidelity proved beyond a peradventure; I could not but think that I was building myself up in an unerring knowledge of Liverpool; especially as I had familiarized myself with the map, and could turn sharp corners on it, with marvelous confidence and celerity.

In imagination, as I lay in my berth on ship-board, I used to take pleasant afternoon rambles through the town; down St. James-street and up Great George's, stopping at various places of interest and attraction. I began to think I had been born in Liverpool, so familiar seemed all the features of the map. And though some of the streets there depicted were thickly involved, endlessly angular and crooked, like the map of Boston, in Massachusetts, yet, I made no doubt, that I could march through them in the darkest night, and even run for the most distant dock upon a pressing emergency.

Dear delusion!

It never occurred to my boyish thoughts, that though a guide-book, fifty years old, might have done good service in its day, yet it would prove but a miserable cicerone to a modern. I little imagined that the Liverpool my father saw, was another Liverpool from that to which I, his son Wellingborough was sailing. No; these things never obtruded; so accustomed had I been to associate my old morocco guide-book with the town it described, that the bare thought of there being any discrepancy, never entered my mind.

While we lay in the Mersey, before entering the dock, I got out my guide-book to see how the map would compare with the identical place itself. But they bore not the slightest resemblance. However, thinks I, this is owing to my taking a horizontal view, instead of a bird's-eye survey. So, never mind old guide-book, *you*, at least, are all right.

But my faith received a severe shock that same evening, when the crew went ashore to supper, as I have previously related.

The men stopped at a curious old tavern, near the Prince's Dock's walls; and having my guide-book in my pocket, I drew it forth to compare notes, when I found, that precisely upon the spot where I and my shipmates were standing, and a cherry-cheeked bar-maid was filling their glasses, my infallible old Morocco, in that very place, located a fort; adding, that it was well worth the intelligent stranger's while to visit it for the purpose of beholding the guard relieved in the evening.

This was a staggerer; for how could a tavern be mistaken for a castle? and this was about the hour mentioned for the guard to turn out; yet not a red coat was to be seen. But for all this, I could not, for one small discrepancy, condemn the old family servant who had so faithfully served my own father before me; and when I learned that this tavern went by the name of *"The Old Fort Tavern;"* and when I was told that many of the old stones were yet in the walls, I almost completely exonerated my guide-book from the half-insinuated charge of misleading me.

The next day was Sunday, and I had it all to myself; and now, thought I, my guide-book and I shall have a famous ramble up street and down lane, even unto the furthest limits of this Liverpool.

I rose bright and early; from head to foot performed my ablutions "with Eastern scrupulosity," and I arrayed myself in my red shirt and shooting-jacket, and the sportsman's pantaloons; and crowned my entire man with the tarpaulin; so that from this curious combination of clothing, and particularly from my red shirt, I must have looked like a very strange compound indeed: three parts sportsman, and two soldier, to one of the sailor.

My shipmates, of course, made merry at my appearance; but I heeded them not; and after breakfast, jumped ashore, full of brilliant anticipations.

My gait was erect, and I was rather tall for my age; and that may have been the reason why, as I was rapidly walking along the dock, a drunken sailor passing, exclaimed, *"Eyes right! quick step there!"*

Another fellow stopped me to know whether I was going fox-hunting; and one of the dock-police, stationed at the gates, after peeping out upon me from his sentry box, a snug little den, furnished with benches and newspapers, and hung round with storm jackets and oiled capes, issued forth in a great hurry, crossed my path as I was emerging into the street, and commanded me to *halt!* I obeyed; when scanning my appearance pertinaciously, he desired to know where I got that tarpaulin hat, not being able to account for the phenomenon of its roofing the head of a broken-down fox-hunter. But I pointed to my ship, which lay at no great distance; when remarking from my voice that I was a Yankee, this faithful functionary permitted me to pass.

It must be known that the police stationed at the gates of the docks are extremely observant of strangers going out; as many thefts are perpetrated on board the ships; and if they chance to see any thing suspicious, they probe into it without mercy. Thus, the old men who buy *"shakings,"* and rubbish from vessels, must turn their bags wrong side out before the police, ere they are allowed to go outside the walls. And often they will search a suspicious looking fellow's clothes, even if he be a very thin man, with attenuated and almost imperceptible pockets.

But where was I going?

I will tell. My intention was in the first place, to visit Riddough's Hotel, where my father had stopped, more than thirty years before: and then, with the map in my hand, follow him through all the town, according to the dotted lines in the diagram. For thus would I be performing a filial pilgrimage to spots which would be hallowed in my eyes.

At last, when I found myself going down Old Hall-street toward Lord-street, where the hotel was situated, according to my authority; and when, taking out my map, I found that Old Hall-street was marked there, through its whole extent with my father's pen; a thousand fond, affectionate emotions rushed around my heart.

Yes, in this very street, thought I, nay, on this very flagging my father walked. Then I almost wept, when I looked down on my sorry apparel, and marked how the people regarded me; the men staring at so grotesque a young stranger, and the old ladies, in beaver hats and ruffles, crossing the walk a little to shun me.

How differently my father must have appeared; perhaps in a blue coat, buff vest, and Hessian boots. And little did he think, that a son of his would ever visit Liverpool as a poor friendless sailor-boy. But I was not born then: no, when he walked this flagging, I was not so much as thought of; I was not included in the census of the universe. My own father did not know me then; and had never seen, or heard, or so much as dreamed of me. And that thought had a touch of sadness to me; for if it had certainly been, that my own parent, at one time, never cast a thought upon me, how might it be with me hereafter? Poor, poor Wellingborough! thought I, miserable boy! you are indeed friendless and forlorn. Here you wander a stranger in a strange town, and the very thought of your father's having been here before you, but carries with it the reflection that, he then knew you not, nor cared for you one whit.

But dispelling these dismal reflections as well as I could, I pushed on my way, till I got to Chapel-street, which I crossed; and then, going under a cloister-like arch of stone, whose gloom and narrowness delighted me, and filled my Yankee soul with romantic thoughts of old Abbeys and Minsters, I emerged into the fine quadrangle of the Merchants' Exchange.

There, leaning against the colonnade, I took out my map, and traced my father right across Chapel-street, and actually through the very arch at my back, into the paved square where I stood.

So vivid was now the impression of his having been here, and so narrow the passage from which he had emerged, that I felt like running on, and overtaking him around the Town Hall adjoining, at the head of Castle-street. But I soon checked myself, when remembering that he had gone whither no son's search could find him in this world. And then I thought of all that must have happened to him since he paced through that arch. What trials and troubles he had encountered; how he had been shaken by many storms of adversity, and at last died a bankrupt. I looked at my own sorry garb, and had much ado to keep from tears.

But I rallied, and gazed round at the sculptured stonework, and turned to my guide-book, and looked at the print of the spot. It was correct to a pillar; but wanted the central ornament of the quadrangle. This, however, was but a slight subsequent erection, which ought not to militate against the general character of my friend for comprehensiveness.

The ornament in question is a group of statuary in bronze, elevated upon a marble pedestal and basement, representing Lord Nelson expiring in the arms of Victory. One foot rests on a rolling foe, and the other on a cannon. Victory is dropping a wreath on the dying admiral's brow; while Death, under the similitude of a hideous skeleton, is insinuating his bony hand under the hero's robe, and groping after his heart. A very striking design, and true to the imagination; I never could look at Death without a shudder.

At uniform intervals round the base of the pedestal, four naked figures in chains, somewhat larger than life, are seated in various attitudes of humiliation and despair. One has his leg recklessly thrown over his knee, and his head bowed over, as if he had given up all hope of ever feeling better. Another has his head buried in despondency, and no doubt looks mournfully out of his eyes, but as his face was averted at the time, I could not catch the expression. These woe-begone figures of captives are emblematic of Nelson's principal victories; but I never could look at their swarthy limbs and manacles, without being involuntarily reminded of four African slaves in the market-place.

And my thoughts would revert to Virginia and Carolina; and also to the historical fact, that the African slave-trade once constituted the principal commerce of Liverpool; and that the prosperity of the town was once supposed to have been indissolubly linked to its prosecution. And I remembered that my father had often spoken to gentlemen visiting our house in New York, of the unhappiness that the discussion of the abolition of this trade had occasioned in Liverpool; that the struggle between sordid interest and humanity had made sad havoc at the fire-sides of the merchants; estranged sons from sires; and even separated husband from wife. And my thoughts reverted to my father's friend, the good and great Roscoe, the intrepid enemy of the trade; who in every way exerted his fine talents toward its suppression; writing a poem *("the Wrongs of Africa")*, several pamphlets; and in his place in Parliament, he delivered a speech against it, which, as coming from a member for Liverpool, was supposed to have turned many votes, and had no small share in the triumph of sound policy and humanity that ensued.

How this group of statuary affected me, may be inferred from the fact, that I never went through Chapel-street without going through the little arch to look at it again. And there, night or day, I was sure to find Lord Nelson still falling back; Victory's wreath still hovering over his swordpoint; and Death grim and grasping as ever; while the four bronze captives still lamented their captivity.

Now, as I lingered about the railing of the statuary, on the Sunday I have mentioned, I noticed several persons going in and out of an apartment, opening from the basement under the colonnade; and, advancing, I perceived that this was a news-room, full of files of papers. My love of literature prompted me to open the door and step in; but a glance at my soiled shooting-jacket prompted a dignified looking personage to step up and shut the door in my face. I deliberated a minute what I should do to him; and at last resolutely determined to let him alone, and pass on; which I did; going down Castle-street (so called from a castle which once stood there, said my guide-book), and turning down into Lord.

Arrived at the foot of the latter street, I in vain looked round for the hotel. How serious a disappointment was this may well be imagined, when it is considered that I was all eagerness to behold the very house at which my father stopped; where he slept and dined, smoked his cigar, opened his letters, and read the papers. I inquired of some gentlemen and ladies where the missing hotel was; but they only stared and passed on; until I met a mechanic, apparently, who very civilly stopped to hear my questions and give me an answer.

"Riddough's Hotel?" said he, "upon my word, I think I have heard of such a place; let me see—yes, yes—that was the hotel where my father broke his arm, helping to pull down the walls. My lad, you surely can't be inquiring for Riddough's Hotel! What do you want to find there?"

"Oh! nothing," I replied, "I am much obliged for your information"—and away I walked.

Then, indeed, a new light broke in upon me concerning my guide-book; and all my previous dim suspicions were almost confirmed. It was nearly half a century behind the age! and no more fit to guide me about the town, than the map of Pompeii.

It was a sad, a solemn, and a most melancholy thought. The book on which I had so much relied; the book in the old morocco cover; the book with the cocked-hat corners; the book full of fine old family associations; the book with seventeen plates, executed in the highest style of art; this precious book was next to useless. Yes, the thing that had guided the father, could not guide the son. And I sat down on a shop step, and gave loose to meditation.

Here, now, oh, Wellingborough, thought I, learn a lesson, and never forget it. This world, my boy, is a moving world; its Riddough's Hotels are forever being pulled down; it never stands still; and its sands are forever shifting. This very harbor of Liverpool is gradually filling up, they say; and who knows what your son (if you ever have one) may behold, when he comes to visit Liverpool, as long after you as you come after his grandfather. And, Wellingborough, as your father's guidebook is no guide for you, neither would yours (could you afford to buy a modern one to-day) be a true guide to those who come after you. Guide-books, Wellingborough, are the least reliable books in all literature; and nearly all literature, in one sense, is made up of guide-books. Old ones tell us the ways our fathers went, through the thoroughfares and courts of old; but how few of those former places can their posterity trace, amid avenues of modem erections; to how few is the old guide-book now a clew! Every age makes its own guidebooks, and the old ones are used for waste paper. But there is one Holy Guide-Book, Wellingborough, that will never lead you astray, if you but follow it aright; and some noble monuments that remain, though the pyramids crumble.

But though I rose from the door-step a sadder and a wiser boy, and though my guide-book had been stripped of its reputation for infallibility, I did not treat with contumely or disdain, those sacred pages which had once been a beacon to my sire.

No.—Poor old guide-book, thought I, tenderly stroking its back, and smoothing the dog-ears with reverence; I will not use you with despite, old Morocco! and you will yet prove a trusty conductor through many old streets in the old parts of this town; even if you are at fault, now and then, concerning a Riddough's Hotel, or some other forgotten thing of the past. As I fondly glanced over the leaves, like one who loves more than he chides, my eye lighted upon a passage concerning *"The Old Dock,"* which much aroused my curiosity. I determined to see the place without delay: and walking on, in what I presumed to be the right direction, at last found myself before a spacious and splendid pile of sculptured brown stone; and entering the porch, perceived from incontrovertible tokens that it must be the Custom-house. After admiring it awhile, I took out my guide-book again; and what was my amazement at discovering that, according to its authority, I was entirely mistaken with regard to this Custom-house; for precisely where I stood, *"The Old Dock"* must be standing, and reading on concerning it, I met with this very apposite passage:—*"The first idea that strikes the stranger in coming to this dock, is the singularity of so great a number of ships afloat in the very heart of the town, without discovering any connection with the sea."*

Here, now, was a poser! Old Morocco confessed that there was a good deal of "singularity" about the thing; nor did he pretend to deny that it was, without question, amazing, that this fabulous dock should seem to have no *connection with the sea!* However, the same author went on to say, that the *"astonished stranger must suspend his wonder for awhile, and turn to the left."* But, right or left, no place answering to the description was to be seen.

This was too confounding altogether, and not to be easily accounted for, even by making ordinary allowances for the growth and general improvement of the town in the course of years. So, guide-book in hand, I accosted a policeman standing by, and begged him to tell me whether he was acquainted with any place in that neighborhood called the *"Old Dock."* The man looked at me wonderingly at first, and then seeing I was apparently sane, and quite civil into the bargain, he whipped his well-polished boot with his rattan, pulled up his silver-laced coat-collar, and initiated me into a knowledge of the following facts.

It seems that in this place originally stood the *"pool,"* from which the town borrows a part of its name, and which originally wound round the greater part of the old settlements; that this pool was made into the "Old Dock," for the benefit of the shipping; but that, years ago, it had been filled up, and furnished the site for the Custom-house before me.

I now eyed the spot with a feeling somewhat akin to the Eastern traveler standing on the brink of the Dead Sea. For here the doom of Gomorrah seemed reversed, and a lake had been converted into substantial stone and mortar.

Well, well, Wellingborough, thought I, you had better put the book into your pocket, and carry it home to the Society of Antiquaries; it is several thousand leagues and odd furlongs behind the march of improvement. Smell its old morocco binding, Wellingborough; does it not smell somewhat mummy-ish? Does it not remind you of Cheops and the Catacombs? I tell you it was written before the lost books of Livy, and is cousin-german to that irrecoverably departed volume, entitled, *"The Wars of the Lord"* quoted by Moses in the Pentateuch. Put it up, Wellingborough, put it up, my dear friend; and hereafter follow your nose throughout Liverpool; it will stick to you through thick and thin: and be your ship's mainmast and St. George's spire your landmarks.

No!—And again I rubbed its back softly, and gently adjusted a loose leaf: No, no, I'll not give you up yet. Forth, old Morocco! and lead me in sight of the venerable Abbey of Birkenhead; and let these eager eyes behold the mansion once occupied by the old earls of Derby!

For the book discoursed of both places, and told how the Abbey was on the Cheshire shore, full in view from a point on the Lancashire side, covered over with ivy, and brilliant with moss! And how the house of the noble Derby's was now a common jail of the town; and how that circumstance was full of suggestions, and pregnant with wisdom!

But, alas! I never saw the Abbey; at least none was in sight from the water: and as for the house of the earls, I never saw that.

Ah me, and ten times alas! am I to visit old England in vain? in the land of Thomas-a-Becket and stout John of Gaunt, not to catch the least glimpse of priory or castle? Is there nothing in all the British empire but these smoky ranges of old shops and warehouses? is Liverpool but a brick-kiln? Why, no buildings here look so ancient as the old gable-pointed mansion of my maternal grandfather at home, whose bricks were brought from Holland long before the revolutionary war! Tis a deceit—a gull—a sham—a hoax! This boasted England is no older than the State of New York: if it is, show me the proofs—point out the vouchers. Where's the tower of Julius Caesar? Where's the Roman wall? Show me Stonehenge!

But, Wellingborough, I remonstrated with myself, you are only in Liverpool; the old monuments lie to the north, south, east, and west of you; you are but a sailor-boy, and you can not expect to be a great tourist, and visit the antiquities, in that preposterous shooting-jacket of yours. Indeed, you can not, my boy.

True, true—that's it. I am not the traveler my father was. I am only a common-carrier across the Atlantic.

After a weary day's walk, I at last arrived at the sign of the Baltimore Clipper to supper; and Handsome Mary poured me out a brimmer of tea, in which, for the time, I drowned all my melancholy.

CHAPTER XXXII
THE DOCKS

For more than six weeks, the ship Highlander lay in Prince's Dock; and during that time, besides making observations upon things immediately around me, I made sundry excursions to the neighboring docks, for I never tired of admiring them.

Previous to this, having only seen the miserable wooden wharves, and slip-shod, shambling piers of New York, the sight of these mighty docks filled my young mind with wonder and delight. In New York, to be sure, I could not but be struck with the long line of shipping, and tangled thicket of masts along the East River; yet, my admiration had been much abated by those irregular, unsightly wharves, which, I am sure, are a reproach and disgrace to the city that tolerates them.

Whereas, in Liverpool, I beheld long China walls of masonry; vast piers of stone; and a succession of granite-rimmed docks, completely inclosed, and many of them communicating, which almost recalled to mind the great American chain of lakes: Ontario, Erie, St. Clair, Huron, Michigan, and Superior. The extent and solidity of these structures, seemed equal to what I had read of the old Pyramids of Egypt.

Liverpool may justly claim to have originated the model of the "Wet Dock," [1] so called, of the present day; and every thing that is connected with its design, construction, regulation, and improvement. Even London was induced to copy after Liverpool, and Havre followed her example. In magnitude, cost, and durability, the docks of Liverpool, even at the present day surpass all others in the world.

> [1] This term—*Wet Dock*—did not originate, (as has been erroneously opined by the otherwise learned Bardoldi); from the fact, that persons falling into one, never escaped without a soaking; but it is simply used, in order to distinguish these docks from the *Dry-Dock*, where the bottoms of ships are repaired.

The first dock built by the town was the *"Old Dock,"* alluded to in my Sunday stroll with my guide-book. This was erected in 1710, since which period has gradually arisen that long line of dock-masonry, now flanking the Liverpool side of the Mersey.

For miles you may walk along that river-side, passing dock after dock, like a chain of immense fortresses:—Prince's, George's, Salt-House, Clarence, Brunswick, Trafalgar, King's, Queen's, and many more.

In a spirit of patriotic gratitude to those naval heroes, who by their valor did so much to protect the commerce of Britain, in which Liverpool held so large a stake; the town, long since, bestowed upon its more modern streets, certain illustrious names, that Broadway might be proud of:—Duncan, Nelson, Rodney, St. Vincent, Nile.

But it is a pity, I think, that they had not bestowed these noble names upon their noble docks; so that they might have been as a rank and file of most fit monuments to perpetuate the names of the heroes, in connection with the commerce they defended.

And how much better would such stirring monuments be; full of life and commotion; than hermit obelisks of Luxor, and idle towers of stone; which, useless to the world in themselves, vainly hope to eternize a name, by having it carved, solitary and alone, in their granite. Such monuments are cenotaphs indeed; founded far away from the true body of the fame of the hero; who, if he be truly a hero, must still be linked with the living interests of his race; for the true fame is something free, easy, social, and companionable. They are but tomb-stones, that commemorate his death, but celebrate not his life. It is well enough that over the inglorious and thrice miserable grave of a Dives, some vast marble column should be reared, recording the fact of his having lived and died; for such records are indispensable to preserve his shrunken memory among men; though that memory must soon crumble away with the marble, and mix with the stagnant oblivion of the mob. But to build such a pompous vanity over the remains of a hero, is a slur upon his fame, and an insult to his ghost. And more enduring monuments are built in the closet with the letters of the alphabet, than even Cheops himself could have founded, with all Egypt and Nubia for his quarry.

Among the few docks mentioned above, occur the names of the *King's* and *Queens.* At the time, they often reminded me of the two principal streets in the village I came from in America, which streets once rejoiced in the same royal appellations. But they had been christened previous to the Declaration of Independence; and some years after, in a fever of freedom, they were abolished, at an enthusiastic town-meeting, where King George and his lady were solemnly declared unworthy of being immortalized by the village of L—. A country antiquary once told me, that a committee of two barbers were deputed to write and inform the distracted old gentleman of the fact.

As the description of any one of these Liverpool docks will pretty much answer for all, I will here endeavor to give some account of Prince's Dock, where the Highlander rested after her passage across the Atlantic.

This dock, of comparatively recent construction, is perhaps the largest of all, and is well known to American sailors, from the fact, that it is mostly frequented by the American shipping. Here lie the noble New York packets, which at home are found at the foot of Wall-street; and here lie the Mobile and Savannah cotton ships and traders.

This dock was built like the others, mostly upon the bed of the river, the earth and rock having been laboriously scooped out, and solidified again as materials for the quays and piers. From the river, Prince's Dock is protected by a long pier of masonry, surmounted by a massive wall; and on the side next the town, it is bounded by similar walls, one of which runs along a thoroughfare. The whole space thus inclosed forms an oblong, and may, at a guess, be presumed to comprise about fifteen or twenty acres; but as I had not the rod of a surveyor when I took it in, I will not be certain.

The area of the dock itself, exclusive of the inclosed quays surrounding it, may be estimated at, say, ten acres. Access to the interior from the streets is had through several gateways; so that, upon their being closed, the whole dock is shut up like a house. From the river, the entrance is through a water-gate, and ingress to ships is only to be had, when the level of the dock coincides with that of the river; that is, about the time of high tide, as the level of the dock is always at that mark. So that when it is low tide in the river, the keels of the ships inclosed by the quays are elevated more than twenty feet above those of the vessels in the stream. This, of course, produces a striking effect to a stranger, to see hundreds of immense ships floating high aloft in the heart of a mass of masonry.

Prince's Dock is generally so filled with shipping, that the entrance of a new-comer is apt to occasion a universal stir among all the older occupants. The dock-masters, whose authority is declared by tin signs worn conspicuously over their hats, mount the poops and forecastles of the various vessels, and hail the surrounding strangers in all directions:—"Highlander ahoy! Cast off your bowline, and sheer alongside the Neptune!"—"Neptune ahoy! get out a stern-line, and sheer alongside the Trident!"—"Trident ahoy! get out a bowline, and drop astern of the Undaunted!" And so it runs round like a shock of electricity; touch one, and you touch all. This kind of work irritates and exasperates the sailors to the last degree; but it is only one of the unavoidable inconveniences of inclosed docks, which are outweighed by innumerable advantages.

Just without the water-gate, is a basin, always connecting with the open river, through a narrow entrance between pierheads. This basin forms a sort of ante-chamber to the dock itself, where vessels lie waiting their turn to enter. During a storm, the necessity of this basin is obvious; for it would be impossible to "*dock*" a ship under full headway from a voyage across the ocean. From the turbulent waves, she first glides into the ante-chamber between the pier-heads and from thence into the docks.

Concerning the cost of the docks, I can only state, that the *King's Dock*, comprehending but a comparatively small area, was completed at an expense of some £20,000.

Our old ship-keeper, a Liverpool man by birth, who had long followed the seas, related a curious story concerning this dock. One of the ships which carried over troops from England to Ireland in King William's war, in 1688, entered the King's Dock on the first day of its being opened in 1788, after an interval of just one century. She was a dark little brig, called the *Port-a-Ferry*. And probably, as her timbers must have been frequently renewed in the course of a hundred years, the name alone could have been all that was left of her at the time. A paved area, very wide, is included within the walls; and along the edge of the quays are ranges of iron sheds, intended as a temporary shelter for the goods unladed from the shipping. Nothing can exceed the bustle and activity displayed along these quays during the day; bales, crates, boxes, and cases are being tumbled about by thousands of laborers; trucks are coming and going; dock-masters are shouting; sailors of all nations are singing out at their ropes; and all this commotion is greatly increased by the resoundings from the lofty walls that hem in the din.

CHAPTER XXXIII
THE SALT-DROGHERS, AND GERMAN EMIGRANT SHIPS

Surrounded by its broad belt of masonry, each Liverpool dock is a walled town, full of life and commotion; or rather, it is a small archipelago, an epitome of the world, where all the nations of Christendom, and even those of Heathendom, are represented. For, in itself, each ship is an island, a floating colony of the tribe to which it belongs.

Here are brought together the remotest limits of the earth; and in the collective spars and timbers of these ships, all the forests of the globe are represented, as in a grand parliament of masts. Canada and New Zealand send their pines; America her live oak; India her teak; Norway her spruce; and the Right Honorable Mahogany, member for Honduras and Campeachy, is seen at his post by the wheel. Here, under the beneficent sway of the Genius of Commerce, all climes and countries embrace; and yard-arm touches yard-arm in brotherly love.

A Liverpool dock is a grand caravansary inn, and hotel, on the spacious and liberal plan of the *Astor House*. Here ships are lodged at a moderate charge, and payment is not demanded till the time of departure. Here they are comfortably housed and provided for; sheltered from all weathers and secured from all calamities. For I can hardly credit a story I have heard, that sometimes, in heavy gales, ships lying in the very middle of the docks have lost their top-gallant-masts. Whatever the toils and hardships encountered on the voyage, whether they come from Iceland or the coast of New Guinea, here their sufferings are ended, and they take their ease in their watery inn.

I know not how many hours I spent in gazing at the shipping in Prince's Dock, and speculating concerning their past voyages and future prospects in life. Some had just arrived from the most distant ports, worn, battered, and disabled; others were all a-taunt-o—spruce, gay, and brilliant, in readiness for sea.

Every day the Highlander had some new neighbor. A black brig from Glasgow, with its crew of sober Scotch caps, and its staid, thrifty-looking skipper, would be replaced by a jovial French hermaphrodite, its forecastle echoing with songs, and its quarter-deck elastic from much dancing.

On the other side, perhaps, a magnificent New York Liner, huge as a seventy-four, and suggesting the idea of a Mivart's or Delmonico's afloat, would give way to a Sidney emigrant ship, receiving on board its live freight of shepherds from the Grampians, ere long to be tending their flocks on the hills and downs of New Holland.

I was particularly pleased and tickled, with a multitude of little salt-droghers, rigged like sloops, and not much bigger than a pilot-boat, but with broad bows painted black, and carrying red sails, which looked as if they had been pickled and stained in a tan-yard. These little fellows were continually coming in with their cargoes for ships bound to America; and lying, five or six together, alongside of those lofty Yankee hulls, resembled a parcel of red ants about the carcass of a black buffalo.

When loaded, these comical little craft are about level with the water; and frequently, when blowing fresh in the river, I have seen them flying through the foam with nothing visible but the mast and sail, and a man at the tiller; their entire cargo being snugly secured under hatches.

It was diverting to observe the self-importance of the skipper of any of these diminutive vessels. He would give himself all the airs of an admiral on a three-decker's poop; and no doubt, thought quite as much of himself. And why not? What could Caesar want more? Though his craft was none of the largest, it was subject to *him;* and though his crew might only consist of himself; yet if he governed it well, he achieved a triumph, which the moralists of all ages have set above the victories of Alexander.

These craft have each a little cabin, the prettiest, charmingest, most delightful little dog-hole in the world; not much bigger than an old-fashioned alcove for a bed. It is lighted by little round glasses placed in the deck; so that to the insider, the ceiling is like a small firmament twinkling with astral radiations. For tall men, nevertheless, the place is but ill-adapted; a sitting, or recumbent position being indispensable to an occupancy of the premises. Yet small, low, and narrow as the cabin is, somehow, it affords accommodations to the skipper and his family. Often, I used to watch the tidy good-wife, seated at the open little scuttle, like a woman at a cottage door, engaged in knitting socks for her husband; or perhaps, cutting his hair, as he kneeled before her. And once, while marveling how a couple like this found room to turn in, below, I was amazed by a noisy irruption of cherry-cheeked young tars from the scuttle, whence they came rolling forth, like so many curly spaniels from a kennel.

Upon one occasion, I had the curiosity to go on board a salt-drogher, and fall into conversation with its skipper, a bachelor, who kept house all alone. I found him a very sociable, comfortable old fellow, who had an eye to having things cozy around him. It was in the evening; and he invited me down into his sanctum to supper; and there we sat together like a couple in a box at an oyster-cellar.

"He, he," he chuckled, kneeling down before a fat, moist, little cask of beer, and holding a cocked-hat pitcher to the faucet—"You see, Jack, I keep every thing down here; and nice times I have by myself. Just before going to bed, it ain't bad to take a nightcap, you know; eh! Jack?—here now, smack your lips over that, my boy—have a pipe?—but stop, let's to supper first."

So he went to a little locker, a fixture against the side, and groping in it awhile, and addressing it with—"*What cheer here, what cheer?*" at last produced a loaf, a small cheese, a bit of ham, and a jar of butter. And then placing a board on his lap, spread the table, the pitcher of beer in the center. "Why that's but a two legged table," said I, "let's make it four."

So we divided the burthen, and supped merrily together on our knees.

He was an old ruby of a fellow, his cheeks toasted brown; and it did my soul good, to see the froth of the beer bubbling at his mouth, and sparkling on his nut-brown beard. He looked so like a great mug of ale, that I almost felt like taking him by the neck and pouring him out.

"Now Jack," said he, when supper was over, "now Jack, my boy, do you smoke?—Well then, load away." And he handed me a seal-skin pouch of tobacco and a pipe. We sat smoking together in this little sea-cabinet of his, till it began to look much like a state-room in Tophet; and notwithstanding my host's rubicund nose, I could hardly see him for the fog.

"He, he, my boy," then said he—"I don't never have any bugs here, I tell ye: I smokes 'em all out every night before going to bed."

"And where may you sleep?" said I, looking round, and seeing no sign of a bed.

"Sleep?" says he, "why I sleep in my jacket, that's the best counterpane; and I use my head for a pillow. He-he, funny, ain't it?"

"Very funny," says I.

"Have some more ale?" says he; "plenty more." "No more, thank you," says I; "I guess I'll go;" for what with the tobacco-smoke and the ale, I began to feel like breathing fresh air. Besides, my conscience smote me for thus freely indulging in the pleasures of the table.

"Now, don't go," said he; "don't go, my boy; don't go out into the damp; take an old Christian's advice," laying his hand on my shoulder; "it won't do. You see, by going out now, you'll shake off the ale, and get broad awake again; but if you stay here, you'll soon be dropping off for a nice little nap."

But notwithstanding these inducements, I shook my host's hand and departed. There was hardly any thing I witnessed in the docks that interested me more than the German emigrants who come on board the large New York ships several days before their sailing, to make every thing comfortable ere starting. Old men, tottering with age, and little infants in arms; laughing girls in bright-buttoned bodices, and astute, middle-aged men with pictured pipes in their mouths, would be seen mingling together in crowds of five, six, and seven or eight hundred in one ship.

Every evening these countrymen of Luther and Melancthon gathered on the forecastle to sing and pray. And it was exalting to listen to their fine ringing anthems, reverberating among the crowded shipping, and rebounding from the lofty walls of the docks. Shut your eyes, and you would think you were in a cathedral.

They keep up this custom at sea; and every night, in the dog-watch, sing the songs of Zion to the roll of the great ocean-organ: a pious custom of a devout race, who thus send over their hallelujahs before them, as they hie to the land of the stranger.

And among these sober Germans, my country counts the most orderly and valuable of her foreign population. It is they who have swelled the census of her Northwestern States; and transferring their ploughs from the hills of Transylvania to the prairies of Wisconsin; and sowing the wheat of the Rhine on the banks of the Ohio, raise the grain, that, a hundred fold increased, may return to their kinsmen in Europe.

There is something in the contemplation of the mode in which America has been settled, that, in a noble breast, should forever extinguish the prejudices of national dislikes. Settled by the people of all nations, all nations may claim her for their own. You can not spill a drop of American blood without spilling the blood of the whole world. Be he Englishman, Frenchman, German, Dane, or Scot; the European who scoffs at an American, calls his own brother *Raca*, and stands in danger of the judgment. We are not a narrow tribe of men, with a bigoted Hebrew nationality—whose blood has been debased in the attempt to ennoble it, by maintaining an exclusive succession among ourselves. No: our blood is as the flood of the Amazon, made up of a thousand noble currents all pouring into one. We are not a nation, so much as a world; for unless we may claim all the world for our sire, like Melchisedec, we are without father or mother.

For who was our father and our mother? Or can we point to any Romulus and Remus for our founders? Our ancestry is lost in the universal paternity; and Caesar and Alfred, St. Paul and Luther, and Homer and Shakespeare are as much ours as Washington, who is as much the world's as our own. We are the heirs of all time, and with all nations we divide our inheritance. On this Western Hemisphere all tribes and people are forming into one federated whole; and there is a future which shall see the estranged children of Adam restored as to the old hearthstone in Eden.

The other world beyond this, which was longed for by the devout before Columbus' time, was found in the New; and the deep-sea-lead, that first struck these soundings, brought up the soil of Earth's Paradise. Not a Paradise then, or now; but to be made so, at God's good pleasure, and in the fullness and mellowness of time. The seed is sown, and the harvest must come; and our children's children, on the world's jubilee morning, shall all go with their sickles to the reaping. Then shall the curse of Babel be revoked, a new Pentecost come, and the language they shall speak shall be the language of Britain. Frenchmen, and Danes, and Scots; and the dwellers on the shores of the Mediterranean, and in the regions round about; Italians, and Indians, and Moors; there shall appear unto them cloven tongues as of fire.

CHAPTER XXXIV
THE IRRAWADDY

Among the various ships lying in Prince's Dock, none interested me more than the Irrawaddy, of Bombay, a *"country ship,"* which is the name bestowed by Europeans upon the large native vessels of India. Forty years ago, these merchantmen were nearly the largest in the world; and they still exceed the generality. They are built of the celebrated teak wood, the oak of the East, or in Eastern phrase, *"the King of the Oaks."* The Irrawaddy had just arrived from Hindostan, with a cargo of cotton. She was manned by forty or fifty Lascars, the native seamen of India, who seemed to be immediately governed by a countryman of theirs of a higher caste. While his inferiors went about in strips of white linen, this dignitary was arrayed in a red army-coat, brilliant with gold lace, a cocked hat, and drawn sword. But the general effect was quite spoiled by his bare feet.

In discharging the cargo, his business seemed to consist in flagellating the crew with the flat of his saber, an exercise in which long practice had made him exceedingly expert. The poor fellows jumped away with the tackle-rope, elastic as cats.

One Sunday, I went aboard of the Irrawaddy, when this oriental usher accosted me at the gangway, with his sword at my throat. I gently pushed it aside, making a sign expressive of the pacific character of my motives in paying a visit to the ship. Whereupon he very considerately let me pass.

I thought I was in Pegu, so strangely woody was the smell of the dark-colored timbers, whose odor was heightened by the rigging of *kayar,* or cocoa-nut fiber.

The Lascars were on the forecastle-deck. Among them were Malays, Mahrattas, Burmese, Siamese, and Cingalese. They were seated round "kids" full of rice, from which, according to their invariable custom, they helped themselves with one hand, the other being reserved for quite another purpose. They were chattering like magpies in Hindostanee, but I found that several of them could also speak very good English. They were a small-limbed, wiry, tawny set; and I was informed made excellent seamen, though ill adapted to stand the hardships of northern voyaging.

They told me that seven of their number had died on the passage from Bombay; two or three after crossing the Tropic of Cancer, and the rest met their fate in the Channel, where the ship had been tost about in violent seas, attended with cold rains, peculiar to that vicinity. Two more had been lost overboard from the flying-jib-boom.

I was condoling with a young English cabin-boy on board, upon the loss of these poor fellows, when he said it was their own fault; they would never wear monkey-jackets, but clung to their thin India robes, even in the bitterest weather. He talked about them much as a farmer would about the loss of so many sheep by the murrain.

The captain of the vessel was an Englishman, as were also the three mates, master and boatswain. These officers lived astern in the cabin, where every Sunday they read the Church of England's prayers, while the heathen at the other end of the ship were left to their false gods and idols. And thus, with Christianity on the quarter-deck, and paganism on the forecastle, the Irrawaddy ploughed the sea.

As if to symbolize this state of things, the *"fancy piece"* astern comprised, among numerous other carved decorations, a cross and a miter; while forward, on the bows, was a sort of devil for a figure-head—a dragon-shaped creature, with a fiery red mouth, and a switchy-looking tail.

After her cargo was discharged, which was done "to the sound of flutes and soft recorders"—something as work is done in the navy to the music of the boatswain's pipe—the Lascars were set to *"stripping the ship"* that is, to sending down all her spars and ropes.

At this time, she lay alongside of us, and the Babel on board almost drowned our own voices. In nothing but their girdles, the Lascars hopped about aloft, chattering like so many monkeys; but, nevertheless, showing much dexterity and seamanship in their manner of doing their work.

Every Sunday, crowds of well-dressed people came down to the dock to see this singular ship; many of them perched themselves in the shrouds of the neighboring craft, much to the wrath of Captain Riga, who left strict orders with our old ship-keeper, to drive all strangers out of the Highlander's rigging. It was amusing at these times, to watch the old women with umbrellas, who stood on the quay staring at the Lascars, even when they desired to be private. These inquisitive old ladies seemed to regard the strange sailors as a species of wild animal, whom they might gaze at with as much impunity, as at leopards in the Zoological Gardens.

One night I was returning to the ship, when just as I was passing through the Dock Gate, I noticed a white figure squatting against the wall outside.

It proved to be one of the Lascars who was smoking, as the regulations of the docks prohibit his indulging this luxury on board his vessel. Struck with the curious fashion of his pipe, and the odor from it, I inquired what he was smoking; he replied *"Joggerry,"* which is a species of weed, used in place of tobacco.

Finding that he spoke good English, and was quite communicative, like most smokers, I sat down by *Dattabdool-mans, as* he called himself, and we fell into conversation. So instructive was his discourse, that when we parted, I had considerably added to my stock of knowledge. Indeed, it is a Godsend to fall in with a fellow like this. He knows things you never dreamed of; his experiences are like a man from the moon—wholly strange, a new revelation. If you want to learn romance, or gain an insight into things quaint, curious, and marvelous, drop your books of travel, and take a stroll along the docks of a great commercial port. Ten to one, you will encounter Crusoe himself among the crowds of mariners from all parts of the globe.

But this is no place for making mention of all the subjects upon which I and my Lascar friend mostly discoursed; I will only try to give his account of the *teakwood* and *kayar rope,* concerning which things I was curious, and sought information.

The *"sagoon"* as he called the tree which produces the teak, grows in its greatest excellence among the mountains of Malabar, whence large quantities are sent to Bombay for shipbuilding. He also spoke of another kind of wood, the *"sissor,"* which supplies most of the *"shin-logs,"* or "knees," and crooked timbers in the *country ships.* The sagoon grows to an immense size; sometimes there is fifty feet of trunk, three feet through, before a single bough is put forth. Its leaves are very large; and to convey some idea of them, my Lascar likened them to elephants' ears. He said a purple dye was extracted from them, for the purpose of staining cottons and silks. The wood is specifically heavier than water; it is easily worked, and extremely strong and durable. But its chief merit lies in resisting the action of the salt water, and the attacks of insects; which resistance is caused by its containing a resinous oil called *"poonja."*

To my surprise, he informed me that the Irrawaddy was wholly built by the native shipwrights of India, who, he modestly asserted, surpassed the European artisans.

The rigging, also, was of native manufacture. As the *kayar,* of which it is composed, is now getting into use both in England and America, as well for ropes and rigging as for mats and rugs, my Lascar friend's account of it, joined to my own observations, may not be uninteresting.

In India, it is prepared very much in the same way as in Polynesia. The cocoa-nut is gathered while the husk is still green, and but partially ripe; and this husk is removed by striking the nut forcibly, with both hands, upon a sharp-pointed stake, planted uprightly in the ground. In this way a boy will strip nearly fifteen hundred in a day. But the *kayar* is not made from the husk, as might be supposed, but from the rind of the nut; which, after being long soaked in water, is beaten with mallets, and rubbed together into fibers. After this being dried in the sun, you may spin it, just like hemp, or any similar substance. The fiber thus produced makes very strong and durable ropes, extremely well adapted, from their lightness and durability, for the running rigging of a ship; while the same causes, united with its great strength and buoyancy, render it very suitable for large cables and hawsers.

But the elasticity of the *kayar* ill fits it for the shrouds and standing-rigging of a ship, which require to be comparatively firm. Hence, as the Irrawaddy's shrouds were all of this substance, the Lascar told me, they were continually setting up or slacking off her standing-rigging, according as the weather was cold or warm. And the loss of a foretopmast, between the tropics, in a squall, he attributed to this circumstance.

After a stay of about two weeks, the Irrawaddy had her heavy Indian spars replaced with Canadian pine, and her *kayar* shrouds with hempen ones. She then mustered her pagans, and hoisted sail for London.

CHAPTER XXXV
GALLIOTS, COAST-OF-GUINEA-MAN, AND FLOATING CHAPEL

Another very curious craft often seen in the Liverpool docks, is the Dutch galliot, an old-fashioned looking gentleman, with hollow waist, high prow and stern, and which, seen lying among crowds of tight Yankee traders, and pert French brigantines, always reminded me of a cocked hat among modish beavers.

The construction of the galliot has not altered for centuries; and the northern European nations, Danes and Dutch, still sail the salt seas in this flat-bottomed salt-cellar of a ship; although, in addition to these, they have vessels of a more modern kind.

They seldom paint the galliot; but scrape and varnish all its planks and spars, so that all over it resembles the *"bright side"* or polished *streak*, usually banding round an American ship.

Some of them are kept scrupulously neat and clean, and remind one of a well-scrubbed wooden platter, or an old oak table, upon which much wax and elbow vigor has been expended. Before the wind, they sail well; but on a bowline, owing to their broad hulls and flat bottoms, they make leeway at a sad rate.

Every day, some strange vessel entered Prince's Dock; and hardly would I gaze my fill at some outlandish craft from Surat or the Levant, ere a still more outlandish one would absorb my attention.

Among others, I remember, was a little brig from the Coast of Guinea. In appearance, she was the ideal of a slaver; low, black, clipper-built about the bows, and her decks in a state of most piratical disorder.

She carried a long, rusty gun, on a swivel, amid-ships; and that gun was a curiosity in itself. It must have been some old veteran, condemned by the government, and sold for any thing it would fetch. It was an antique, covered with half-effaced inscriptions, crowns, anchors, eagles; and it had two handles near the trunnions, like those of a tureen. The knob on the breach was fashioned into a dolphin's head; and by a comical conceit, the touch-hole formed the orifice of a human ear; and a stout tympanum it must have had, to have withstood the concussions it had heard.

The brig, heavily loaded, lay between two large ships in ballast; so that its deck was at least twenty feet below those of its neighbors. Thus shut in, its hatchways looked like the entrance to deep vaults or mines; especially as her men were wheeling out of her hold some kind of ore, which might have been gold ore, so scrupulous were they in evening the bushel measures, in which they transferred it to the quay; and so particular was the captain, a dark-skinned whiskerando, in a Maltese cap and tassel, in standing over the sailors, with his pencil and memorandum-book in hand.

The crew were a buccaneering looking set; with hairy chests, purple shirts, and arms wildly tattooed. The mate had a wooden leg, and hobbled about with a crooked cane like a spiral staircase. There was a deal of swearing on board of this craft, which was rendered the more reprehensible when she came to moor alongside the Floating Chapel.

This was the hull of an old sloop-of-war, which had been converted into a mariner's church. A house had been built upon it, and a steeple took the place of a mast. There was a little balcony near the base of the steeple, some twenty feet from the water; where, on week-days, I used to see an old pensioner of a tar, sitting on a camp-stool, reading his Bible. On Sundays he hoisted the Bethel flag, and like the *muezzin* or cryer of prayers on the top of a Turkish mosque, would call the strolling sailors to their devotions; not officially, but on his own account; conjuring them not to make fools of themselves, but muster round the pulpit, as they did about the capstan on a man-of-war. This old worthy was the sexton. I attended the chapel several times, and found there a very orderly but small congregation. The first time I went, the chaplain was discoursing on future punishments, and making allusions to the Tartarean Lake; which, coupled with the pitchy smell of the old hull, summoned up the most forcible image of the thing which I ever experienced.

The floating chapels which are to be found in some of the docks, form one of the means which have been tried to induce the seamen visiting Liverpool to turn their thoughts toward serious things. But as very few of them ever think of entering these chapels, though they might pass them twenty times in the day, some of the clergy, of a Sunday, address them in the open air, from the corners of the quays, or wherever they can procure an audience.

Whenever, in my Sunday strolls, I caught sight of one of these congregations, I always made a point of joining it; and would find myself surrounded by a motley crowd of seamen from all quarters of the globe, and women, and lumpers, and dock laborers of all sorts. Frequently the clergyman would be standing upon an old cask, arrayed in full canonicals, as a divine of the Church of England. Never have I heard religious discourses better adapted to an audience of men, who, like sailors, are chiefly, if not only, to be moved by the plainest of precepts, and demonstrations of the misery of sin, as conclusive and undeniable as those of Euclid. No mere rhetoric avails with such men; fine periods are vanity. You can not touch them with tropes. They need to be pressed home by plain facts.

And such was generally the mode in which they were addressed by the clergy in question: who, taking familiar themes for their discourses, which were leveled right at the wants of their auditors, always succeeded in fastening their attention. In particular, the two great vices to which sailors are most addicted, and which they practice to the ruin of both body and soul; these things, were the most enlarged upon. And several times on the docks, I have seen a robed clergyman addressing a large audience of women collected from the notorious lanes and alleys in the neighborhood.

Is not this as it ought to be? since the true calling of the reverend clergy is like their divine Master's;—not to bring the righteous, but sinners to repentance. Did some of them leave the converted and comfortable congregations, before whom they have ministered year after year; and plunge at once, like St. Paul, into the infected centers and hearts of vice: *then* indeed, would they find a strong enemy to cope with; and a victory gained over *him*, would entitle them to a conqueror's wreath. Better to save one sinner from an obvious vice that is destroying him, than to indoctrinate ten thousand saints. And as from every corner, in Catholic towns, the shrines of Holy Mary and the Child Jesus perpetually remind the commonest wayfarer of his heaven; even so should Protestant pulpits be founded in the market-places, and at street corners, where the men of God might be heard by all of His children.

CHAPTER XXXVI
THE OLD CHURCH OF ST. NICHOLAS, AND THE DEAD-HOUSE

The floating chapel recalls to mind the *"Old Church,"* well known to the seamen of many generations, who have visited Liverpool. It stands very near the docks, a venerable mass of brown stone, and by the town's people is called the Church of St. Nicholas. I believe it is the best preserved piece of antiquity in all Liverpool.

Before the town rose to any importance, it was the only place of worship on that side of the Mersey; and under the adjoining Parish of Walton was a *chapel-of-ease;* though from the straight backed pews, there could have been but little comfort taken in it.

In old times, there stood in front of the church a statue of St. Nicholas, the patron of mariners; to which all pious sailors made offerings, to induce his saintship to grant them short and prosperous voyages. In the tower is a fine chime of bells; and I well remember my delight at first hearing them on the first Sunday morning after our arrival in the dock. It seemed to carry an admonition with it; something like the premonition conveyed to young Whittington by Bow Bells. *"Wellingborough! Wellingborough! you must not forget to go to church, Wellingborough! Don't forget, Wellingborough! Wellingborough! don't forget."*

Thirty or forty years ago, these bells were rung upon the arrival of every Liverpool ship from a foreign voyage. How forcibly does this illustrate the increase of the commerce of the town! Were the same custom now observed, the bells would seldom have a chance to cease.

What seemed the most remarkable about this venerable old church, and what seemed the most barbarous, and grated upon the veneration with which I regarded this time-hallowed structure, was the condition of the grave-yard surrounding it. From its close vicinity to the haunts of the swarms of laborers about the docks, it is crossed and re-crossed by thoroughfares in all directions; and the tomb-stones, not being erect, but horizontal (indeed, they form a complete flagging to the spot), multitudes are constantly walking over the dead; their heels erasing the death's-heads and crossbones, the last mementos of the departed. At noon, when the lumpers employed in loading and unloading the shipping, retire for an hour to snatch a dinner, many of them resort to the grave-yard; and seating themselves upon a tomb-stone use the adjoining one for a table. Often, I saw men stretched out in a drunken sleep upon these slabs; and once, removing a fellow's arm, read the following inscription, which, in a manner, was true to the life, if not to the death:—

HERE LYETH YE BODY OF
TOBIAS DRINKER.

For two memorable circumstances connected with this church, I am indebted to my excellent friend, Morocco, who tells me that in 1588 the Earl of Derby, coming to his residence, and waiting for a passage to the Isle of Man, the corporation erected and adorned a sumptuous stall in the church for his reception. And moreover, that in the time of Cromwell's wars, when the place was taken by that mad nephew of King Charles, Prince Rupert, he converted the old church into a military prison and stable; when, no doubt, another *"sumptuous stall"* was erected for the benefit of the steed of some noble cavalry officer.

In the basement of the church is a Dead House, like the Morgue in Paris, where the bodies of the drowned are exposed until claimed by their friends, or till buried at the public charge.

From the multitudes employed about the shipping, this dead-house has always more or less occupants. Whenever I passed up Chapel-street, I used to see a crowd gazing through the grim iron grating of the door, upon the faces of the drowned within. And once, when the door was opened, I saw a sailor stretched out, stark and stiff, with the sleeve of his frock rolled up, and showing his name and date of birth tattooed upon his arm. It was a sight full of suggestions; he seemed his own headstone.

I was told that standing rewards are offered for the recovery of persons falling into the docks; so much, if restored to life, and a less amount if irrecoverably drowned. Lured by this, several horrid old men and women are constantly prying about the docks, searching after bodies. I observed them principally early in the morning, when they issued from their dens, on the same principle that the rag-rakers, and rubbish-pickers in the streets, sally out bright and early; for then, the night-harvest has ripened.

There seems to be no calamity overtaking man, that can not be rendered merchantable. Undertakers, sextons, tomb-makers, and hearse-drivers, get their living from the dead; and in times of plague most thrive. And these miserable old men and women hunted after corpses to keep from going to the church-yard themselves; for they were the most wretched of starvelings.

CHAPTER XXXVII
WHAT REDBURN SAW IN LAUNCELOTT'S-HEY

The dead-house reminds me of other sad things; for in the vicinity of the docks are many very painful sights.

In going to our boarding-house, the sign of the Baltimore Clipper, I generally passed through a narrow street called "Launcelott's-Hey," lined with dingy, prison-like cotton warehouses. In this street, or rather alley, you seldom see any one but a truck-man, or some solitary old warehouse-keeper, haunting his smoky den like a ghost.

Once, passing through this place, I heard a feeble wail, which seemed to come out of the earth. It was but a strip of crooked side-walk where I stood; the dingy wall was on every side, converting the mid-day into twilight; and not a soul was in sight. I started, and could almost have run, when I heard that dismal sound. It seemed the low, hopeless, endless wail of some one forever lost. At last I advanced to an opening which communicated downward with deep tiers of cellars beneath a crumbling old warehouse; and there, some fifteen feet below the walk, crouching in nameless squalor, with her head bowed over, was the figure of what had been a woman. Her blue arms folded to her livid bosom two shrunken things like children, that leaned toward her, one on each side. At first, I knew not whether they were alive or dead. They made no sign; they did not move or stir; but from the vault came that soul-sickening wail.

I made a noise with my foot, which, in the silence, echoed far and near; but there was no response. Louder still; when one of the children lifted its head, and cast upward a faint glance; then closed its eyes, and lay motionless. The woman also, now gazed up, and perceived me; but let fall her eye again. They were dumb and next to dead with want. How they had crawled into that den, I could not tell; but there they had crawled to die. At that moment I never thought of relieving them; for death was so stamped in their glazed and unimploring eyes, that I almost regarded them as already no more. I stood looking down on them, while my whole soul swelled within me; and I asked myself, What right had any body in the wide world to smile and be glad, when sights like this were to be seen? It was enough to turn the heart to gall; and make a man-hater of a Howard. For who were these ghosts that I saw? Were they not human beings? A woman and two girls? With eyes, and lips, and ears like any queen? with hearts which, though they did not bound with blood, yet beat with a dull, dead ache that was their life.

At last, I walked on toward an open lot in the alley, hoping to meet there some ragged old women, whom I had daily noticed groping amid foul rubbish for little particles of dirty cotton, which they washed out and sold for a trifle.

I found them; and accosting one, I asked if she knew of the persons I had just left. She replied, that she did not; nor did she want to. I then asked another, a miserable, toothless old woman, with a tattered strip of coarse baling stuff round her body. Looking at me for an instant, she resumed her raking in the rubbish, and said that she knew who it was that I spoke of; but that she had no time to attend to beggars and their brats. Accosting still another, who seemed to know my errand, I asked if there was no place to which the woman could be taken. "Yes," she replied, "to the church-yard." I said she was alive, and not dead.

"Then she'll never die," was the rejoinder. "She's been down there these three days, with nothing to eat;—that I know myself."

"She desarves it," said an old hag, who was just placing on her crooked shoulders her bag of pickings, and who was turning to totter off, "that Betsy Jennings desarves it—was she ever married? tell me that."

Leaving Launcelott's-Hey, I turned into a more frequented street; and soon meeting a policeman, told him of the condition of the woman and the girls.

"It's none of my business, Jack," said he. "I don't belong to that street."

"Who does then?"

"I don't know. But what business is it of yours? Are you not a Yankee?"

"Yes," said I, "but come, I will help you remove that woman, if you say so."

"There, now, Jack, go on board your ship and stick to it; and leave these matters to the town."

I accosted two more policemen, but with no better success; they would not even go with me to the place. The truth was, it was out of the way, in a silent, secluded spot; and the misery of the three outcasts, hiding away in the ground, did not obtrude upon any one.

Returning to them, I again stamped to attract their attention; but this time, none of the three looked up, or even stirred. While I yet stood irresolute, a voice called to me from a high, iron-shuttered window in a loft over the way; and asked what I was about. I beckoned to the man, a sort of porter, to come down, which he did; when I pointed down into the vault.

"Well," said he, "what of it?"

"Can't we get them out?" said I, "haven't you some place in your warehouse where you can put them? have you nothing for them to eat?"

"You're crazy, boy," said he; "do you suppose, that Parkins and Wood want their warehouse turned into a hospital?"

I then went to my boarding-house, and told Handsome Mary of what I had seen; asking her if she could not do something to get the woman and girls removed; or if she could not do that, let me have some food for them. But though a kind person in the main, Mary replied that she gave away enough to beggars in her own street (which was true enough) without looking after the whole neighborhood.

Going into the kitchen, I accosted the cook, a little shriveled-up old Welshwoman, with a saucy tongue, whom the sailors called *Brandy-Nan*; and begged her to give me some cold victuals, if she had nothing better, to take to the vault. But she broke out in a storm of swearing at the miserable occupants of the vault, and refused. I then stepped into the room where our dinner was being spread; and waiting till the girl had gone out, I snatched some bread and cheese from a stand, and thrusting it into the bosom of my frock, left the house. Hurrying to the lane, I dropped the food down into the vault. One of the girls caught at it convulsively, but fell back, apparently fainting; the sister pushed the other's arm aside, and took the bread in her hand; but with a weak uncertain grasp like an infant's. She placed it to her mouth; but letting it fall again, murmuring faintly something like "water." The woman did not stir; her head was bowed over, just as I had first seen her.

Seeing how it was, I ran down toward the docks to a mean little sailor tavern, and begged for a pitcher; but the cross old man who kept it refused, unless I would pay for it. But I had no money. So as my boarding-house was some way off, and it would be lost time to run to the ship for my big iron pot; under the impulse of the moment, I hurried to one of the Boodle Hydrants, which I remembered having seen running near the scene of a still smoldering fire in an old rag house; and taking off a new tarpaulin hat, which had been loaned me that day, filled it with water.

With this, I returned to Launcelott's-Hey; and with considerable difficulty, like getting down into a well, I contrived to descend with it into the vault; where there was hardly space enough left to let me stand. The two girls drank out of the hat together; looking up at me with an unalterable, idiotic expression, that almost made me faint. The woman spoke not a word, and did not stir. While the girls were breaking and eating the bread, I tried to lift the woman's head; but, feeble as she was, she seemed bent upon holding it down. Observing her arms still clasped upon her bosom, and that something seemed hidden under the rags there, a thought crossed my mind, which impelled me forcibly to withdraw her hands for a moment; when I caught a glimpse of a meager little babe—the lower part of its body thrust into an old bonnet. Its face was dazzlingly white, even in its squalor; but the closed eyes looked like balls of indigo. It must have been dead some hours.

The woman refusing to speak, eat, or drink, I asked one of the girls who they were, and where they lived; but she only stared vacantly, muttering something that could not be understood.

The air of the place was now getting too much for me; but I stood deliberating a moment, whether it was possible for me to drag them out of the vault. But if I did, what then? They would only perish in the street, and here they were at least protected from the rain; and more than that, might die in seclusion.

I crawled up into the street, and looking down upon them again, almost repented that I had brought them any food; for it would only tend to prolong their misery, without hope of any permanent relief: for die they must very soon; they were too far gone for any medicine to help them. I hardly know whether I ought to confess another thing that occurred to me as I stood there; but it was this—I felt an almost irresistible impulse to do them the last mercy, of in some way putting an end to their horrible lives; and I should almost have done so, I think, had I not been deterred by thoughts of the law. For I well knew that the law, which would let them perish of themselves without giving them one cup of water, would spend a thousand pounds, if necessary, in convicting him who should so much as offer to relieve them from their miserable existence.

The next day, and the next, I passed the vault three times, and still met the same sight. The girls leaning up against the woman on each side, and the woman with her arms still folding the babe, and her head bowed. The first evening I did not see the bread that I had dropped down in the morning; but the second evening, the bread I had dropped that morning remained untouched. On the third morning the smell that came from the vault was such, that I accosted the same policeman I had accosted before, who was patrolling the same street, and told him that the persons I had spoken to him about were dead, and he had better have them removed. He looked as if he did not believe me, and added, that it was not his street.

When I arrived at the docks on my way to the ship, I entered the guard-house within the walls, and asked for one of the captains, to whom I told the story; but, from what he said, was led to infer that the Dock Police was distinct from that of the town, and this was not the right place to lodge my information.

I could do no more that morning, being obliged to repair to the ship; but at twelve o'clock, when I went to dinner, I hurried into Launcelott's-Hey, when I found that the vault was empty. In place of the women and children, a heap of quick-lime was glistening.

I could not learn who had taken them away, or whither they had gone; but my prayer was answered—they were dead, departed, and at peace.

But again I looked down into the vault, and in fancy beheld the pale, shrunken forms still crouching there. Ah! what are our creeds, and how do we hope to be saved? Tell me, oh Bible, that story of Lazarus again, that I may find comfort in my heart for the poor and forlorn. Surrounded as we are by the wants and woes of our fellowmen, and yet given to follow our own pleasures, regardless of their pains, are we not like people sitting up with a corpse, and making merry in the house of the dead?

CHAPTER XXXVIII
THE DOCK-WALL BEGGARS

I might relate other things which befell me during the six weeks and more that I remained in Liverpool, often visiting the cellars, sinks, and hovels of the wretched lanes and courts near the river. But to tell of them, would only be to tell over again the story just told; so I return to the docks.

The old women described as picking dirty fragments of cotton in the empty lot, belong to the same class of beings who at all hours of the day are to be seen within the dock walls, raking over and over the heaps of rubbish carried ashore from the holds of the shipping.

As it is against the law to throw the least thing overboard, even a rope yarn; and as this law is very different from similar laws in New York, inasmuch as it is rigidly enforced by the dock-masters; and, moreover, as after discharging a ship's cargo, a great deal of dirt and worthless dunnage remains in the hold, the amount of rubbish accumulated in the appointed receptacles for depositing it within the walls is extremely large, and is constantly receiving new accessions from every vessel that unlades at the quays.

Standing over these noisome heaps, you will see scores of tattered wretches, armed with old rakes and picking-irons, turning over the dirt, and making as much of a rope-yarn as if it were a skein of silk. Their findings, nevertheless, are but small; for as it is one of the immemorial perquisites of the second mate of a merchant ship to collect, and sell on his own account, all the condemned "old junk" of the vessel to which he belongs, he generally takes good heed that in the buckets of rubbish carried ashore, there shall be as few rope-yarns as possible.

In the same way, the cook preserves all the odds and ends of pork-rinds and beef-fat, which he sells at considerable profit; upon a six months' voyage frequently realizing thirty or forty dollars from the sale, and in large ships, even more than that. It may easily be imagined, then, how desperately driven to it must these rubbish-pickers be, to ransack heaps of refuse which have been previously gleaned.

Nor must I omit to make mention of the singular beggary practiced in the streets frequented by sailors; and particularly to record the remarkable army of paupers that beset the docks at particular hours of the day.

At twelve o'clock the crews of hundreds and hundreds of ships issue in crowds from the dock gates to go to their dinner in the town. This hour is seized upon by multitudes of beggars to plant themselves against the outside of the walls, while others stand upon the curbstone to excite the charity of the seamen. The first time that I passed through this long lane of pauperism, it seemed hard to believe that such an array of misery could be furnished by any town in the world.

Every variety of want and suffering here met the eye, and every vice showed here its victims. Nor were the marvelous and almost incredible shifts and stratagems of the professional beggars, wanting to finish this picture of all that is dishonorable to civilization and humanity.

Old women, rather mummies, drying up with slow starving and age; young girls, incurably sick, who ought to have been in the hospital; sturdy men, with the gallows in their eyes, and a whining lie in their mouths; young boys, hollow-eyed and decrepit; and puny mothers, holding up puny babes in the glare of the sun, formed the main features of the scene.

But these were diversified by instances of peculiar suffering, vice, or art in attracting charity, which, to me at least, who had never seen such things before, seemed to the last degree uncommon and monstrous.

I remember one cripple, a young man rather decently clad, who sat huddled up against the wall, holding a painted board on his knees. It was a picture intending to represent the man himself caught in the machinery of some factory, and whirled about among spindles and cogs, with his limbs mangled and bloody. This person said nothing, but sat silently exhibiting his board. Next him, leaning upright against the wall, was a tall, pallid man, with a white bandage round his brow, and his face cadaverous as a corpse. He, too, said nothing; but with one finger silently pointed down to the square of flagging at his feet, which was nicely swept, and stained blue, and bore this inscription in chalk:—

> "I have had no food for three days;
> My wife and children are dying."

Further on lay a man with one sleeve of his ragged coat removed, showing an unsightly sore; and above it a label with some writing.

In some places, for the distance of many rods, the whole line of flagging immediately at the base of the wall, would be completely covered with inscriptions, the beggars standing over them in silence.

But as you passed along these horrible records, in an hour's time destined to be obliterated by the feet of thousands and thousands of wayfarers, you were not left unassailed by the clamorous petitions of the more urgent applicants for charity. They beset you on every hand; catching you by the coat; hanging on, and following you along; and, *for Heaven's sake,* and *for God's sake,* and *for Christ's sake,* beseeching of you but *one ha'penny.* If you so much as glanced your eye on one of them, even for an instant, it was perceived like lightning, and the person never left your side until you turned into another street, or satisfied his demands. Thus, at least, it was with the sailors; though I observed that the beggars treated the town's people differently.

I can not say that the seamen did much to relieve the destitution which three times every day was presented to their view. Perhaps habit had made them callous; but the truth might have been that very few of them had much money to give. Yet the beggars must have had some inducement to infest the dock walls as they did.

As an example of the caprice of sailors, and their sympathy with suffering among members of their own calling, I must mention the case of an old man, who every day, and all day long, through sunshine and rain, occupied a particular corner, where crowds of tars were always passing. He was an uncommonly large, plethoric man, with a wooden leg, and dressed in the nautical garb; his face was red and round; he was continually merry; and with his wooden stump thrust forth, so as almost to trip up the careless wayfarer, he sat upon a great pile of monkey jackets, with a little depression in them between his knees, to receive the coppers thrown him. And plenty of pennies were tost into his poor-box by the sailors, who always exchanged a pleasant word with the old man, and passed on, generally regardless of the neighboring beggars.

The first morning I went ashore with my shipmates, some of them greeted him as an old acquaintance; for that corner he had occupied for many long years. He was an old man-of-war's man, who had lost his leg at the battle of Trafalgar; and singular to tell, he now exhibited his wooden one as a genuine specimen of the oak timbers of Nelson's ship, the Victory.

Among the paupers were several who wore old sailor hats and jackets, and claimed to be destitute tars; and on the strength of these pretensions demanded help from their brethren; but Jack would see through their disguise in a moment, and turn away, with no benediction.

As I daily passed through this lane of beggars, who thronged the docks as the Hebrew cripples did the Pool of Bethesda, and as I thought of my utter inability in any way to help them, I could not but offer up a prayer, that some angel might descend, and turn the waters of the docks into an elixir, that would heal all their woes, and make them, man and woman, healthy and whole as their ancestors, Adam and Eve, in the garden.

Adam and Eve! If indeed ye are yet alive and in heaven, may it be no part of your immortality to look down upon the world ye have left. For as all these sufferers and cripples are as much your family as young Abel, so, to you, the sight of the world's woes would be a parental torment indeed.

CHAPTER XXXIX
THE BOOBLE-ALLEYS OF THE TOWN

The same sights that are to be met with along the dock walls at noon, in a less degree, though diversified with other scenes, are continually encountered in the narrow streets where the sailor boarding-houses are kept.

In the evening, especially when the sailors are gathered in great numbers, these streets present a most singular spectacle, the entire population of the vicinity being seemingly turned into them. Hand-organs, fiddles, and cymbals, plied by strolling musicians, mix with the songs of the seamen, the babble of women and children, and the groaning and whining of beggars. From the various boarding-houses, each distinguished by gilded emblems outside—an anchor, a crown, a ship, a windlass, or a dolphin—proceeds the noise of revelry and dancing; and from the open casements lean young girls and old women, chattering and laughing with the crowds in the middle of the street. Every moment strange greetings are exchanged between old sailors who chance to stumble upon a shipmate, last seen in Calcutta or Savannah; and the invariable courtesy that takes place upon these occasions, is to go to the next spirit-vault, and drink each other's health.

There are particular paupers who frequent particular sections of these streets, and who, I was told, resented the intrusion of mendicants from other parts of the town.

Chief among them was a white-haired old man, stone-blind; who was led up and down through the long tumult by a woman holding a little saucer to receive contributions. This old man sang, or rather chanted, certain words in a peculiarly long-drawn, guttural manner, throwing back his head, and turning up his sightless eyeballs to the sky. His chant was a lamentation upon his infirmity; and at the time it produced the same effect upon me, that my first reading of Milton's Invocation to the Sun did, years afterward. I can not recall it all; but it was something like this, drawn out in an endless groan—

"Here goes the blind old man; blind, blind, blind; no more will he see sun nor moon—no more see sun nor moon!" And thus would he pass through the middle of the street; the woman going on in advance, holding his hand, and dragging him through all obstructions; now and then leaving him standing, while she went among the crowd soliciting coppers.

But one of the most curious features of the scene is the number of sailor ballad-singers, who, after singing their verses, hand you a printed copy, and beg you to buy. One of these persons, dressed like a man-of-war's-man, I observed every day standing at a corner in the middle of the street. He had a full, noble voice, like a church-organ; and his notes rose high above the surrounding din. But the remarkable thing about this ballad-singer was one of his arms, which, while singing, he somehow swung vertically round and round in the air, as if it revolved on a pivot. The feat was unnaturally unaccountable; and he performed it with the view of attracting sympathy; since he said that in falling from a frigate's mast-head to the deck, he had met with an injury, which had resulted in making his wonderful arm what it was.

I made the acquaintance of this man, and found him no common character. He was full of marvelous adventures, and abounded in terrific stories of pirates and sea murders, and all sorts of nautical enormities. He was a monomaniac upon these subjects; he was a Newgate Calendar of the robberies and assassinations of the day, happening in the sailor quarters of the town; and most of his ballads were upon kindred subjects. He composed many of his own verses, and had them printed for sale on his own account. To show how expeditious he was at this business, it may be mentioned, that one evening on leaving the dock to go to supper, I perceived a crowd gathered about the *Old Fort Tavern;* and mingling with the rest, I learned that a woman of the town had just been killed at the bar by a drunken Spanish sailor from Cadiz. The murderer was carried off by the police before my eyes, and the very next morning the ballad-singer with the miraculous arm, was singing the tragedy in front of the boarding-houses, and handing round printed copies of the song, which, of course, were eagerly bought up by the seamen.

This passing allusion to the murder will convey some idea of the events which take place in the lowest and most abandoned neighborhoods frequented by sailors in Liverpool. The pestilent lanes and alleys which, in their vocabulary, go by the names of Rotten-row, Gibraltar-place, and Booble-alley, are putrid with vice and crime; to which, perhaps, the round globe does not furnish a parallel. The sooty and begrimed bricks of the very houses have a reeking, Sodomlike, and murderous look; and well may the shroud of coal-smoke, which hangs over this part of the town, more than any other, attempt to hide the enormities here practiced. These are the haunts from which sailors sometimes disappear forever; or issue in the morning, robbed naked, from the broken doorways. These are the haunts in which cursing, gambling, pickpocketing, and common iniquities, are virtues too lofty for the infected gorgons and hydras to practice. Propriety forbids that I should enter into details; but kidnappers, burkers, and resurrectionists are almost saints and angels to them. They seem leagued together, a company of miscreant misanthropes, bent upon doing all the malice to mankind in their power. With sulphur and brimstone they ought to be burned out of their arches like vermin.

CHAPTER XL
PLACARDS, BRASS-JEWELERS, TRUCK-HORSES, AND STEAMERS

As I wish to group together what fell under my observation concerning the Liverpool docks, and the scenes roundabout, I will try to throw into this chapter various minor things that I recall.

The advertisements of pauperism chalked upon the flagging round the dock walls, are singularly accompanied by a multitude of quite different announcements, placarded upon the walls themselves. They are principally notices of the approaching departure of *"superior, fast-sailing, coppered and copper-fastened ships,"* for the United States, Canada, New South Wales, and other places. Interspersed with these, are the advertisements of Jewish clothesmen, informing the judicious seamen where he can procure of the best and the cheapest; together with ambiguous medical announcements of the tribe of quacks and empirics who prey upon all seafaring men. Not content with thus publicly giving notice of their whereabouts, these indefatigable Sangrados and pretended Samaritans hire a parcel of shabby workhouse-looking knaves, whose business consists in haunting the dock walls about meal times, and silently thrusting mysterious little billets—duodecimo editions of the larger advertisements—into the astonished hands of the tars.

They do this, with such a mysterious hang-dog wink; such a sidelong air; such a villainous assumption of your necessities; that, at first, you are almost tempted to knock them down for their pains.

Conspicuous among the notices on the walls, are huge Italic inducements to all seamen disgusted with the merchant service, to accept a round bounty, and embark in her Majesty's navy.

In the British armed marine, in time of peace, they do not ship men for the general service, as in the American navy; but for particular ships, going upon particular cruises. Thus, the frigate Thetis may be announced as about to sail under the command of that fine old sailor, and noble father to his crew, *Lord George Flagstaff.*

Similar announcements may be seen upon the walls concerning enlistments in the army. And never did auctioneer dilate with more rapture upon the charms of some country-seat put up for sale, than the authors of these placards do, upon the beauty and salubrity of the distant climes, for which the regiments wanting recruits are about to sail. Bright lawns, vine-clad hills, endless meadows of verdure, here make up the landscape; and adventurous young gentlemen, fond of travel, are informed, that here is a chance for them to see the world at their leisure, and be paid for enjoying themselves into the bargain. The regiments for India are promised plantations among valleys of palms; while to those destined for New Holland, a novel sphere of life and activity is opened; and the companies bound to Canada and Nova Scotia are lured by tales of summer suns, that ripen grapes in December. No word of war is breathed; hushed is the clang of arms in these announcements; and the sanguine recruit is almost tempted to expect that pruning-hooks, instead of swords, will be the weapons he will wield.

Alas! is not this the cruel stratagem of Bruce at Bannockburn, who decoyed to his war-pits by covering them over with green boughs? For instead of a farm at the blue base of the Himalayas, the Indian recruit encounters the keen saber of the Sikh; and instead of basking in sunny bowers, the Canadian soldier stands a shivering sentry upon the bleak ramparts of Quebec, a lofty mark for the bitter blasts from Baffin's Bay and Labrador. There, as his eye sweeps down the St. Lawrence, whose every billow is bound for the main that laves the shore of Old England; as he thinks of his long term of enlistment, which sells him to the army as Doctor Faust sold himself to the devil; how the poor fellow must groan in his grief, and call to mind the church-yard stile, and his Mary.

These army announcements are well fitted to draw recruits in Liverpool. Among the vast number of emigrants, who daily arrive from all parts of Britain to embark for the United States or the colonies, there are many young men, who, upon arriving at Liverpool, find themselves next to penniless; or, at least, with only enough money to carry them over the sea, without providing for future contingencies. How easily and naturally, then, may such youths be induced to enter upon the military life, which promises them a free passage to the most distant and flourishing colonies, and certain pay for doing nothing; besides holding out hopes of vineyards and farms, to be verified in the fullness of time. For in a moneyless youth, the decision to leave home at all, and embark upon a long voyage to reside in a remote clime, is a piece of adventurousness only one removed from the spirit that prompts the army recruit to enlist.

I never passed these advertisements, surrounded by crowds of gaping emigrants, without thinking of rattraps.

Besides the mysterious agents of the quacks, who privily thrust their little notes into your hands, folded up like a powder; there are another set of rascals prowling about the docks, chiefly at dusk; who make strange motions to you, and beckon you to one side, as if they had some state secret to disclose, intimately connected with the weal of the commonwealth. They nudge you with an elbow full of indefinite hints and intimations; they glitter upon you an eye like a Jew's or a pawnbroker's; they dog you like Italian assassins. But if the blue coat of a policeman chances to approach, how quickly they strive to look completely indifferent, as to the surrounding universe; how they saunter off, as if lazily wending their way to an affectionate wife and family.

The first time one of these mysterious personages accosted me, I fancied him crazy, and hurried forward to avoid him. But arm in arm with my shadow, he followed after; till amazed at his conduct, I turned round and paused.

He was a little, shabby, old man, with a forlorn looking coat and hat; and his hand was fumbling in his vest pocket, as if to take out a card with his address. Seeing me stand still he made a sign toward a dark angle of the wall, near which we were; when taking him for a cunning foot-pad, I again wheeled about, and swiftly passed on. But though I did not look round, I *felt* him following me still; so once more I stopped. The fellow now assumed so mystic and admonitory an air, that I began to fancy he came to me on some warning errand; that perhaps a plot had been laid to blow up the Liverpool docks, and he was some Monteagle bent upon accomplishing my flight. I was determined to see what he was. With all my eyes about me, I followed him into the arch of a warehouse; when he gazed round furtively, and silently showing me a ring, whispered, "You may have it for a shilling; it's pure gold—I found it in the gutter—hush! don't speak! give me the money, and it's yours."

"My friend," said I, "I don't trade in these articles; I don't want your ring."

"Don't you? Then take that," he whispered, in an intense hushed passion; and I fell flat from a blow on the chest, while this infamous jeweler made away with himself out of sight. This business transaction was conducted with a counting-house promptitude that astonished me.

After that, I shunned these scoundrels like the leprosy: and the next time I was pertinaciously followed, I stopped, and in a loud voice, pointed out the man to the passers-by; upon which he absconded; rapidly turning up into sight a pair of obliquely worn and battered boot-heels. I could not help thinking that these sort of fellows, so given to running away upon emergencies, must furnish a good deal of work to the shoemakers; as they might, also, to the growers of hemp and gallows-joiners.

Belonging to a somewhat similar fraternity with these irritable merchants of brass jewelry just mentioned, are the peddlers of Sheffield razors, mostly boys, who are hourly driven out of the dock gates by the police; nevertheless, they contrive to saunter back, and board the vessels, going among the sailors and privately exhibiting their wares. Incited by the extreme cheapness of one of the razors, and the gilding on the case containing it, a shipmate of mine purchased it on the spot for a commercial equivalent of the price, in tobacco. On the following Sunday, he used that razor; and the result was a pair of tormented and tomahawked cheeks, that almost required a surgeon to dress them. In old times, by the way, it was not a bad thought, that suggested the propriety of a barber's practicing surgery in connection with the chin-harrowing vocation.

Another class of knaves, who practice upon the sailors in Liverpool, are the pawnbrokers, inhabiting little rookeries among the narrow lanes adjoining the dock. I was astonished at the multitude of gilded balls in these streets, emblematic of their calling. They were generally next neighbors to the gilded grapes over the spirit-vaults; and no doubt, mutually to facilitate business operations, some of these establishments have connecting doors inside, so as to play their customers into each other's hands. I often saw sailors in a state of intoxication rushing from a spirit-vault into a pawnbroker's; stripping off their boots, hats, jackets, and neckerchiefs, and sometimes even their pantaloons on the spot, and offering to pawn them for a song. Of course such applications were never refused. But though on shore, at Liverpool, poor Jack finds more sharks than at sea, he himself is by no means exempt from practices, that do not savor of a rigid morality; at least according to law. In tobacco smuggling he is an adept: and when cool and collected, often manages to evade the Customs completely, and land goodly packages of the weed, which owing to the immense duties upon it in England, commands a very high price.

As soon as we came to anchor in the river, before reaching the dock, three Custom-house underlings boarded us, and coming down into the forecastle, ordered the men to produce all the tobacco they had. Accordingly several pounds were brought forth.

"Is that all?" asked the officers.

"All," said the men.

"We will see," returned the others.

And without more ado, they emptied the chests right and left; tossed over the bunks and made a thorough search of the premises; but discovered nothing. The sailors were then given to understand, that while the ship lay in dock, the tobacco must remain in the cabin, under custody of the chief mate, who every morning would dole out to them one plug per head, as a security against their carrying it ashore.

"Very good," said the men.

But several of them had secret places in the ship, from whence they daily drew pound after pound of tobacco, which they smuggled ashore in the manner following.

When the crew went to meals, each man carried at least one plug in his pocket; *that* he had a right to; and as many more were hidden about his person as he dared. Among the great crowds pouring out of the dock-gates at such hours, of course these smugglers stood little chance of detection; although vigilant looking policemen were always standing by. And though these *"Charlies"* might suppose there were tobacco smugglers passing; yet to hit the right man among such a throng, would be as hard, as to harpoon a speckled porpoise, one of ten thousand darting under a ship's bows.

Our forecastle was often visited by foreign sailors, who knowing we came from America, were anxious to purchase tobacco at a cheap rate; for in Liverpool it is about an American penny per pipe-full. Along the docks they sell an English pennyworth, put up in a little roll like confectioners' mottoes, with poetical lines, or instructive little moral precepts printed in red on the back.

Among all the sights of the docks, the noble truck-horses are not the least striking to a stranger. They are large and powerful brutes, with such sleek and glossy coats, that they look as if brushed and put on by a valet every morning. They march with a slow and stately step, lifting their ponderous hoofs like royal Siam elephants. Thou shalt not lay stripes upon these Roman citizens; for their docility is such, they are guided without rein or lash; they go or come, halt or march on, at a whisper. So grave, dignified, gentlemanly, and courteous did these fine truck-horses look—so full of calm intelligence and sagacity, that often I endeavored to get into conversation with them, as they stood in contemplative attitudes while their loads were preparing. But all I could get from them was the mere recognition of a friendly neigh; though I would stake much upon it that, could I have spoken in their language, I would have derived from them a good deal of valuable information touching the docks, where they passed the whole of their dignified lives.

There are unknown worlds of knowledge in brutes; and whenever you mark a horse, or a dog, with a peculiarly mild, calm, deep-seated eye, be sure he is an Aristotle or a Kant, tranquilly speculating upon the mysteries in man. No philosophers so thoroughly comprehend us as dogs and horses. They see through us at a glance. And after all, what is a horse but a species of four-footed dumb man, in a leathern overall, who happens to live upon oats, and toils for his masters, half-requited or abused, like the biped hewers of wood and drawers of water? But there is a touch of divinity even in brutes, and a special halo about a horse, that should forever exempt him from indignities. As for those majestic, magisterial truck-horses of the docks, I would as soon think of striking a judge on the bench, as to lay violent hand upon their holy hides.

It is wonderful what loads their majesties will condescend to draw. The truck is a large square platform, on four low wheels; and upon this the lumpers pile bale after bale of cotton, as if they were filling a large warehouse, and yet a procession of three of these horses will tranquilly walk away with the whole.

The truckmen themselves are almost as singular a race as their animals. Like the Judiciary in England, they wear gowns,—not of the same cut and color though,—which reach below their knees; and from the racket they make on the pavements with their hob-nailed brogans, you would think they patronized the same shoemaker with their horses. I never could get any thing out of these truckmen. They are a reserved, sober-sided set, who, with all possible solemnity, march at the head of their animals; now and then gently advising them to sheer to the right or the left, in order to avoid some passing vehicle. Then spending so much of their lives in the high-bred company of their horses, seems to have mended their manners and improved their taste, besides imparting to them something of the dignity of their animals; but it has also given to them a sort of refined and uncomplaining aversion to human society.

There are many strange stories told of the truck-horse. Among others is the following: There was a parrot, that from having long been suspended in its cage from a low window fronting a dock, had learned to converse pretty fluently in the language of the stevedores and truckmen. One day a truckman left his vehicle standing on the quay, with its back to the water. It was noon, when an interval of silence falls upon the docks; and Poll, seeing herself face to face with the horse, and having a mind for a chat, cried out to him, *"Back! back! back!"*

Backward went the horse, precipitating himself and truck into the water.

Brunswick Dock, to the west of Prince's, is one of the most interesting to be seen. Here lie the various black steamers (so unlike the American boats, since they have to navigate the boisterous Narrow Seas) plying to all parts of the three kingdoms. Here you see vast quantities of produce, imported from starving Ireland; here you see the decks turned into pens for oxen and sheep; and often, side by side with these inclosures, Irish deck-passengers, thick as they can stand, seemingly penned in just like the cattle. It was the beginning of July when the Highlander arrived in port; and the Irish laborers were daily coming over by thousands, to help harvest the English crops.

One morning, going into the town, I heard a tramp, as of a drove of buffaloes, behind me; and turning round, beheld the entire middle of the street filled by a great crowd of these men, who had just emerged from Brunswick Dock gates, arrayed in long-tailed coats of hoddin-gray, corduroy knee-breeches, and shod with shoes that raised a mighty dust. Flourishing their Donnybrook shillelahs, they looked like an irruption of barbarians. They were marching straight out of town into the country; and perhaps out of consideration for the finances of the corporation, took the middle of the street, to save the side-walks.

"Sing *Langolee, and the Lakes of Killarney,*" cried one fellow, tossing his stick into the air, as he danced in his brogans at the head of the rabble. And so they went! capering on, merry as pipers.

When I thought of the multitudes of Irish that annually land on the shores of the United States and Canada, and, to my surprise, witnessed the additional multitudes embarking from Liverpool to New Holland; and when, added to all this, I daily saw these hordes of laborers, descending, thick as locusts, upon the English corn-fields; I could not help marveling at the fertility of an island, which, though her crop of potatoes may fail, never yet failed in bringing her annual crop of men into the world.

CHAPTER XLI
REDBURN ROVES ABOUT HITHER AND THITHER

I do not know that any other traveler would think it worth while to mention such a thing; but the fact is, that during the summer months in Liverpool, the days are exceedingly lengthy; and the first evening I found myself walking in the twilight after nine o'clock, I tried to recall my astronomical knowledge, in order to account satisfactorily for so curious a phenomenon. But the days in summer, and the nights in winter, are just as long in Liverpool as at Cape Horn; for the latitude of the two places very nearly corresponds.

These Liverpool days, however, were a famous thing for me; who, thereby, was enabled after my day's work aboard the Highlander, to ramble about the town for several hours. After I had visited all the noted places I could discover, of those marked down upon my father's map, I began to extend my rovings indefinitely; forming myself into a committee of one, to investigate all accessible parts of the town; though so many years have elapsed, ere I have thought of bringing in my report.

This was a great delight to me: for wherever I have been in the world, I have always taken a vast deal of lonely satisfaction in wandering about, up and down, among out-of-the-way streets and alleys, and speculating upon the strangers I have met. Thus, in Liverpool I used to pace along endless streets of dwelling-houses, looking at the names on the doors, admiring the pretty faces in the windows, and invoking a passing blessing upon the chubby children on the door-steps. I was stared at myself, to be sure: but what of that? We must give and take on such occasions. In truth, I and my shooting-jacket produced quite a sensation in Liverpool: and I have no doubt, that many a father of a family went home to his children with a curious story, about a wandering phenomenon they had encountered, traversing the side-walks that day. In the words of the old song, *"I cared for nobody, no not I, and nobody cared for me."* I stared my fill with impunity, and took all stares myself in good part.

Once I was standing in a large square, gaping at a splendid chariot drawn up at a portico. The glossy horses quivered with good-living, and so did the sumptuous calves of the gold-laced coachman and footmen in attendance. I was particularly struck with the red cheeks of these men: and the many evidences they furnished of their enjoying this meal with a wonderful relish.

While thus standing, I all at once perceived, that the objects of my curiosity, were making me an object of their own; and that they were gazing at me, as if I were some unauthorized intruder upon the British soil. Truly, they had reason: for when I now think of the figure I must have cut in those days, I only marvel that, in my many strolls, my passport was not a thousand times demanded.

Nevertheless, I was only a forlorn looking mortal among tens of thousands of rags and tatters. For in some parts of the town, inhabited by laborers, and poor people generally; I used to crowd my way through masses of squalid men, women, and children, who at this evening hour, in those quarters of Liverpool, seem to empty themselves into the street, and live there for the time. I had never seen any thing like it in New York. Often, I witnessed some curious, and many very sad scenes; and especially I remembered encountering a pale, ragged man, rushing along frantically, and striving to throw off his wife and children, who clung to his arms and legs; and, in God's name, conjured him not to desert them. He seemed bent upon rushing down to the water, and drowning himself, in some despair, and craziness of wretchedness. In these haunts, beggary went on before me wherever I walked, and dogged me unceasingly at the heels. Poverty, poverty, poverty, in almost endless vistas: and want and woe staggered arm in arm along these miserable streets.

And here, I must not omit one thing, that struck me at the time. It was the absence of negroes; who in the large towns in the "free states" of America, almost always form a considerable portion of the destitute. But in these streets, not a negro was to be seen. All were whites; and with the exception of the Irish, were natives of the soil: even Englishmen; as much Englishmen, as the dukes in the House of Lords. This conveyed a strange feeling: and more than any thing else, reminded me that I was not in my own land. For *there*, such a being as a native beggar is almost unknown; and to be a born American citizen seems a guarantee against pauperism; and this, perhaps, springs from the virtue of a vote.

Speaking of negroes, recalls the looks of interest with which negro-sailors are regarded when they walk the Liverpool streets. In Liverpool indeed the negro steps with a prouder pace, and lifts his head like a man; for here, no such exaggerated feeling exists in respect to him, as in America. Three or four times, I encountered our black steward, dressed very handsomely, and walking arm in arm with a good-looking English woman. In New York, such a couple would have been mobbed in three minutes; and the steward would have been lucky to escape with whole limbs. Owing to the friendly reception extended to them, and the unwonted immunities they enjoy in Liverpool, the black cooks and stewards of American ships are very much attached to the place and like to make voyages to it.

Being so young and inexperienced then, and unconsciously swayed in some degree by those local and social prejudices, that are the marring of most men, and from which, for the mass, there seems no possible escape; at first I was surprised that a colored man should be treated as he is in this town; but a little reflection showed that, after all, it was but recognizing his claims to humanity and normal equality; so that, in some things, we Americans leave to other countries the carrying out of the principle that stands at the head of our Declaration of Independence.

During my evening strolls in the wealthier quarters, I was subject to a continual mortification. It was the humiliating fact, wholly unforeseen by me, that upon the whole, and barring the poverty and beggary, Liverpool, away from the docks, was very much such a place as New York. There were the same sort of streets pretty much; the same rows of houses with stone steps; the same kind of side-walks and curbs; and the same elbowing, heartless-looking crowd as ever.

I came across the Leeds Canal, one afternoon; but, upon my word, no one could have told it from the Erie Canal at Albany. I went into St. John's Market on a Saturday night; and though it was strange enough to see that great roof supported by so many pillars, yet the most discriminating observer would not have been able to detect any difference between the articles exposed for sale, and the articles exhibited in Fulton Market, New York.

I walked down Lord-street, peering into the jewelers' shops; but I thought I was walking down a block in Broadway. I began to think that all this talk about travel was a humbug; and that he who lives in a nut-shell, lives in an epitome of the universe, and has but little to see beyond him.

It is true, that I often thought of London's being only seven or eight hours' travel by railroad from where I was; and that *there,* surely, must be a world of wonders waiting my eyes: but more of London anon.

Sundays were the days upon which I made my longest explorations. I rose bright and early, with my whole plan of operations in my head. First walking into some dock hitherto unexamined, and then to breakfast. Then a walk through the more fashionable streets, to see the people going to church; and then I myself went to church, selecting the goodliest edifice, and the tallest Kentuckian of a spire I could find.

For I am an admirer of church architecture; and though, perhaps, the sums spent in erecting magnificent cathedrals might better go to the founding of charities, yet since these structures are built, those who disapprove of them in one sense, may as well have the benefit of them in another.

It is a most Christian thing, and a matter most sweet to dwell upon and simmer over in solitude, that any poor sinner may go to church wherever he pleases; and that even St. Peter's in Rome is open to him, as to a cardinal; that St. Paul's in London is not shut against him; and that the Broadway Tabernacle, in New York, opens all her broad aisles to him, and will not even have doors and thresholds to her pews, the better to allure him by an unbounded invitation. I say, this consideration of the hospitality and democracy in churches, is a most Christian and charming thought. It speaks whole volumes of folios, and Vatican libraries, for Christianity; it is more eloquent, and goes farther home than all the sermons of Massillon, Jeremy Taylor, Wesley, and Archbishop Tillotson.

Nothing daunted, therefore, by thinking of my being a stranger in the land; nothing daunted by the architectural superiority and costliness of any Liverpool church; or by the streams of silk dresses and fine broadcloth coats flowing into the aisles, I used humbly to present myself before the sexton, as a candidate for admission. He would stare a little, perhaps (one of them once hesitated), but in the end, what could he do but show me into a pew; not the most commodious of pews, to be sure; nor commandingly located; nor within very plain sight or hearing of the pulpit. No; it was remarkable, that there was always some confounded pillar or obstinate angle of the wall in the way; and I used to think, that the sextons of Liverpool must have held a secret meeting on my account, and resolved to apportion me the most inconvenient pew in the churches under their charge. However, they always gave me a seat of some sort or other; sometimes even on an oaken bench in the open air of the aisle, where I would sit, dividing the attention of the congregation between myself and the clergyman. The whole congregation seemed to know that I was a foreigner of distinction.

It was sweet to hear the service read, the organ roll, the sermon preached—just as the same things were going on three thousand five hundred miles off, at home! But then, the prayer in behalf of her majesty the Queen, somewhat threw me back. Nevertheless, I joined in that prayer, and invoked for the lady the best wishes of a poor Yankee.

How I loved to sit in the holy hush of those brown old monastic aisles, thinking of Harry the Eighth, and the Reformation! How I loved to go a roving with my eye, all along the sculptured walls and buttresses; winding in among the intricacies of the pendent ceiling, and wriggling my fancied way like a wood-worm. I could have sat there all the morning long, through noon, unto night. But at last the benediction would come; and appropriating my share of it, I would slowly move away, thinking how I should like to go home with some of the portly old gentlemen, with high-polished boots and Malacca canes, and take a seat at their cosy and comfortable dinner-tables. But, alas! there was no dinner for me except at the sign of the Baltimore Clipper.

Yet the Sunday dinners that Handsome Mary served up were not to be scorned. The roast beef of Old England abounded; and so did the immortal plum-puddings, and the unspeakably capital gooseberry pies. But to finish off with that abominable *"swipes"* almost spoiled all the rest: not that I myself patronized *"swipes"* but my shipmates did; and every cup I saw them drink, I could not choose but taste in imagination, and even then the flavor was bad.

On Sundays, at dinner-time, as, indeed, on every other day, it was curious to watch the proceedings at the sign of the Clipper. The servant girls were running about, mustering the various crews, whose dinners were spread, each in a separate apartment; and who were collectively known by the names of their ships.

"Where are the *Arethusas?*—Here's their beef been smoking this half-hour."—"Fly, Betty, my dear, here come the *Splendids.*"— "Run, Molly, my love; get the salt-cellars for the *Highlanders* ."—"You Peggy, where's the *Siddons' pickle-pat?*"—"I say, Judy, are you never coming with that pudding for the *Lord Nelsons?*"

On week days, we did not fare quite so well as on Sundays; and once we came to dinner, and found two enormous bullock hearts smoking at each end of the Highlanders' table. Jackson was indignant at the outrage.

He always sat at the head of the table; and this time he squared himself on his bench, and erecting his knife and fork like flag-staffs, so as to include the two hearts between them, he called out for Danby, the boarding-house keeper; for although his wife Mary was in fact at the head of the establishment, yet Danby himself always came in for the fault-findings.

Danby obsequiously appeared, and stood in the doorway, well knowing the philippics that were coming. But he was not prepared for the peroration of Jackson's address to him; which consisted of the two bullock hearts, snatched bodily off the dish, and flung at his head, by way of a recapitulation of the preceding arguments. The company then broke up in disgust, and dined elsewhere.

Though I almost invariably attended church on Sunday mornings, yet the rest of the day I spent on my travels; and it was on one of these afternoon strolls, that on passing through St. George's-square, I found myself among a large crowd, gathered near the base of George the Fourth's equestrian statue.

The people were mostly mechanics and artisans in their holiday clothes; but mixed with them were a good many soldiers, in lean, lank, and dinnerless undresses, and sporting attenuated rattans. These troops belonged to the various regiments then in town. Police officers, also, were conspicuous in their uniforms. At first perfect silence and decorum prevailed.

Addressing this orderly throng was a pale, hollow-eyed young man, in a snuff-colored surtout, who looked worn with much watching, or much toil, or too little food. His features were good, his whole air was respectable, and there was no mistaking the fact, that he was strongly in earnest in what he was saying.

In his hand was a soiled, inflammatory-looking pamphlet, from which he frequently read; following up the quotations with nervous appeals to his hearers, a rolling of his eyes, and sometimes the most frantic gestures. I was not long within hearing of him, before I became aware that this youth was a Chartist.

Presently the crowd increased, and some commotion was raised, when I noticed the police officers augmenting in number; and by and by, they began to glide through the crowd, politely hinting at the propriety of dispersing. The first persons thus accosted were the soldiers, who accordingly sauntered off, switching their rattans, and admiring their high-polished shoes. It was plain that the Charter did not hang very heavy round their hearts. For the rest, they also gradually broke up; and at last I saw the speaker himself depart.

I do not know why, but I thought he must be some despairing elder son, supporting by hard toil his mother and sisters; for of such many political desperadoes are made.

That same Sunday afternoon, I strolled toward the outskirts of the town, and attracted by the sight of two great Pompey's pillars, in the shape of black steeples, apparently rising directly from the soil, I approached them with much curiosity. But looking over a low parapet connecting them, what was my surprise to behold at my feet a smoky hollow in the ground, with rocky walls, and dark holes at one end, carrying out of view several lines of iron railways; while far beyond, straight out toward the open country, ran an endless railroad. Over the place, a handsome Moorish arch of stone was flung; and gradually, as I gazed upon it, and at the little side arches at the bottom of the hollow, there came over me an undefinable feeling, that I had previously seen the whole thing before. Yet how could that be? Certainly, I had never been in Liverpool before: but then, that Moorish arch! surely I remembered that very well. It was not till several months after reaching home in America, that my perplexity upon this matter was cleared away. In glancing over an old number of the Penny Magazine, there I saw a picture of the place to the life; and remembered having seen the same print years previous. It was a representation of the spot where the Manchester railroad enters the outskirts of the town.

CHAPTER XLII
HIS ADVENTURE WITH THE CROSS OLD GENTLEMAN

My adventure in the News-Room in the Exchange, which I have related in a previous chapter, reminds me of another, at the Lyceum, some days after, which may as well be put down here, before I forget it.

I was strolling down Bold-street, I think it was, when I was struck by the sight of a brown stone building, very large and handsome. The windows were open, and there, nicely seated, with their comfortable legs crossed over their comfortable knees, I beheld several sedate, happy-looking old gentlemen reading the magazines and papers, and one had a fine gilded volume in his hand.

Yes, this must be the Lyceum, thought I; let me see. So I whipped out my guide-book, and opened it at the proper place; and sure enough, the building before me corresponded stone for stone. I stood awhile on the opposite side of the street, gazing at my picture, and then at its original; and often dwelling upon the pleasant gentlemen sitting at the open windows; till at last I felt an uncontrollable impulse to step in for a moment, and run over the news.

I'm a poor, friendless sailor-boy, thought I, and they can not object; especially as I am from a foreign land, and strangers ought to be treated with courtesy. I turned the matter over again, as I walked across the way; and with just a small tapping of a misgiving at my heart, I at last scraped my feet clean against the curb-stone, and taking off my hat while I was yet in the open air, slowly sauntered in.

But I had not got far into that large and lofty room, filled with many agreeable sights, when a crabbed old gentleman lifted up his eye from the *London Times*, which words I saw boldly printed on the back of the large sheet in his hand, and looking at me as if I were a strange dog with a muddy hide, that had stolen out of the gutter into this fine apartment, he shook his silver-headed cane at me fiercely, till the spectacles fell off his nose. Almost at the same moment, up stepped a terribly cross man, who looked as if he had a mustard plaster on his back, that was continually exasperating him; who throwing down some papers which he had been filing, took me by my innocent shoulders, and then, putting his foot against the broad part of my pantaloons, wheeled me right out into the street, and dropped me on the walk, without so much as offering an apology for the affront. I sprang after him, but in vain; the door was closed upon me.

These Englishmen have no manners, that's plain, thought I; and I trudged on down the street in a reverie.

CHAPTER XLIII
HE TAKES A DELIGHTFUL RAMBLE INTO THE COUNTRY; AND MAKES THE ACQUAINTANCE OF THREE ADORABLE CHARMERS

Who that dwells in America has not heard of the bright fields and green hedges of England, and longed to behold them? Even so had it been with me; and now that I was actually in England, I resolved not to go away without having a good, long look at the open fields.

On a Sunday morning I started, with a lunch in my pocket. It was a beautiful day in July; the air was sweet with the breath of buds and flowers, and there was a green splendor in the landscape that ravished me. Soon I gained an elevation commanding a wide sweep of view; and meadow and mead, and woodland and hedge, were all around me.

Ay, ay! this was old England, indeed! I had found it at last—there it was in the country! Hovering over the scene was a soft, dewy air, that seemed faintly tinged with the green of the grass; and I thought, as I breathed my breath, that perhaps I might be inhaling the very particles once respired by Rosamond the Fair.

On I trudged along the London road—smooth as an entry floor—and every white cottage I passed, embosomed in honeysuckles, seemed alive in the landscape.

But the day wore on; and at length the sun grew hot; and the long road became dusty. I thought that some shady place, in some shady field, would be very pleasant to repose in. So, coming to a charming little dale, undulating down to a hollow, arched over with foliage, I crossed over toward it; but paused by the road-side at a frightful announcement, nailed against an old tree, used as a gate-post—

"MAN-TRAPS AND SPRING-GUNS!"

In America I had never heard of the like. What could it mean? They were not surely *cannibals*, that dwelt down in that beautiful little dale, and lived by catching men, like weasels and beavers in Canada!

"A *man-trap!*" It must be so. The announcement could bear but one meaning—that there was something near by, intended to catch human beings; some species of mechanism, that would suddenly fasten upon the unwary rover, and hold him by the leg like a dog; or, perhaps, devour him on the spot.

Incredible! In a Christian land, too! Did that sweet lady, Queen Victoria, permit such diabolical practices? Had her gracious majesty ever passed by this way, and seen the announcement?

And who put it there?

The proprietor, probably.

And what right had he to do so?

Why, he owned the soil.

And where are his title-deeds?

In his strong-box, I suppose.

Thus I stood wrapt in cogitations.

You are a pretty fellow, Wellingborough, thought I to myself; you are a mighty traveler, indeed:—stopped on your travels by a *man-trap!* Do you think Mungo Park was so served in Africa? Do you think Ledyard was so entreated in Siberia? Upon my word, you will go home not very much wiser than when you set out; and the only excuse you can give, for not having seen more sights, will be *man-traps—mantraps, my masters!* that frightened you!

And then, in my indignation, I fell back upon first principles. What right has this man to the soil he thus guards with dragons? What excessive effrontery, to lay sole claim to a solid piece of this planet, right down to the earth's axis, and, perhaps, straight through to the antipodes! For a moment I thought I would test his traps, and enter the forbidden Eden.

But the grass grew so thickly, and seemed so full of sly things, that at last I thought best to pace off.

Next, I came to a hawthorn lane, leading down very prettily to a nice little church; a mossy little church; a beautiful little church; just such a church as I had always dreamed to be in England. The porch was viny as an arbor; the ivy was climbing about the tower; and the bees were humming about the hoary old head-stones along the walls.

Any man-traps here? thought I—any spring-guns?

No.

So I walked on, and entered the church, where I soon found a seat. No Indian, red as a deer, could have startled the simple people more. They gazed and they gazed; but as I was all attention to the sermon, and conducted myself with perfect propriety, they did not expel me, as at first I almost imagined they might.

Service over, I made my way through crowds of children, who stood staring at the marvelous stranger, and resumed my stroll along the London Road.

My next stop was at an inn, where under a tree sat a party of rustics, drinking ale at a table.

"Good day," said I.

"Good day; from Liverpool?"

"I guess so."

"For London?"

"No; not this time. I merely come to see the country."

At this, they gazed at each other; and I, at myself; having doubts whether I might not look something like a horse-thief.

"Take a seat," said the landlord, a fat fellow, with his wife's apron on, I thought.

"Thank you."

And then, little by little, we got into a long talk: in the course of which, I told who I was, and where I was from. I found these rustics a good-natured, jolly set; and I have no doubt they found me quite a sociable youth. They treated me to ale; and I treated them to stories about America, concerning which, they manifested the utmost curiosity. One of them, however, was somewhat astonished that I had not made the acquaintance of a brother of his, who had resided somewhere on the banks of the Mississippi for several years past; but among twenty millions of people, I had never happened to meet him, at least to my knowledge.

At last, leaving this party, I pursued my way, exhilarated by the lively conversation in which I had shared, and the pleasant sympathies exchanged: and perhaps, also, by the ale I had drunk:—fine old ale; yes, English ale, ale brewed in England! And I trod English soil; and breathed English air; and every blade of grass was an Englishman born. Smoky old Liverpool, with all its pitch and tar was now far behind; nothing in sight but open meadows and fields.

Come, Wellingborough, why not push on for London?— Hurra! what say you? let's have a peep at St. Paul's? Don't you want to see the queen?

Have you no longing to behold the duke? Think of Westminster Abbey, and the Tunnel under the Thames! Think of Hyde Park, and the ladies!

But then, thought I again, with my hands wildly groping in my two vacuums of pockets—who's to pay the bill?—You can't beg your way, Wellingborough; that would never do; for you are your father's son, Wellingborough; and you must not disgrace your family in a foreign land; you must not turn pauper.

Ah! Ah! it was indeed too true; there was no St. Paul's or Westminster Abbey for me; that was flat.

Well, well, up heart, you'll see it one of these days.

But think of it! here I am on the very road that leads to the Thames—think of *that!*—here I am—ay, treading in the wheel-tracks of coaches that are bound for the metropolis!—It was too bad; too bitterly bad. But I shoved my old hat over my brows, and walked on; till at last I came to a green bank, deliriously shaded by a fine old tree with broad branching arms, that stretched themselves over the road, like a hen gathering her brood under her wings. Down on the green grass I threw myself and there lay my head, like a last year's nut. People passed by, on foot and in carriages, and little thought that the sad youth under the tree was the great-nephew of a late senator in the American Congress.

Presently, I started to my feet, as I heard a gruff voice behind me from the field, crying out—"What are you doing there, you young rascal?—run away from the work'us, have ye? Tramp, or I'll set Blucher on ye!"

And who was Blucher? A cut-throat looking dog, with his black bull-muzzle thrust through a gap in the hedge. And his master? A sturdy farmer, with an alarming cudgel in his hand.

"Come, are you going to start?" he cried.

"Presently," said I, making off with great dispatch. When I had got a few yards into the middle of the highroad (which belonged as much to me as it did to the queen herself), I turned round, like a man on his own premises, and said— "Stranger! if you ever visit America, just call at our house, and you'll always find there a dinner and a bed. Don't fail."

I then walked on toward Liverpool, full of sad thoughts concerning the cold charities of the world, and the infamous reception given to hapless young travelers, in broken-down shooting-jackets.

On, on I went, along the skirts of forbidden green fields; until reaching a cottage, before which I stood rooted.

So sweet a place I had never seen: no palace in Persia could be pleasanter; there were flowers in the garden; and six red cheeks, like six moss-roses, hanging from the casement. At the embowered doorway, sat an old man, confidentially communing with his pipe: while a little child, sprawling on the ground, was playing with his shoestrings. A hale matron, but with rather a prim expression, was reading a journal by his side: and three charmers, three Peris, three Houris! were leaning out of the window close by.

Ah! Wellingborough, don't you wish you could step in?

With a heavy heart at his cheerful sigh, I was turning to go, when—is it possible? the old man called me back, and invited me in.

"Come, come," said he, "you look as if you had walked far; come, take a bowl of milk. Matilda, my dear" (how my heart jumped), "go fetch some from the dairy." And the white-handed angel did meekly obey, and handed *me—me*, the vagabond, a bowl of bubbling milk, which I could hardly drink down, for gazing at the dew on her lips.

As I live, I could have married that charmer on the spot!

She was by far the most beautiful rosebud I had yet seen in England. But I endeavored to dissemble my ardent admiration; and in order to do away at once with any unfavorable impressions arising from the close scrutiny of my miserable shooting-jacket, which was now taking place, I declared myself a Yankee sailor from Liverpool, who was spending a Sunday in the country.

"And have you been to church to-day, young man?" said the old lady, looking daggers.

"Good madam, I have; the little church down yonder, you know—a most excellent sermon—I am much the better for it."

I wanted to mollify this severe looking old lady; for even my short experience of old ladies had convinced me that they are the hereditary enemies of all strange young men.

I soon turned the conversation toward America, a theme which I knew would be interesting, and upon which I could be fluent and agreeable. I strove to talk in Addisonian English, and ere long could see very plainly that my polished phrases were making a surprising impression, though that miserable shooting-jacket of mine was a perpetual drawback to my claims to gentility.

Spite of all my blandishments, however, the old lady stood her post like a sentry; and to my inexpressible chagrin, kept the three charmers in the background, though the old man frequently called upon them to advance. This fine specimen of an old Englishman seemed to be quite as free from ungenerous suspicions as his vinegary spouse was full of them. But I still lingered, snatching furtive glances at the young ladies, and vehemently talking to the old man about Illinois, and the river Ohio, and the fine farms in the Genesee country, where, in harvest time, the laborers went into the wheat fields a thousand strong.

Stick to it, Wellingborough, thought I; don't give the old lady time to think; stick to it, my boy, and an invitation to tea will reward you. At last it came, and the old lady abated her frowns.

It was the most delightful of meals; the three charmers sat all on one side, and I opposite, between the old man and his wife. The middle charmer poured out the souchong, and handed me the buttered muffins; and such buttered muffins never were spread on the other side of the Atlantic. The butter had an aromatic flavor; by Jove, it was perfectly delicious.

And there they sat—the charmers, I mean—eating these buttered muffins in plain sight. I wished I was a buttered muffin myself. Every minute they grew handsomer and handsomer; and I could not help thinking what a fine thing it would be to carry home a beautiful English wife! how my friends would stare! a lady from England!

I might have been mistaken; but certainly I thought that Matilda, the one who had handed me the milk, sometimes looked rather benevolently in the direction where I sat. She certainly *did* look at my jacket; and I am constrained to think at my face. Could it be possible she had fallen in love at first sight? Oh, rapture! But oh, misery! that was out of the question; for what a looking suitor was Wellingborough?

At length, the old lady glanced toward the door, and made some observations about its being yet a long walk to town. She handed me the buttered muffins, too, as if performing a final act of hospitality; and in other fidgety ways vaguely hinted her desire that I should decamp.

Slowly I rose, and murmured my thanks, and bowed, and tried to be off; but as quickly I turned, and bowed, and thanked, and lingered again and again. Oh, charmers! oh, Peris! thought I, must I go? Yes, Wellingborough, you must; so I made one desperate congee, and darted through the door.

I have never seen them since: no, nor heard of them; but to this day I live a bachelor on account of those ravishing charmers.

As the long twilight was waning deeper and deeper into the night, I entered the town; and, plodding my solitary way to the same old docks, I passed through the gates, and scrambled my way among tarry smells, across the tiers of ships between the quay and the Highlander. My only resource was my bunk; in I turned, and, wearied with my long stroll, was soon fast asleep, dreaming of red cheeks and roses.

CHAPTER XLIV
REDBURN INTRODUCES MASTER HARRY BOLTON TO THE FAVORABLE CONSIDERATION OF THE READER

It was the day following my Sunday stroll into the country, and when I had been in England four weeks or more, that I made the acquaintance of a handsome, accomplished, but unfortunate youth, young Harry Bolton. He was one of those small, but perfectly formed beings, with curling hair, and silken muscles, who seem to have been born in cocoons. His complexion was a mantling brunette, feminine as a girl's; his feet were small; his hands were white; and his eyes were large, black, and womanly; and, poetry aside, his voice was as the sound of a harp.

But where, among the tarry docks, and smoky sailor-lanes and by-ways of a seaport, did I, a battered Yankee boy, encounter this courtly youth?

Several evenings I had noticed him in our street of boarding-houses, standing in the doorways, and silently regarding the animated scenes without. His beauty, dress, and manner struck me as so out of place in such a street, that I could not possibly divine what had transplanted this delicate exotic from the conservatories of some Regent-street to the untidy potato-patches of Liverpool.

At last I suddenly encountered him at the sign of the Baltimore Clipper. He was speaking to one of my shipmates concerning America; and from something that dropped, I was led to imagine that he contemplated a voyage to my country. Charmed with his appearance, and all eagerness to enjoy the society of this incontrovertible son of a gentleman—a kind of pleasure so long debarred me—I smoothed down the skirts of my jacket, and at once accosted him; declaring who I was, and that nothing would afford me greater delight than to be of the least service, in imparting any information concerning America that he needed.

He glanced from my face to my jacket, and from my jacket to my face, and at length, with a pleased but somewhat puzzled expression, begged me to accompany him on a walk.

We rambled about St. George's Pier until nearly midnight; but before we parted, with uncommon frankness, he told me many strange things respecting his history.

According to his own account, Harry Bolton was a native of Bury St. Edmunds, a borough of Suffolk, not very far from London, where he was early left an orphan, under the charge of an only aunt. Between his aunt and himself, his mother had divided her fortune; and young Harry thus fell heir to a portion of about five thousand pounds.

Being of a roving mind, as he approached his majority he grew restless of the retirement of a country place; especially as he had no profession or business of any kind to engage his attention.

In vain did Bury, with all its fine old monastic attractions, lure him to abide on the beautiful banks of her Larke, and under the shadow of her stately and storied old Saxon tower.

By all my rare old historic associations, breathed Bury; by my Abbey-gate, that bears to this day the arms of Edward the Confessor; by my carved roof of the old church of St. Mary's, which escaped the low rage of the bigoted Puritans; by the royal ashes of Mary Tudor, that sleep in my midst; by my Norman ruins, and by all the old abbots of Bury, do not, oh Harry! abandon me. Where will you find shadier walks than under my lime-trees? where lovelier gardens than those within the old walls of my monastery, approached through my lordly Gate? Or if, oh Harry! indifferent to my historic mosses, and caring not for my annual verdure, thou must needs be lured by other tassels, and wouldst fain, like the Prodigal, squander thy patrimony, then, go not away from old Bury to do it. For here, on Angel-Hill, are my coffee and card-rooms, and billiard saloons, where you may lounge away your mornings, and empty your glass and your purse as you list.

In vain. Bury was no place for the adventurous Harry, who must needs hie to London, where in one winter, in the company of gambling sportsmen and dandies, he lost his last sovereign.

What now was to be done? His friends made interest for him in the requisite quarters, and Harry was soon embarked for Bombay, as a midshipman in the East India service; in which office he was known as a "*guinea-pig,*" a humorous appellation then bestowed upon the middies of the Company. And considering the perversity of his behavior, his delicate form, and soft complexion, and that gold guineas had been his bane, this appellation was not altogether, in poor Harry's case, inapplicable.

He made one voyage, and returned; another, and returned; and then threw up his warrant in disgust. A few weeks' dissipation in London, and again his purse was almost drained; when, like many prodigals, scorning to return home to his aunt, and amend—though she had often written him the kindest of letters to that effect—Harry resolved to precipitate himself upon the New World, and there carve out a fresh fortune. With this object in view, he packed his trunks, and took the first train for Liverpool. Arrived in that town, he at once betook himself to the docks, to examine the American shipping, when a new crotchet entered his brain, born of his old sea reminiscences. It was to assume duck browsers and tarpaulin, and gallantly cross the Atlantic as a sailor. There was a dash of romance in it; a taking abandonment; and scorn of fine coats, which exactly harmonized with his reckless contempt, at the time, for all past conventionalities.

Thus determined, he exchanged his trunk for a mahogany chest; sold some of his superfluities; and moved his quarters to the sign of the Gold Anchor in Union-street.

After making his acquaintance, and learning his intentions, I was all anxiety that Harry should accompany me home in the Highlander, a desire to which he warmly responded.

Nor was I without strong hopes that he would succeed in an application to the captain; inasmuch as during our stay in the docks, three of our crew had left us, and their places would remain unsupplied till just upon the eve of our departure.

And here, it may as well be related, that owing to the heavy charges to which the American ships long staying in Liverpool are subjected, from the obligation to continue the wages of their seamen, when they have little or no work to employ them, and from the necessity of boarding them ashore, like lords, at their leisure, captains interested in the ownership of their vessels, are not at all indisposed to let their sailors abscond, if they please, and thus forfeit their money; for they well know that, when wanted, a new crew is easily to be procured, through the crimps of the port.

Though he spake English with fluency, and from his long service in the vessels of New York, was almost an American to behold, yet Captain Riga was in fact a Russian by birth, though this was a fact that he strove to conceal. And though extravagant in his personal expenses, and even indulging in luxurious habits, costly as Oriental dissipation, yet Captain Riga was a niggard to others; as, indeed, was evinced in the magnificent stipend of three dollars, with which he requited my own valuable services. Therefore, as it was agreed between Harry and me, that he should offer to ship as a *"boy,"* at the same rate of compensation with myself, I made no doubt that, incited by the cheapness of the bargain, Captain Riga would gladly close with him; and thus, instead of paying sixteen dollars a month to a thorough-going tar, who would consume all his rations, buy up my young blade of Bury, at the rate of half a dollar a week; with the cheering prospect, that by the end of the voyage, his fastidious palate would be the means of leaving a handsome balance of salt beef and pork in the *harness-cask.*

With part of the money obtained by the sale of a few of his velvet vests, Harry, by my advice, now rigged himself in a Guernsey frock and man-of-war browsers; and thus equipped, he made his appearance, one fine morning, on the quarterdeck of the Highlander, gallantly doffing his virgin tarpaulin before the redoubtable Riga.

No sooner were his wishes made known, than I perceived in the captain's face that same bland, benevolent, and bewitchingly merry expression, that had so charmed, but deceived me, when, with Mr. Jones, I had first accosted him in the cabin.

Alas, Harry! thought I,—as I stood upon the forecastle looking astern where they stood,—that *"gallant, gay deceiver"* shall not altogether cajole you, if Wellingborough can help it. Rather than that should be the case, indeed, I would forfeit the pleasure of your society across the Atlantic.

At this interesting interview the captain expressed a sympathetic concern touching the sad necessities, which he took upon himself to presume must have driven Harry to sea; he confessed to a warm interest in his future welfare; and did not hesitate to declare that, in going to America, under such circumstances, to seek his fortune, he was acting a manly and spirited part; and that the voyage thither, as a sailor, would be an invigorating preparative to the landing upon a shore, where he must battle out his fortune with Fate.

He engaged him at once; but was sorry to say, that he could not provide him a home on board till the day previous to the sailing of the ship; and during the interval, he could not honor any drafts upon the strength of his wages.

However, glad enough to conclude the agreement upon any terms at all, my young blade of Bury expressed his satisfaction; and full of admiration at so urbane and gentlemanly a sea-captain, he came forward to receive my congratulations.

"Harry," said I, "be not deceived by the fascinating Riga—that gay Lothario of all inexperienced, sea-going youths, from the capital or the country; he has a Janus-face, Harry; and you will not know him when he gets you out of sight of land, and mouths his cast-off coats and browsers. For *then* he is another personage altogether, and adjusts his character to the shabbiness of his integuments. No more condolings and sympathy then; no more blarney; he will hold you a little better than his boots, and would no more think of addressing you than of invoking wooden Donald, the figure-head on our bows."

And I further admonished my friend concerning our crew, particularly of the diabolical Jackson, and warned him to be cautious and wary. I told him, that unless he was somewhat accustomed to the rigging, and could furl a royal in a squall, he would be sure to subject himself to a sort of treatment from the sailors, in the last degree ignominious to any mortal who had ever crossed his legs under mahogany.

And I played the inquisitor, in cross-questioning Harry respecting the precise degree in which he was a practical sailor;—whether he had a giddy head; whether his arms could bear the weight of his body; whether, with but one hand on a shroud, a hundred feet aloft in a tempest, he felt he could look right to windward and beard it.

To all this, and much more, Harry rejoined with the most off-hand and confident air; saying that in his *"guinea-pig"* days, he had often climbed the masts and handled the sails in a gentlemanly and amateur way; so he made no doubt that he would very soon prove an expert tumbler in the Highlander's rigging.

His levity of manner, and sanguine assurance, coupled with the constant sight of his most unseamanlike person—more suited to the Queen's drawing-room than a ship's forecastle-bred many misgivings in my mind. But after all, every one in this world has his own fate intrusted to himself; and though we may warn, and forewarn, and give sage advice, and indulge in many apprehensions touching our friends; yet our friends, for the most part, will *"gang their ain gate;"* and the most we can do is, to hope for the best. Still, I suggested to Harry, whether he had not best cross the sea as a steerage passenger, since he could procure enough money for that; but no, he was bent upon going as a sailor.

I now had a comrade in my afternoon strolls, and Sunday excursions; and as Harry was a generous fellow, he shared with me his purse and his heart. He sold off several more of his fine vests and browsers, his silver-keyed flute and enameled guitar; and a portion of the money thus furnished was pleasantly spent in refreshing ourselves at the road-side inns in the vicinity of the town.

Reclining side by side in some agreeable nook, we exchanged our experiences of the past. Harry enlarged upon the fascinations of a London life; described the curricle he used to drive in Hyde Park; gave me the measurement of Madame Vestris' ankle; alluded to his first introduction at a club to the madcap Marquis of Waterford; told over the sums he had lost upon the turf on a Derby day; and made various but enigmatical allusions to a certain Lady Georgiana Theresa, the noble daughter of an anonymous earl.

Even in conversation, Harry was a prodigal; squandering his aristocratic narrations with a careless hand; and, perhaps, sometimes spending funds of reminiscences not his own.

As for me, I had only my poor old uncle the senator to fall back upon; and I used him upon all emergencies, like the knight in the game of chess; making him hop about, and stand stiffly up to the encounter, against all my fine comrade's array of dukes, lords, curricles, and countesses.

In these long talks of ours, I frequently expressed the earnest desire I cherished, to make a visit to London; and related how strongly tempted I had been one Sunday, to walk the whole way, without a penny in my pocket. To this, Harry rejoined, that nothing would delight him more, than to show me the capital; and he even meaningly but mysteriously hinted at the possibility of his doing so, before many days had passed. But this seemed so idle a thought, that I only imputed it to my friend's good-natured, rattling disposition, which sometimes prompted him to out with any thing, that he thought would be agreeable. Besides, would this fine blade of Bury be seen, by his aristocratic acquaintances, walking down Oxford-street, say, arm in arm with the sleeve of my shooting-jacket? The thing was preposterous; and I began to think, that Harry, after all, was a little bit disposed to impose upon my Yankee credulity.

Luckily, my Bury blade had no acquaintance in Liverpool, where, indeed, he was as much in a foreign land, as if he were already on the shores of Lake Erie; so that he strolled about with me in perfect abandonment; reckless of the cut of my shooting-jacket; and not caring one whit who might stare at so singular a couple.

But once, crossing a square, faced on one side by a fashionable hotel, he made a rapid turn with me round a corner; and never stopped, till the square was a good block in our rear. The cause of this sudden retreat, was a remarkably elegant coat and pantaloons, standing upright on the hotel steps, and containing a young buck, tapping his teeth with an ivory-headed riding-whip.

"Who was he, Harry?" said I.

"My old chum, Lord Lovely," said Harry, with a careless air, "and Heaven only knows what brings Lovely from London."

"A lord?" said I starting; "then I must look at him again;" for lords are very scarce in Liverpool.

Unmindful of my companion's remonstrances, I ran back to the corner; and slowly promenaded past the upright coat and pantaloons on the steps.

It was not much of a lord to behold; very thin and limber about the legs, with small feet like a doll's, and a small, glossy head like a seal's. I had seen just such looking lords standing in sentimental attitudes in front of Palmo's in Broadway.

However, he and I being mutual friends of Harry's, I thought something of accosting him, and taking counsel concerning what was best to be done for the young prodigal's welfare; but upon second thoughts I thought best not to intrude; especially, as just then my lord Lovely stepped to the open window of a flashing carriage which drew up; and throwing himself into an interesting posture, with the sole of one boot vertically exposed, so as to show the stamp on it—a coronet—fell into a sparkling conversation with a magnificent white satin hat, surmounted by a regal marabou feather, inside.

I doubted not, this lady was nothing short of a peeress; and thought it would be one of the pleasantest and most charming things in the world, just to seat myself beside her, and order the coachman to take us a drive into the country.

But, as upon further consideration, I imagined that the peeress might decline the honor of my company, since I had no formal card of introduction; I marched on, and rejoined my companion, whom I at once endeavored to draw out, touching Lord Lovely; but he only made mysterious answers; and turned off the conversation, by allusions to his visits to Ickworth in Suffolk, the magnificent seat of the Most Noble Marquis of Bristol, who had repeatedly assured Harry that he might consider Ickworth his home.

Now, all these accounts of marquises and Ickworths, and Harry's having been hand in glove with so many lords and ladies, began to breed some suspicions concerning the rigid morality of my friend, as a teller of the truth. But, after all, thought I to myself, who can prove that Harry has fibbed? Certainly, his manners are polished, he has a mighty easy address;

and there is nothing altogether impossible about his having consorted with the master of Ickworth, and the daughter of the anonymous earl. And what right has a poor Yankee, like me, to insinuate the slightest suspicion against what he says? What little money he has, he spends freely; he can not be a polite blackleg, for I am no pigeon to pluck; so *that* is out of the question;—perish such a thought, concerning my own bosom friend!

But though I drowned all my suspicions as well as I could, and ever cherished toward Harry a heart, loving and true; yet, spite of all this, I never could entirely digest some of his imperial reminiscences of high life. I was very sorry for this; as at times it made me feel ill at ease in his company; and made me hold back my whole soul from him; when, in its loneliness, it was yearning to throw itself into the unbounded bosom of some immaculate friend.

CHAPTER XLV
HARRY BOLTON KIDNAPS REDBURN, AND CARRIES HIM OFF TO LONDON

It might have been a week after our glimpse of Lord Lovely, that Harry, who had been expecting a letter, which, he told me, might possibly alter his plans, one afternoon came bounding on board the ship, and sprang down the hatchway into the *between-decks,* where, in perfect solitude, I was engaged picking oakum; at which business the mate had set me, for want of any thing better.

"Hey for London, Wellingborough!" he cried. "Off tomorrow! first train—be there the same night—come! I have money to rig you all out—drop that hangman's stuff there, and away! Pah! how it smells here! Come; up you jump!"

I trembled with amazement and delight.

London? it could not be!—and Harry—how kind of him! he was then indeed what he seemed. But instantly I thought of all the circumstances of the case, and was eager to know what it was that had induced this sudden departure.

In reply my friend told me, that he had received a remittance, and had hopes of recovering a considerable sum, lost in some way that he chose to conceal.

"But how am I to leave the ship, Harry?" said I; "they will not let me go, will they? You had better leave me behind, after all; I don't care very much about going; and besides, I have no money to share the expenses."

This I said, only pretending indifference, for my heart was jumping all the time.

"Tut! my Yankee bantam," said Harry; "look here!" and he showed me a handful of gold.

"But they are *yours,* and not *mine,* Harry," said I.

"Yours *and* mine, my sweet fellow," exclaimed Harry. "Come, sink the ship, and let's go!"

"But you don't consider, if I quit the ship, they'll be sending a constable after me, won't they?"

"What! and do you think, then, they value your services so highly? Ha! ha!-Up, up, Wellingborough: I can't wait."

True enough. I well knew that Captain Riga would not trouble himself much, if I *did* take French leave of him. So, without further thought of the matter, I told Harry to wait a few moments, till the ship's bell struck four; at which time I used to go to supper, and be free for the rest of the day.

The bell struck; and off we went. As we hurried across the quay, and along the dock walls, I asked Harry all about his intentions. He said, that go to London he must, and to Bury St. Edmunds; but that whether he should for any time remain at either place, he could not now tell; and it was by no means impossible, that in less than a week's time we would be back again in Liverpool, and ready for sea. But all he said was enveloped in a mystery that I did not much like; and I hardly know whether I have repeated correctly what he said at the time.

Arrived at the *Golden Anchor*, where Harry put up, he at once led me to his room, and began turning over the contents of his chest, to see what clothing he might have, that would fit me.

Though he was some years my senior, we were about the same size—if any thing, I was larger than he; so, with a little stretching, a shirt, vest, and pantaloons were soon found to suit. As for a coat and hat, those Harry ran out and bought without delay; returning with a loose, stylish sack-coat, and a sort of foraging cap, very neat, genteel, and unpretending.

My friend himself soon doffed his Guernsey frock, and stood before me, arrayed in a perfectly plain suit, which he had bought on purpose that very morning. I asked him why he had gone to that unnecessary expense, when he had plenty of other clothes in his chest. But he only winked, and looked knowing. This, again, I did not like. But I strove to drown ugly thoughts.

Till quite dark, we sat talking together; when, locking his chest, and charging his landlady to look after it well, till he called, or sent for it; Harry seized my arm, and we sallied into the street.

Pursuing our way through crowds of frolicking sailors and fiddlers, we turned into a street leading to the Exchange. There, under the shadow of the colonnade, Harry told me to stop, while he left me, and went to finish his toilet. Wondering what he meant, I stood to one side; and presently was joined by a stranger in whiskers and mustache.

"It's *me*" said the stranger; and who was *me* but Harry, who had thus metamorphosed himself? I asked him the reason; and in a faltering voice, which I tried to make humorous, expressed a hope that he was not going to turn gentleman forger.

He laughed, and assured me that it was only a precaution against being recognized by his own particular friends in London, that he had adopted this mode of disguising himself.

"And why afraid of your friends?" asked I, in astonishment, "and we are not in London yet."

"Pshaw! what a Yankee you are, Wellingborough. Can't you see very plainly that I have a plan in my head? And this disguise is only for a short time, you know. But I'll tell you all by and by."

I acquiesced, though not feeling at ease; and we walked on, till we came to a public house, in the vicinity of the place at which the cars are taken.

We stopped there that night, and next day were off, whirled along through boundless landscapes of villages, and meadows, and parks: and over arching viaducts, and through wonderful tunnels; till, half delirious with excitement, I found myself dropped down in the evening among gas-lights, under a great roof in Euston Square.

London at last, and in the West-End!

CHAPTER XLVI
A MYSTERIOUS NIGHT IN LONDON

"No time to lose," said Harry, "come along."

He called a cab: in an undertone mentioned the number of a house in some street to the driver; we jumped in, and were off.

As we rattled over the boisterous pavements, past splendid squares, churches, and shops, our cabman turning corners like a skater on the ice, and all the roar of London in my ears, and no end to the walls of brick and mortar; I thought New York a hamlet, and Liverpool a coal-hole, and myself somebody else: so unreal seemed every thing about me. My head was spinning round like a top, and my eyes ached with much gazing; particularly about the corners, owing to my darting them so rapidly, first this side, and then that, so as not to miss any thing; though, in truth, I missed much.

"Stop," cried Harry, after a long while, putting his head out of the window, all at once—"stop! do you hear, you deaf man? you have passed the house—No. 40 I told you—that's it—the high steps there, with the purple light!"

The cabman being paid, Harry adjusting his whiskers and mustache, and bidding me assume a lounging look, pushed his hat a little to one side, and then locking arms, we sauntered into the house; myself feeling not a little abashed; it was so long since I had been in any courtly society.

It was some semi-public place of opulent entertainment; and far surpassed any thing of the kind I had ever seen before.

The floor was tesselated with snow-white, and russet-hued marbles; and echoed to the tread, as if all the Paris catacombs were underneath. I started with misgivings at that hollow, boding sound, which seemed sighing with a subterraneous despair, through all the magnificent spectacle around me; mocking it, where most it glared.

The walls were painted so as to deceive the eye with interminable colonnades; and groups of columns of the finest Scagliola work of variegated marbles—emerald-green and gold, St. Pons veined with silver, Sienna with porphyry—supported a resplendent fresco ceiling, arched like a bower, and thickly clustering with mimic grapes. Through all the East of this foliage, you spied in a crimson dawn, Guide's ever youthful Apollo, driving forth the horses of the sun. From sculptured stalactites of vine-boughs, here and there pendent hung galaxies of gas lights, whose vivid glare was softened by pale, cream-colored, porcelain spheres, shedding over the place a serene, silver flood; as if every porcelain sphere were a moon; and this superb apartment was the moon-lit garden of Portia at Belmont; and the gentle lovers, Lorenzo and Jessica, lurked somewhere among the vines.

At numerous Moorish looking tables, supported by Caryatides of turbaned slaves, sat knots of gentlemanly men, with cut decanters and taper-waisted glasses, journals and cigars, before them.

To and fro ran obsequious waiters, with spotless napkins thrown over their arms, and making a profound salaam, and hemming deferentially, whenever they uttered a word.

At the further end of this brilliant apartment, was a rich mahogany turret-like structure, partly built into the wall, and communicating with rooms in the rear. Behind, was a very handsome florid old man, with snow-white hair and whiskers, and in a snow-white jacket—he looked like an almond tree in blossom—who seemed to be standing, a polite sentry over the scene before him; and it was he, who mostly ordered about the waiters; and with a silent salute, received the silver of the guests.

Our entrance excited little or no notice; for every body present seemed exceedingly animated about concerns of their own; and a large group was gathered around one tall, military looking gentleman, who was reading some India war-news from the Times, and commenting on it, in a very loud voice, condemning, in toto, the entire campaign.

We seated ourselves apart from this group, and Harry, rapping on the table, called for wine; mentioning some curious foreign name.

The decanter, filled with a pale yellow wine, being placed before us, and my comrade having drunk a few glasses; he whispered me to remain where I was, while he withdrew for a moment.

I saw him advance to the turret-like place, and exchange a confidential word with the almond tree there, who immediately looked very much surprised,—I thought, a little disconcerted,—and then disappeared with him.

While my friend was gone, I occupied myself with looking around me, and striving to appear as indifferent as possible, and as much used to all this splendor as if I had been born in it. But, to tell the truth, my head was almost dizzy with the strangeness of the sight, and the thought that I was really in London. What would my brother have said? What would Tom Legare, the treasurer of the Juvenile Temperance Society, have thought?

But I almost began to fancy I had no friends and relatives living in a little village three thousand five hundred miles off, in America; for it was hard to unite such a humble reminiscence with the splendid animation of the London-like scene around me.

And in the delirium of the moment, I began to indulge in foolish golden visions of the counts and countesses to whom Harry might introduce me; and every instant I expected to hear the waiters addressing some gentleman as *"My Lord,"* or *"four Grace."* But if there were really any lords present, the waiters omitted their titles, at least in my hearing.

Mixed with these thoughts were confused visions of St. Paul's and the Strand, which I determined to visit the very next morning, before breakfast, or perish in the attempt. And I even longed for Harry's return, that we might immediately sally out into the street, and see some of the sights, before the shops were all closed for the night.

While I thus sat alone, I observed one of the waiters eying me a little impertinently, as I thought, and as if he saw something queer about me. So I tried to assume a careless and lordly air, and by way of helping the thing, threw one leg over the other, like a young Prince Esterhazy; but all the time I felt my face burning with embarrassment, and for the time, I must have looked very guilty of something. But spite of this, I kept looking boldly out of my eyes, and straight through my blushes, and observed that every now and then little parties were made up among the gentlemen, and they retired into the rear of the house, as if going to a private apartment. And I overheard one of them drop the word *Rouge;* but he could not have used rouge, for his face was exceedingly pale. Another said something about *Loo.*

At last Harry came back, his face rather flushed.

"Come along, Redburn," said he.

So making no doubt we were off for a ramble, perhaps to Apsley House, in the Park, to get a sly peep at the old Duke before he retired for the night, for Harry had told me the Duke always went to bed early, I sprang up to follow him; but what was my disappointment and surprise, when he only led me into the passage, toward a staircase lighted by three marble Graces, unitedly holding a broad candelabra, like an elk's antlers, over the landing.

We rambled up the long, winding slope of those aristocratic stairs, every step of which, covered with Turkey rugs, looked gorgeous as the hammer-cloth of the Lord Mayor's coach; and Harry hied straight to a rosewood door, which, on magical hinges, sprang softly open to his touch.

As we entered the room, methought I was slowly sinking in some reluctant, sedgy sea; so thick and elastic the Persian carpeting, mimicking parterres of tulips, and roses, and jonquils, like a bower in Babylon.

Long lounges lay carelessly disposed, whose fine damask was interwoven, like the Gobelin tapestry, with pictorial tales of tilt and tourney. And oriental ottomans, whose cunning warp and woof were wrought into plaited serpents, undulating beneath beds of leaves, from which, here and there, they flashed out sudden splendors of green scales and gold.

In the broad bay windows, as the hollows of King Charles' oaks, were Laocoon-like chairs, in the antique taste, draped with heavy fringes of bullion and silk.

The walls, covered with a sort of tartan-French paper, variegated with bars of velvet, were hung round with mythological oil-paintings, suspended by tasseled cords of twisted silver and blue.

They were such pictures as the high-priests, for a bribe, showed to Alexander in the innermost shrine of the white temple in the Libyan oasis: such pictures as the pontiff of the sun strove to hide from Cortez, when, sword in hand, he burst open the sanctorum of the pyramid-fane at Cholula: such pictures as you may still see, perhaps, in the central alcove of the excavated mansion of Pansa, in Pompeii—in that part of it called by Varro *the hollow of the house:* such pictures as Martial and Seutonius mention as being found in the private cabinet of the Emperor Tiberius: such pictures as are delineated on the bronze medals, to this day dug up on the ancient island of Capreas: such pictures as you might have beheld in an arched recess, leading from the left hand of the secret side-gallery of the temple of Aphrodite in Corinth.

In the principal pier was a marble bracket, sculptured in the semblance of a dragon's crest, and supporting a bust, most wonderful to behold. It was that of a bald-headed old man, with a mysteriously-wicked expression, and imposing silence by one thin finger over his lips. His marble mouth seemed tremulous with secrets.

"Sit down, Wellingborough," said Harry; "don't be frightened, we are at home.—Ring the bell, will you? But stop;"— and advancing to the mysterious bust, he whispered something in its ear.

"He's a knowing mute, Wellingborough," said he; "who stays in this one place all the time, while he is yet running of errands. But mind you don't breathe any secrets in his ear."

In obedience to a summons so singularly conveyed, to my amazement a servant almost instantly appeared, standing transfixed in the attitude of a bow.

"Cigars," said Harry. When they came, he drew up a small table into the middle of the room, and lighting his cigar, bade me follow his example, and make myself happy.

Almost transported with such princely quarters, so undreamed of before, while leading my dog's life in the filthy forecastle of the Highlander, I twirled round a chair, and seated myself opposite my friend.

But all the time, I felt ill at heart; and was filled with an undercurrent of dismal forebodings. But I strove to dispel them; and turning to my companion, exclaimed, "And pray, do you live here, Harry, in this Palace of Aladdin?"

"Upon my soul," he cried, "you have hit it:—you must have been here before! Aladdin's Palace! Why, Wellingborough, it goes by that very name."

Then he laughed strangely: and for the first time, I thought he had been quaffing too freely: yet, though he looked wildly from his eyes, his general carriage was firm.

"Who are you looking at so hard, Wellingborough?" said he.

"I am afraid, Harry," said I, "that when you left me just now, you must have been drinking something stronger than wine."

"Hear him now," said Harry, turning round, as if addressing the bald-headed bust on the bracket,—"a parson 'pon honor!—But remark you, Wellingborough, my boy, I must leave you again, and for a considerably longer time than before:—I may not be back again to-night."

"What?" said I.

"Be still," he cried, "hear me, I know the old duke here, and—"

"Who? not the Duke of Wellington," said I, wondering whether Harry was really going to include *him* too, in his long list of confidential friends and acquaintances.

"Pooh!" cried Harry, "I mean the white-whiskered old man you saw below; they call him *the Duke:—he* keeps the house. I say, I know him well, and he knows *me;* and he knows what brings me here, also. Well; we have arranged every thing about you; you are to stay in this room, and sleep here tonight, and—and—" continued he, speaking low—"you must guard this letter—" slipping a sealed one into my hand—"and, if I am not back by morning, you must post right on to Bury, and leave the letter there;—

here, take this paper—it's all set down here in black and white—where you are to go, and what you are to do. And after that's done—mind, this is all in case I don't return—then you may do what you please: stay here in London awhile, or go back to Liverpool. And here's enough to pay all your expenses."

All this was a thunder stroke. I thought Harry was crazy. I held the purse in my motionless hand, and stared at him, till the tears almost started from my eyes.

"What's the matter, Redburn?" he cried, with a wild sort of laugh—"you are not afraid of me, are you?—No, no! I believe in you, my boy, or you would not hold that purse in your hand; no, nor that letter."

"What in heaven's name do you mean?" at last I exclaimed, "you don't really intend to desert me in this strange place, do you, Harry?" and I snatched him by the hand.

"Pooh, pooh," he cried, "let me go. I tell you, it's all right: do as I say: that's all. Promise me now, will you? Swear it!—no, no," he added, vehemently, as I conjured him to tell me more—"no, I won't: I have nothing more to tell you—not a word. Will you swear?"

"But one sentence more for your own sake, Harry: hear me!"

"Not a syllable! Will you swear?—you will not? then here, give me that purse:—there—there—take that—and that—and that;—that will pay your fare back to Liverpool; good-by to you: you are not my friend," and he wheeled round his back.

I know not what flashed through my mind, but something suddenly impelled me; and grasping his hand, I swore to him what he demanded.

Immediately he ran to the bust, whispered a word, and the white-whiskered old man appeared: whom he clapped on the shoulder, and then introduced me as his friend—young Lord Stormont; and bade the almond tree look well to the comforts of his lordship, while he—Harry—was gone.

The almond tree blandly bowed, and grimaced, with a peculiar expression, that I hated on the spot. After a few words more, he withdrew. Harry then shook my hand heartily, and without giving me a chance to say one word, seized his cap, and darted out of the room, saying, "Leave not this room tonight; and remember the letter, and Bury!"

I fell into a chair, and gazed round at the strange-looking walls and mysterious pictures, and up to the chandelier at the ceiling; then rose, and opened the door, and looked down the lighted passage; but only heard the hum from the roomful below, scattered voices, and a hushed ivory rattling from the closed apartments adjoining. I stepped back into the room, and a terrible revulsion came over me: I would have given the world had I been safe back in Liverpool, fast asleep in my old bunk in Prince's Dock.

I shuddered at every footfall, and almost thought it must be some assassin pursuing me. The whole place seemed infected; and a strange thought came over me, that in the very damasks around, some eastern plague had been imported. And was that pale yellow wine, that I drank below, drugged? thought I. This must be some house whose foundations take hold on the pit. But these fearful reveries only enchanted me fast to my chair; so that, though I then wished to rush forth from the house, my limbs seemed manacled.

While thus chained to my seat, something seemed suddenly flung open; a confused sound of imprecations, mixed with the ivory rattling, louder than before, burst upon my ear, and through the partly open door of the room where I was, I caught sight of a tall, frantic man, with clenched hands, wildly darting through the passage, toward the stairs.

And all the while, Harry ran through my soul—in and out, at every door, that burst open to his vehement rush.

At that moment my whole acquaintance with him passed like lightning through my mind, till I asked myself why he had come here, to London, to do this thing?—why would not Liverpool have answered? and what did he want of me? But, every way, his conduct was unaccountable. From the hour he had accosted me on board the ship, his manner seemed gradually changed; and from the moment we had sprung into the cab, he had seemed almost another person from what he had seemed before.

But what could I do? He was gone, that was certain;—would he ever come back? But he might still be somewhere in the house; and with a shudder, I thought of that ivory rattling, and was almost ready to dart forth, search every room, and save him. But that would be madness, and I had sworn not to do so. There seemed nothing left, but to await his return. Yet, if he did not return, what then? I took out the purse, and counted over the money, and looked at the letter and paper of memoranda.

Though I vividly remember it all, I will not give the superscription of the letter, nor the contents of the paper. But after I had looked at them attentively, and considered that Harry could have no conceivable object in deceiving me, I thought to myself, Yes, he's in earnest; and here I am—yes, even in London! And here in this room will I stay, come what will. I will implicitly follow his directions, and so see out the last of this thing.

But spite of these thoughts, and spite of the metropolitan magnificence around me, I was mysteriously alive to a dreadful feeling, which I had never before felt, except when penetrating into the lowest and most squalid haunts of sailor iniquity in Liverpool. All the mirrors and marbles around me seemed crawling over with lizards; and I thought to myself, that though gilded and golden, the serpent of vice is a serpent still.

It was now grown very late; and faint with excitement, I threw myself upon a lounge; but for some time tossed about restless, in a sort of nightmare. Every few moments, spite of my oath, I was upon the point of starting up, and rushing into the street, to inquire where I was; but remembering Harry's injunctions, and my own ignorance of the town, and that it was now so late, I again tried to be composed.

At last, I fell asleep, dreaming about Harry fighting a duel of dice-boxes with the military-looking man below; and the next thing I knew, was the glare of a light before my eyes, and Harry himself, very pale, stood before me.

"The letter and paper," he cried.

I fumbled in my pockets, and handed them to him.

"There! there! there! thus I tear you," he cried, wrenching the letter to pieces with both hands like a madman, and stamping upon the fragments. "I am off for America; the game is up."

"For God's sake explain," said I, now utterly bewildered, and frightened. "Tell me, Harry, what is it? You have not been gambling?"

"Ha, ha," he deliriously laughed. "Gambling? red and white, you mean?—cards?—dice?—the bones?—Ha, ha!—Gambling? gambling?" he ground out between his teeth—"what two devilish, stiletto-sounding syllables they are!"

"Wellingborough," he added, marching up to me slowly, but with his eyes blazing into mine—"Wellingborough"—and fumbling in his breast-pocket, he drew forth a dirk—"Here, Wellingborough, take it—take it, I say—are you stupid?—there, there"—and he pushed it into my hands. "Keep it away from me—keep it out of my sight—I don't want it near me, while I feel as I do. They serve suicides scurvily here, Wellingborough; they don't bury them decently. See that bell-rope! By Heaven, it's an invitation to hang myself"—and seizing it by the gilded handle at the end, he twitched it down from the wall.

"In God's name, what ails you?" I cried.

"Nothing, oh nothing," said Harry, now assuming a treacherous, tropical calmness—"nothing, Redburn; nothing in the world. I'm the serenest of men."

"But give me that dirk," he suddenly cried—"let me have it, I say. Oh! I don't mean to murder myself—I'm past that now—give it me"—and snatching it from my hand, he flung down an empty purse, and with a terrific stab, nailed it fast with the dirk to the table.

"There now," he cried, "there's something for the old duke to see to-morrow morning; that's about all that's left of me— that's my skeleton, Wellingborough. But come, don't be downhearted; there's a little more gold yet in Golconda; I have a guinea or two left. Don't stare so, my boy; we shall be in Liverpool to-morrow night; we start in the morning"—and turning his back, he began to whistle very fiercely.

"And this, then," said I, "is your showing me London, is it, Harry? I did not think this; but tell me your secret, whatever it is, and I will not regret not seeing the town."

He turned round upon me like lightning, and cried, "Red-burn! you must swear another oath, and instantly."

"And why?" said I, in alarm, "what more would you have me swear?"

"Never to question me again about this infernal trip to London!" he shouted, with the foam at his lips—"never to breathe it! swear!"

"I certainly shall not trouble you, Harry, with questions, if you do not desire it," said I, "but there's no need of swearing."

"Swear it, I say, as you love me, Redburn," he added, imploringly.

"Well, then, I solemnly do. Now lie down, and let us forget ourselves as soon as we can; for me, you have made me the most miserable dog alive."

"And what am I?" cried Harry; "but pardon me, Redburn, I did not mean to offend; if you knew all—but no, no!—never mind, never mind!" And he ran to the bust, and whispered in its ear. A waiter came.

"Brandy," whispered Harry, with clenched teeth.

"Are you not going to sleep, then?" said I, more and more alarmed at his wildness, and fearful of the effects of his drinking still more, in such a mood.

"No sleep for me! sleep if *you* can—I mean to sit up with a decanter!—let me see"—looking at the ormolu clock on the mantel—"it's only two hours to morning."

The waiter, looking very sleepy, and with a green shade on his brow, appeared with the decanter and glasses on a salver, and was told to leave it and depart.

Seeing that Harry was not to be moved, I once more threw myself on the lounge. I did not sleep; but, like a somnambulist, only dozed now and then; starting from my dreams; while Harry sat, with his hat on, at the table; the brandy before him; from which he occasionally poured into his glass. Instead of exciting him, however, to my amazement, the spirits seemed to soothe him down; and, ere long, he was comparatively calm.

At last, just as I had fallen into a deep sleep, I was wakened by his shaking me, and saying our cab was at the door.

"Look! it is broad day," said he, brushing aside the heavy hangings of the window.

We left the room; and passing through the now silent and deserted hall of pillars, which, at this hour, reeked as with blended roses and cigar-stumps decayed; a dumb waiter; rubbing his eyes, flung open the street door; we sprang into the cab; and soon found ourselves whirled along northward by railroad, toward Prince's Dock and the Highlander.

CHAPTER XLVII
HOMEWARD BOUND

Once more in Liverpool; and wending my way through the same old streets to the sign of the Golden Anchor; I could scarcely credit the events of the last thirty-six hours.

So unforeseen had been our departure in the first place; so rapid our journey; so unaccountable the conduct of Harry; and so sudden our return; that all united to overwhelm me. That I had been at all in London seemed impossible; and that I had been there, and come away little the wiser, was almost distracting to one who, like me, had so longed to behold that metropolis of marvels.

I looked hard at Harry as he walked in silence at my side; I stared at the houses we passed; I thought of the cab, the gas lighted hall in the Palace of Aladdin, the pictures, the letter, the oath, the dirk; the mysterious place where all these mysteries had occurred; and then, was almost ready to conclude, that the pale yellow wine had been drugged.

As for Harry, stuffing his false whiskers and mustache into his pocket, he now led the way to the boarding-house; and saluting the landlady, was shown to his room; where we immediately shifted our clothes, appearing once more in our sailor habiliments.

"Well, what do you propose to do now, Harry?" said I, with a heavy heart.

"Why, visit your Yankee land in the Highlander, of course—what else?" he replied.

"And is it to be a visit, or a long stay?" asked I.

"That's as it may turn out," said Harry; "but I have now more than ever resolved upon the sea. There is nothing like the sea for a fellow like me, Redburn; a desperate man can not get any further than the wharf, you know; and the next step must be a long jump. But come, let's see what they have to eat here, and then for a cigar and a stroll. I feel better already. Never say die, is my motto."

We went to supper; after that, sallied out; and walking along the quay of Prince's Dock, heard that the ship Highlander had that morning been advertised to sail in two days' time.

"Good!" exclaimed Harry; and I was glad enough myself.

Although I had now been absent from the ship a full forty-eight hours, and intended to return to her, yet I did not anticipate being called to any severe account for it from the officers; for several of our men had absented themselves longer than I had, and upon their return, little or nothing was said to them. Indeed, in some cases, the mate seemed to know nothing about it. During the whole time we lay in Liverpool, the discipline of the ship was altogether relaxed; and I could hardly believe they were the same officers who were so dictatorial at sea. The reason of this was, that we had nothing important to do; and although the captain might now legally refuse to receive me on board, yet I was not afraid of that, as I was as stout a lad for my years, and worked as cheap, as any one he could engage to take my place on the homeward passage.

Next morning we made our appearance on board before the rest of the crew; and the mate perceiving me, said with an oath, "Well, sir, you have thought best to return then, have you? Captain Riga and I were flattering ourselves that you had made a run of it for good."

Then, thought I, the captain, who seems to affect to know nothing of the proceedings of the sailors, has been aware of my absence.

"But turn to, sir, turn to," added the mate; "here! aloft there, and free that pennant; it's foul of the backstay—jump!"

The captain coming on board soon after, looked very benevolently at Harry; but, as usual, pretended not to take the slightest notice of myself.

We were all now very busy in getting things ready for sea. The cargo had been already stowed in the hold by the stevedores and lumpers from shore; but it became the crew's business to clear away the *between-decks*, extending from the cabin bulkhead to the forecastle, for the reception of about five hundred emigrants, some of whose boxes were already littering the decks.

To provide for their wants, a far larger supply of water was needed than upon the outward-bound passage. Accordingly, besides the usual number of casks on deck, rows of immense tierces were lashed amid-ships, all along the *between-decks*, forming a sort of aisle on each side, furnishing access to four rows of bunks,—three tiers, one above another,—against the ship's sides; two tiers being placed over the tierces of water in the middle. These bunks were rapidly knocked together with coarse planks. They looked more like dog-kennels than any thing else; especially as the place was so gloomy and dark; no light coming down except through the fore and after hatchways, both of which were covered with little houses called *"booby-hatches."* Upon the main-hatches, which were well calked and covered over with heavy tarpaulins, the *"passengers-galley"* was solidly lashed down.

This *galley* was a large open stove, or iron range—made expressly for emigrant ships, wholly unprotected from the weather, and where alone the emigrants are permitted to cook their food while at sea.

After two days' work, every thing was in readiness; most of the emigrants on board; and in the evening we worked the ship close into the outlet of Prince's Dock, with the bow against the water-gate, to go out with the tide in the morning.

In the morning, the bustle and confusion about us was indescribable. Added to the ordinary clamor of the docks, was the hurrying to and fro of our five hundred emigrants, the last of whom, with their baggage, were now coming on board; the appearance of the cabin passengers, following porters with their trunks; the loud orders of the dock-masters, ordering the various ships behind us to preserve their order of going out; the leave-takings, and good-by's, and God-bless-you's, between the emigrants and their friends; and the cheers of the surrounding ships.

At this time we lay in such a way, that no one could board us except by the bowsprit, which overhung the quay. Staggering along that bowsprit, now came a one-eyed *crimp* leading a drunken tar by the collar, who had been shipped to sail with us the day previous. It has been stated before, that two or three of our men had left us for good, while in port. When the crimp had got this man and another safely lodged in a bunk below, he returned on shore; and going to a miserable cab, pulled out still another apparently drunken fellow, who proved completely helpless. However, the ship now swinging her broadside more toward the quay, this stupefied sailor, with a Scotch cap pulled down over his closed eyes, only revealing a sallow Portuguese complexion, was lowered on board by a rope under his arms, and passed forward by the crew, who put him likewise into a bunk in the forecastle, the crimp himself carefully tucking him in, and bidding the bystanders not to disturb him till the ship was away from the land.

This done, the confusion increased, as we now glided out of the dock. Hats and handkerchiefs were waved; hurrahs were exchanged; and tears were shed; and the last thing I saw, as we shot into the stream, was a policeman collaring a boy, and walking him off to the guard-house.

A steam-tug, the *Goliath*, now took us by the arm, and gallanted us down the river past the fort.

The scene was most striking.

Owing to a strong breeze, which had been blowing up the river for four days past, holding wind-bound in the various docks a multitude of ships for all parts of the world; there was now under weigh, a vast fleet of merchantmen, all steering broad out to sea. The white sails glistened in the clear morning air like a great Eastern encampment of sultans; and from many a forecastle, came the deep mellow old song *Ho-o-he-yo, cheerily men!* as the crews called their anchors.

The wind was fair; the weather mild; the sea most smooth; and the poor emigrants were in high spirits at so auspicious a beginning of their voyage. They were reclining all over the decks, talking of soon seeing America, and relating how the agent had told them, that twenty days would be an uncommonly long voyage.

Here it must be mentioned, that owing to the great number of ships sailing to the Yankee ports from Liverpool, the competition among them in obtaining emigrant passengers, who as a cargo are much more remunerative than crates and bales, is exceedingly great; so much so, that some of the agents they employ, do not scruple to deceive the poor applicants for passage, with all manner of fables concerning the short space of time, in which their ships make the run across the ocean.

This often induces the emigrants to provide a much smaller stock of provisions than they otherwise would; the effect of which sometimes proves to be in the last degree lamentable; as will be seen further on. And though benevolent societies have been long organized in Liverpool, for the purpose of keeping offices, where the emigrants can obtain reliable information and advice, concerning their best mode of embarkation, and other matters interesting to them; and though the English authorities have imposed a law, providing that every captain of an emigrant ship bound for any port of America shall see to it, that each passenger is provided with rations of food for sixty days; yet, all this has not deterred mercenary ship-masters and unprincipled agents from practicing the grossest deception; nor exempted the emigrants themselves, from the very sufferings intended to be averted.

No sooner had we fairly gained the expanse of the Irish Sea, and, one by one, lost sight of our thousand consorts, than the weather changed into the most miserable cold, wet, and cheerless days and nights imaginable. The wind was tempestuous, and dead in our teeth; and the hearts of the emigrants fell. Nearly all of them had now hied below, to escape the uncomfortable and perilous decks: and from the two *"booby-hatches"* came the steady hum of a subterranean wailing and weeping. That irresistible wrestler, sea-sickness, had overthrown the stoutest of their number, and the women and children were embracing and sobbing in all the agonies of the poor emigrant's first storm at sea.

Bad enough is it at such times with ladies and gentlemen in the cabin, who have nice little state-rooms; and plenty of privacy; and stewards to run for them at a word, and put pillows under their heads, and tenderly inquire how they are getting along, and mix them a posset: and even then, in the abandonment of this soul and body subduing malady, such ladies and gentlemen will often give up life itself as unendurable, and put up the most pressing petitions for a speedy annihilation; all of which, however, only arises from their intense anxiety to preserve their valuable lives.

How, then, with the friendless emigrants, stowed away like bales of cotton, and packed like slaves in a slave-ship; confined in a place that, during storm time, must be closed against both light and air; who can do no cooking, nor warm so much as a cup of water; for the drenching seas would instantly flood their fire in their exposed galley on deck? How, then, with these men, and women, and children, to whom a first voyage, under the most advantageous circumstances, must come just as hard as to the Honorable De Lancey Fitz Clarence, lady, daughter, and seventeen servants.

Nor is this all: for in some of these ships, as in the case of the Highlander, the emigrant passengers are cut off from the most indispensable conveniences of a civilized dwelling. This forces them in storm time to such extremities, that no wonder fevers and plagues are the result. We had not been at sea one week, when to hold your head down the fore hatchway was like holding it down a suddenly opened cesspool.

But still more than this. Such is the aristocracy maintained on board some of these ships, that the most arbitrary measures are enforced, to prevent the emigrants from intruding upon the most holy precincts of the quarter-deck, the only completely open space on ship-board. Consequently—even in fine weather—when they come up from below, they are crowded in the waist of the ship, and jammed among the boats, casks, and spars; abused by the seamen, and sometimes cuffed by the officers, for unavoidably standing in the way of working the vessel.

The cabin-passengers of the Highlander numbered some fifteen in all; and to protect this detachment of gentility from the barbarian incursions of the *"wild Irish"* emigrants, ropes were passed athwart-ships, by the mainmast, from side to side: which defined the boundary line between those who had paid three pounds passage-money, from those who had paid twenty guineas. And the cabin-passengers themselves were the most urgent in having this regulation maintained.

Lucky would it be for the pretensions of some parvenus, whose souls are deposited at their banker's, and whose bodies but serve to carry about purses, knit of poor men's heartstrings, if thus easily they could precisely define, ashore, the difference between them and the rest of humanity.

But, I, Redburn, am a poor fellow, who have hardly ever known what it is to have five silver dollars in my pocket at one time; so, no doubt, this circumstance has something to do with my slight and harmless indignation at these things.

CHAPTER XLVIII
A LIVING CORPSE

It was destined that our departure from the English strand, should be marked by a tragical event, akin to the sudden end of the suicide, which had so strongly impressed me on quitting the American shore.

Of the three newly shipped men, who in a state of intoxication had been brought on board at the dock gates, two were able to be engaged at their duties, in four or five hours after quitting the pier. But the third man yet lay in his bunk, in the self-same posture in which his limbs had been adjusted by the crimp, who had deposited him there.

His name was down on the ship's papers as Miguel Saveda, and for Miguel Saveda the chief mate at last came forward, shouting down the forecastle-scuttle, and commanding his instant presence on deck. But the sailors answered for their new comrade; giving the mate to understand that Miguel was still fast locked in his trance, and could not obey him; when, muttering his usual imprecation, the mate retired to the quarterdeck.

This was in the first dog-watch, from four to six in the evening. At about three bells, in the next watch, Max the Dutchman, who, like most old seamen, was something of a physician in cases of drunkenness, recommended that Miguel's clothing should be removed, in order that he should lie more comfortably. But Jackson, who would seldom let any thing be done in the forecastle that was not proposed by himself, capriciously forbade this proceeding.

So the sailor still lay out of sight in his bunk, which was in the extreme angle of the forecastle, behind the *bowsprit-bitts*—two stout timbers rooted in the ship's keel. An hour or two afterward, some of the men observed a strange odor in the forecastle, which was attributed to the presence of some dead rat among the hollow spaces in the side planks; for some days before, the forecastle had been smoked out, to extirpate the vermin overrunning her. At midnight, the larboard watch, to which I belonged, turned out; and instantly as every man waked, he exclaimed at the now intolerable smell, supposed to be heightened by the shaking up the bilge-water, from the ship's rolling.

"Blast that rat!" cried the Greenlander.

"He's blasted already," said Jackson, who in his drawers had crossed over to the bunk of Miguel. "It's a water-rat, shipmates, that's dead; and here he is"—and with that, he dragged forth the sailor's arm, exclaiming, "Dead as a timber-head!"

Upon this the men rushed toward the bunk, Max with the light, which he held to the man's face.

"No, he's not dead," he cried, as the yellow flame wavered for a moment at the seaman's motionless mouth. But hardly had the words escaped, when, to the silent horror of all, two threads of greenish fire, like a forked tongue, darted out between the lips; and in a moment, the cadaverous face was crawled over by a swarm of wormlike flames.

The lamp dropped from the hand of Max, and went out; while covered all over with spires and sparkles of flame, that faintly crackled in the silence, the uncovered parts of the body burned before us, precisely like phosphorescent shark in a midnight sea.

The eyes were open and fixed; the mouth was curled like a scroll, and every lean feature firm as in life; while the whole face, now wound in curls of soft blue flame, wore an aspect of grim defiance, and eternal death. Prometheus, blasted by fire on the rock.

One arm, its red shirt-sleeve rolled up, exposed the man's name, tattooed in vermilion, near the hollow of the middle joint; and as if there was something peculiar in the painted flesh, every vibrating letter burned so white, that you might read the flaming name in the flickering ground of blue.

"Where's that d—d Miguel?" was now shouted down among us from the scuttle by the mate, who had just come on deck, and was determined to have every man up that belonged to his watch.

"He's gone to the harbor where they never weigh anchor," coughed Jackson. "Come you down, sir, and look."

Thinking that Jackson intended to beard him, the mate sprang down in a rage; but recoiled at the burning body as if he had been shot by a bullet. "My God!" he cried, and stood holding fast to the ladder.

"Take hold of it," said Jackson, at last, to the Greenlander; "it must go overboard. Don't stand shaking there, like a dog; take hold of it, I say! But stop"—and smothering it all in the blankets, he pulled it partly out of the bunk.

A few minutes more, and it fell with a bubble among the phosphorescent sparkles of the damp night sea, leaving a coruscating wake as it sank.

This event thrilled me through and through with unspeakable horror; nor did the conversation of the watch during the next four hours on deck at all serve to soothe me.

But what most astonished me, and seemed most incredible, was the infernal opinion of Jackson, that the man had been actually dead when brought on board the ship; and that knowingly, and merely for the sake of the month's advance, paid into his hand upon the strength of the bill he presented, the body-snatching crimp had knowingly shipped a corpse on board of the Highlander, under the pretense of its being a live body in a drunken trance. And I heard Jackson say, that he had known of such things having been done before. But that a really dead body ever burned in that manner, I can not even yet believe. But the sailors seemed familiar with such things; or at least with the stories of such things having happened to others.

For me, who at that age had never so much as happened to hear of a case like this, of animal combustion, in the horrid mood that came over me, I almost thought the burning body was a premonition of the hell of the Calvinists, and that Miguel's earthly end was a foretaste of his eternal condemnation.

Immediately after the burial, an iron pot of red coals was placed in the bunk, and in it two handfuls of coffee were roasted. This done, the bunk was nailed up, and was never opened again during the voyage; and strict orders were given to the crew not to divulge what had taken place to the emigrants; but to this, they needed no commands.

After the event, no one sailor but Jackson would stay alone in the forecastle, by night or by noon; and no more would they laugh or sing, or in any way make merry there, but kept all their pleasantries for the watches on deck. All but Jackson: who, while the rest would be sitting silently smoking on their chests, or in their bunks, would look toward the fatal spot, and cough, and laugh, and invoke the dead man with incredible scoffs and jeers. He froze my blood, and made my soul stand still.

CHAPTER XLIX
CARLO

There was on board our ship, among the emigrant passengers, a rich-cheeked, chestnut-haired Italian boy, arrayed in a faded, olive-hued velvet jacket, and tattered trowsers rolled up to his knee. He was not above fifteen years of age; but in the twilight pensiveness of his full morning eyes, there seemed to sleep experiences so sad and various, that his days must have seemed to him years. It was not an eye like Harry's tho' Harry's was large and womanly. It shone with a soft and spiritual radiance, like a moist star in a tropic sky; and spoke of humility, deep-seated thoughtfulness, yet a careless endurance of all the ills of life.

The head was if any thing small; and heaped with thick clusters of tendril curls, half overhanging the brows and delicate ears, it somehow reminded you of a classic vase, piled up with Falernian foliage.

From the knee downward, the naked leg was beautiful to behold as any lady's arm; so soft and rounded, with infantile ease and grace. His whole figure was free, fine, and indolent; he was such a boy as might have ripened into life in a Neapolitan vineyard; such a boy as gipsies steal in infancy; such a boy as Murillo often painted, when he went among the poor and outcast, for subjects wherewith to captivate the eyes of rank and wealth; such a boy, as only Andalusian beggars are, full of poetry, gushing from every rent.

Carlo was his name; a poor and friendless son of earth, who had no sire; and on life's ocean was swept along, as spoon-drift in a gale.

Some months previous, he had landed in Prince's Dock, with his hand-organ, from a Messina vessel; and had walked the streets of Liverpool, playing the sunny airs of southern climes, among the northern fog and drizzle. And now, having laid by enough to pay his passage over the Atlantic, he had again embarked, to seek his fortunes in America.

From the first, Harry took to the boy.

"Carlo," said Harry, "how did you succeed in England?"

He was reclining upon an old sail spread on the long-boat; and throwing back his soiled but tasseled cap, and caressing one leg like a child, he looked up, and said in his broken English—that seemed like mixing the potent wine of Oporto with some delicious syrup:—said he, "Ah! I succeed very well!—for I have tunes for the young and the old, the gay and the sad. I have marches for military young men, and love-airs for the ladies, and solemn sounds for the aged. I never draw a crowd, but I know from their faces what airs will best please them; I never stop before a house, but I judge from its portico for what tune they will soonest toss me some silver. And I ever play sad airs to the merry, and merry airs to the sad; and most always the rich best fancy the sad, and the poor the merry."

"But do you not sometimes meet with cross and crabbed old men," said Harry, "who would much rather have your room than your music?"

"Yes, sometimes," said Carlo, playing with his foot, "sometimes I do."

"And then, knowing the value of quiet to unquiet men, I suppose you never leave them under a shilling?"

"No," continued the boy, "I love my organ as I do myself, for it is my only friend, poor organ! it sings to me when I am sad, and cheers me; and I never play before a house, on purpose to be paid for leaving off, not I; would I, poor organ?"— looking down the hatchway where it was. "No, that I never have done, and never will do, though I starve; for when people drive me away, I do not think my organ is to blame, but they themselves are to blame; for such people's musical pipes are cracked, and grown rusted, that no more music can be breathed into their souls."

"No, Carlo; no music like yours, perhaps," said Harry, with a laugh.

"Ah! there's the mistake. Though my organ is as full of melody, as a hive is of bees; yet no organ can make music in unmusical breasts; no more than my native winds can, when they breathe upon a harp without chords."

Next day was a serene and delightful one; and in the evening when the vessel was just rippling along impelled by a gentle yet steady breeze, and the poor emigrants, relieved from their late sufferings, were gathered on deck; Carlo suddenly started up from his lazy reclinings; went below, and, assisted by the emigrants, returned with his organ.

Now, music is a holy thing, and its instruments, however humble, are to be loved and revered. Whatever has made, or does make, or may make music, should be held sacred as the golden bridle-bit of the Shah of Persia's horse, and the golden hammer, with which his hoofs are shod. Musical instruments should be like the silver tongs, with which the high-priests tended the Jewish altars—never to be touched by a hand profane. Who would bruise the poorest reed of Pan, though plucked from a beggar's hedge, would insult the melodious god himself.

And there is no humble thing with music in it, not a fife, not a negro-fiddle, that is not to be reverenced as much as the grandest architectural organ that ever rolled its flood-tide of harmony down a cathedral nave. For even a Jew's-harp may be so played, as to awaken all the fairies that are in us, and make them dance in our souls, as on a moon-lit sward of violets.

But what subtle power is this, residing in but a bit of steel, which might have made a tenpenny nail, that so enters, without knocking, into our inmost beings, and shows us all hidden things?

Not in a spirit of foolish speculation altogether, in no merely transcendental mood, did the glorious Greek of old fancy the human soul to be essentially a harmony. And if we grant that theory of Paracelsus and Campanella, that every man has four souls within him; then can we account for those banded sounds with silver links, those quartettes of melody, that sometimes sit and sing within us, as if our souls were baronial halls, and our music were made by the hoarest old harpers of Wales.

But look! here is poor Carlo's organ; and while the silent crowd surrounds him, there he stands, looking mildly but inquiringly about him; his right hand pulling and twitching the ivory knobs at one end of his instrument.

Behold the organ!

Surely, if much virtue lurk in the old fiddles of Cremona, and if their melody be in proportion to their antiquity, what divine ravishments may we not anticipate from this venerable, embrowned old organ, which might almost have played the Dead March in Saul, when King Saul himself was buried.

A fine old organ! carved into fantastic old towers, and turrets, and belfries; its architecture seems somewhat of the Gothic, monastic order; in front, it looks like the West-Front of York Minster.

What sculptured arches, leading into mysterious intricacies!—what mullioned windows, that seem as if they must look into chapels flooded with devotional sunsets!—what flying buttresses, and gable-ends, and niches with saints!—But stop! 'tis a Moorish iniquity; for here, as I live, is a Saracenic arch; which, for aught I know, may lead into some interior Alhambra.

Ay, it does; for as Carlo now turns his hand, I hear the gush of the Fountain of Lions, as he plays some thronged Italian air—a mixed and liquid sea of sound, that dashes its spray in my face.

Play on, play on, Italian boy! what though the notes be broken, here's that within that mends them. Turn hither your pensive, morning eyes; and while I list to the organs twain— one yours, one mine—let me gaze fathoms down into thy fathomless eye;—'tis good as gazing down into the great South Sea, and seeing the dazzling rays of the dolphins there.

Play on, play on! for to every note come trooping, now, triumphant standards, armies marching—all the pomp of sound. Methinks I am Xerxes, the nucleus of the martial neigh of all the Persian studs. Like gilded damask-flies, thick clustering on some lofty bough, my satraps swarm around me.

But now the pageant passes, and I droop; while Carlo taps his ivory knobs; and plays some flute-like saraband—soft, dulcet, dropping sounds, like silver cans in bubbling brooks. And now a clanging, martial air, as if ten thousand brazen trumpets, forged from spurs and swordhilts, called North, and South, and East, to rush to West!

Again—what blasted heath is this?—what goblin sounds of Macbeth's witches?—Beethoven's Spirit Waltz! the muster-call of sprites and specters. Now come, hands joined, Medusa, Hecate, she of Endor, and all the Blocksberg's, demons dire.

Once more the ivory knobs are tapped; and long-drawn, golden sounds are heard—some ode to Cleopatra; slowly loom, and solemnly expand, vast, rounding orbs of beauty; and before me float innumerable queens, deep dipped in silver gauzes.

All this could Carlo do—make, unmake me; build me up; to pieces take me; and join me limb to limb. He is the architect of domes of sound, and bowers of song.

And all is done with that old organ! Reverenced, then, be all street organs; more melody is at the beck of my Italian boy, than lurks in squadrons of Parisian orchestras.

But look! Carlo has that to feast the eye as well as ear; and the same wondrous magic in me, magnifies them into grandeur; though every figure greatly needs the artist's repairing hand, and sadly needs a dusting.

His York Minster's West-Front opens; and like the gates of Milton's heaven, it turns on golden hinges.

What have we here? The inner palace of the Great Mogul? Group and gilded columns, in confidential clusters; fixed fountains; canopies and lounges; and lords and dames in silk and spangles.

The organ plays a stately march; and presto! wide open arches; and out come, two and two, with nodding plumes, in crimson turbans, a troop of martial men; with jingling scimiters, they pace the hall; salute, pass on, and disappear.

Now, ground and lofty tumblers; jet black Nubian slaves. They fling themselves on poles; stand on their heads; and downward vanish.

And now a dance and masquerade of figures, reeling from the side-doors, among the knights and dames. Some sultan leads a sultaness; some emperor, a queen; and jeweled sword-hilts of carpet knights fling back the glances tossed by coquettes of countesses.

On this, the curtain drops; and there the poor old organ stands, begrimed, and black, and rickety.

Now, tell me, Carlo, if at street corners, for a single penny, I may thus transport myself in dreams Elysian, who so rich as I? Not he who owns a million.

And Carlo! ill betide the voice that ever greets thee, my Italian boy, with aught but kindness; cursed the slave who ever drives thy wondrous box of sights and sounds forth from a lordling's door!

CHAPTER L
HARRY BOLTON AT SEA

As yet I have said nothing about how my friend, Harry, got along as a sailor.

Poor Harry! a feeling of sadness, never to be comforted, comes over me, even now when I think of you. For this voyage that you went, but carried you part of the way to that ocean grave, which has buried you up with your secrets, and whither no mourning pilgrimage can be made.

But why this gloom at the thought of the dead? And why should we not be glad? Is it, that we ever think of them as departed from all joy? Is it, that we believe that indeed they are dead? They revisit us not, the departed; their voices no more ring in the air; summer may come, but it is winter with them; and even in our own limbs we feel not the sap that every spring renews the green life of the trees.

But Harry! you live over again, as I recall your image before me. I see you, plain and palpable as in life; and can make your existence obvious to others. Is he, then, dead, of whom this may be said?

But Harry! you are mixed with a thousand strange forms, the centaurs of fancy; half real and human, half wild and grotesque. Divine imaginings, like gods, come down to the groves of our Thessalies, and there, in the embrace of wild, dryad reminiscences, beget the beings that astonish the world.

But Harry! though your image now roams in my Thessaly groves, it is the same as of old; and among the droves of mixed beings and centaurs, you show like a zebra, banding with elks.

And indeed, in his striped Guernsey frock, dark glossy skin and hair, Harry Bolton, mingling with the Highlander's crew, looked not unlike the soft, silken quadruped-creole, that, pursued by wild Bushmen, bounds through Caffrarian woods.

How they hunted you, Harry, my zebra! those ocean barbarians, those unimpressible, uncivilized sailors of ours! How they pursued you from bowsprit to mainmast, and started you out of your every retreat!

Before the day of our sailing, it was known to the seamen that the girlish youth, whom they daily saw near the sign of the Clipper in Union-street, would form one of their homeward-bound crew. Accordingly, they cast upon him many a critical glance; but were not long in concluding that Harry would prove no very great accession to their strength; that the hoist of so tender an arm would not tell many hundred-weight on the maintop-sail halyards. Therefore they disliked him before they became acquainted with him; and such dislikes, as every one knows, are the most inveterate, and liable to increase. But even sailors are not blind to the sacredness that hallows a stranger; and for a time, abstaining from rudeness, they only maintained toward my friend a cold and unsympathizing civility.

As for Harry, at first the novelty of the scene filled up his mind; and the thought of being bound for a distant land, carried with it, as with every one, a buoyant feeling of undefinable expectation. And though his money was now gone again, all but a sovereign or two, yet that troubled him but little, in the first flush of being at sea.

But I was surprised, that one who had certainly seen much of life, should evince such an incredible ignorance of what was wholly inadmissible in a person situated as he was. But perhaps his familiarity with lofty life, only the less qualified him for understanding the other extreme. Will you believe me, this Bury blade once came on deck in a brocaded dressing-gown, embroidered slippers, and tasseled smoking-cap, to stand his morning watch.

As soon as I beheld him thus arrayed, a suspicion, which had previously crossed my mind, again recurred, and I almost vowed to myself that, spite his protestations, Harry Bolton never could have been at sea before, even as a *Guinea-pig* in an Indiaman; for the slightest acquaintance with the sea-life and sailors, should have prevented him, it would seem, from enacting this folly.

"Who's that Chinese mandarin?" cried the mate, who had made voyages to Canton. "Look you, my fine fellow, douse that mainsail now, and furl it in a trice."

"Sir?" said Harry, starting back. "Is not this the morning watch, and is not mine a morning gown?"

But though, in my refined friend's estimation, nothing could be more appropriate; in the mate's, it was the most monstrous of incongruities; and the offensive gown and cap were removed.

"It is too bad!" exclaimed Harry to me; "I meant to lounge away the watch in that gown until coffee time;—and I suppose your Hottentot of a mate won't permit a gentleman to smoke his Turkish pipe of a morning; but by gad, I'll wear straps to my pantaloons to spite him!"

Oh! that was the rock on which you split, poor Harry! Incensed at the want of polite refinement in the mates and crew, Harry, in a pet and pique, only determined to provoke them the more; and the storm of indignation he raised very soon overwhelmed him.

The sailors took a special spite to his chest, a large mahogany one, which he had had made to order at a furniture warehouse. It was ornamented with brass screw-heads, and other devices; and was well filled with those articles of the wardrobe in which Harry had sported through a London season; for the various vests and pantaloons he had sold in Liverpool, when in want of money, had not materially lessened his extensive stock.

It was curious to listen to the various hints and opinings thrown out by the sailors at the occasional glimpses they had of this collection of silks, velvets, broadcloths, and satins. I do not know exactly what they thought Harry had been; but they seemed unanimous in believing that, by abandoning his country, Harry had left more room for the gamblers. Jackson even asked him to lift up the lower hem of his browsers, to test the color of his calves.

It is a noteworthy circumstance, that whenever a slender made youth, of easy manners and polite address happens to form one of a ship's company, the sailors almost invariably impute his sea-going to an irresistible necessity of decamping from terra-firma in order to evade the constables.

These white-fingered gentry must be light-fingered too, they say to themselves, or they would not be after putting their hands into our tar. What else can bring them to sea?

Cogent and conclusive this; and thus Harry, from the very beginning, was put down for a very equivocal character.

Sometimes, however, they only made sport of his appearance; especially one evening, when his monkey jacket being wet through, he was obliged to mount one of his swallow-tailed coats. They said he carried two mizzen-peaks at his stern; declared he was a broken-down quill-driver, or a footman to a Portuguese running barber, or some old maid's tobacco-boy. As for the captain, it had become all the same to Harry as if there were no gentlemanly and complaisant Captain Riga on board. For to his no small astonishment, — but just as I had predicted, — Captain Riga never noticed him now, but left the business of indoctrinating him into the little experiences of a greenhorn's career solely in the hands of his officers and crew.

But the worst was to come. For the first few days, whenever there was any running aloft to be done, I noticed that Harry was indefatigable in coiling away the slack of the rigging about decks; ignoring the fact that his shipmates were springing into the shrouds. And when all hands of the watch would be engaged *clewing up a t'-gallant-sail,* that is, pulling the proper ropes on deck that wrapped the sail up on the yard aloft, Harry would always manage to get near the *belaying-pin, so* that when the time came for two of us to spring into the rigging, he would be inordinately fidgety in making fast the *clew-lines,* and would be so absorbed in that occupation, and would so elaborate the hitchings round the pin, that it was quite impossible for him, after doing so much, to mount over the bulwarks before his comrades had got there. However, after securing the clew-lines beyond a possibility of their getting loose, Harry would always make a feint of starting in a prodigious hurry for the shrouds; but suddenly looking up, and seeing others in advance, would retreat, apparently quite chagrined that he had been cut off from the opportunity of signalizing his activity.

At this I was surprised, and spoke to my friend; when the alarming fact was confessed, that he had made a private trial of it, and it never would do: *he could not go aloft;* his nerves would not hear of it.

"Then, Harry," said I, "better you had never been born. Do you know what it is that you are coming to? Did you not tell me that you made no doubt you would acquit yourself well in the rigging? Did you not say that you had been two voyages to Bombay? Harry, you were mad to ship. But you only imagine it: try again; and my word for it, you will very soon find yourself as much at home among the spars as a bird in a tree."

But he could not be induced to try it over again; the fact was, *his nerves could not stand it;* in the course of his courtly career, he had drunk too much strong Mocha coffee and gunpowder tea, and had smoked altogether too many Havannas.

At last, as I had repeatedly warned him, the mate singled him out one morning, and commanded him to mount to the main-truck, and unreeve the short signal halyards.

"Sir?" said Harry, aghast.

"Away you go!" said the mate, snatching a whip's end.

"Don't strike me!" screamed Harry, drawing himself up.

"Take that, and along with you," cried the mate, laying the rope once across his back, but lightly.

"By heaven!" cried Harry, wincing—not with the blow, but the insult: and then making a dash at the mate, who, holding out his long arm, kept him lazily at bay, and laughed at him, till, had I not feared a broken head, I should infallibly have pitched my boy's bulk into the officer.

"Captain Riga!" cried Harry.

"Don't call upon *him*" said the mate; "he's asleep, and won't wake up till we strike Yankee soundings again. Up you go!" he added, flourishing the rope's end.

Harry looked round among the grinning tars with a glance of terrible indignation and agony; and then settling his eye on me, and seeing there no hope, but even an admonition of obedience, as his only resource, he made one bound into the rigging, and was up at the main-top in a trice. I thought a few more springs would take him to the truck, and was a little fearful that in his desperation he might then jump overboard; for I had heard of delirious greenhorns doing such things at sea, and being lost forever. But no; he stopped short, and looked down from the top. Fatal glance! it unstrung his every fiber; and I saw him reel, and clutch the shrouds, till the mate shouted out for him not to squeeze the tar out of the ropes. "Up you go, sir." But Harry said nothing.

"You Max," cried the mate to the Dutch sailor, "spring after him, and help him; you understand?"

Max went up the rigging hand over hand, and brought his red head with a bump against the base of Harry's back. Needs must when the devil drives; and higher and higher, with Max bumping him at every step, went my unfortunate friend. At last he gained the royal yard, and the thin signal halyards—, hardly bigger than common twine—were flying in the wind. "Unreeve!" cried the mate.

I saw Harry's arm stretched out—his legs seemed shaking in the rigging, even to us, down on deck; and at last, thank heaven! the deed was done.

He came down pale as death, with bloodshot eyes, and every limb quivering. From that moment he never put foot in rattlin; never mounted above the bulwarks; and for the residue of the voyage, at least, became an altered person.

At the time, he went to the mate—since he could not get speech of the captain—and conjured him to intercede with Riga, that his name might be stricken off from the list of the ship's company, so that he might make the voyage as a steerage passenger; for which privilege, he bound himself to pay, as soon as he could dispose of some things of his in New York, over and above the ordinary passage-money. But the mate gave him a blunt denial; and a look of wonder at his effrontery. Once a sailor on board a ship, and *always* a sailor for that voyage, at least; for within so brief a period, no officer can bear to associate on terms of any thing like equality with a person whom he has ordered about at his pleasure.

Harry then told the mate solemnly, that he might do what he pleased, but go aloft again he *could* not, and *would* not. He would do any thing else but that.

This affair sealed Harry's fate on board of the Highlander; the crew now reckoned him fair play for their worst jibes and jeers, and he led a miserable life indeed.

Few landsmen can imagine the depressing and self-humiliating effects of finding one's self, for the first time, at the beck of illiterate sea-tyrants, with no opportunity of exhibiting any trait about you, but your ignorance of every thing connected with the sea-life that you lead, and the duties you are constantly called upon to perform. In such a sphere, and under such circumstances, Isaac Newton and Lord Bacon would be sea-clowns and bumpkins; and Napoleon Bonaparte be cuffed and kicked without remorse. In more than one instance I have seen the truth of this; and Harry, poor Harry, proved no exception. And from the circumstances which exempted me from experiencing the bitterest of these evils, I only the more felt for one who, from a strange constitutional nervousness, before unknown even to himself, was become as a hunted hare to the merciless crew.

But how was it that Harry Bolton, who spite of his effeminacy of appearance, had evinced, in our London trip, such unmistakable flashes of a spirit not easily tamed—how was it, that he could now yield himself up to the almost passive reception of contumely and contempt? Perhaps his spirit, for the time, had been broken. But I will not undertake to explain; we are curious creatures, as every one knows; and there are passages in the lives of all men, so out of keeping with the common tenor of their ways, and so seemingly contradictory of themselves, that only He who made us can expound them.

CHAPTER LI
THE EMIGRANTS

After the first miserable weather we experienced at sea, we had intervals of foul and fair, mostly the former, however, attended with head winds, till at last, after a three days' fog and rain, the sun rose cheerily one morning, and showed us Cape Clear. Thank heaven, we were out of the weather emphatically called *"Channel weather,"* and the last we should see of the eastern hemisphere was now in plain sight, and all the rest was broad ocean.

Land ho! was cried, as the dark purple headland grew out of the north. At the cry, the Irish emigrants came rushing up the hatchway, thinking America itself was at hand.

"Where is it?" cried one of them, running out a little way on the bowsprit. "Is *that* it?"

"Aye, it doesn't look much like *ould* Ireland, does it?" said Jackson.

"Not a bit, honey:—and how long before we get there? to-night?"

Nothing could exceed the disappointment and grief of the emigrants, when they were at last informed, that the land to the north was their own native island, which, after leaving three or four weeks previous in a steamboat for Liverpool, was now close to them again; and that, after newly voyaging so many days from the Mersey, the Highlander was only bringing them in view of the original home whence they started.

They were the most simple people I had ever seen. They seemed to have no adequate idea of distances; and to them, America must have seemed as a place just over a river. Every morning some of them came on deck, to see how much nearer we were: and one old man would stand for hours together, looking straight off from the bows, as if he expected to see New York city every minute, when, perhaps, we were yet two thousand miles distant, and steering, moreover, against a head wind.

The only thing that ever diverted this poor old man from his earnest search for land, was the occasional appearance of porpoises under the bows;

when he would cry out at the top of his voice—"Look, look, ye divils! look at the great pigs of the sea!"

At last, the emigrants began to think, that the ship had played them false; and that she was bound for the East Indies, or some other remote place; and one night, Jackson set a report going among them, that Riga purposed taking them to Barbary, and selling them all for slaves; but though some of the old women almost believed it, and a great weeping ensued among the children, yet the men knew better than to believe such a ridiculous tale.

Of all the emigrants, my Italian boy Carlo, seemed most at his ease. He would lie all day in a dreamy mood, sunning himself in the long boat, and gazing out on the sea. At night, he would bring up his organ, and play for several hours; much to the delight of his fellow voyagers, who blessed him and his organ again and again; and paid him for his music by furnishing him his meals. Sometimes, the steward would come forward, when it happened to be very much of a moonlight, with a message from the cabin, for Carlo to repair to the quarterdeck, and entertain the gentlemen and ladies.

There was a fiddler on board, as will presently be seen; and sometimes, by urgent entreaties, he was induced to unite his music with Carlo's, for the benefit of the cabin occupants; but this was only twice or thrice: for this fiddler deemed himself considerably elevated above the other steerage-passengers; and did not much fancy the idea of fiddling to strangers; and thus wear out his elbow, while persons, entirely unknown to him, and in whose welfare he felt not the slightest interest, were curveting about in famous high spirits. So for the most part, the gentlemen and ladies were fain to dance as well as they could to my little Italian's organ.

It was the most accommodating organ in the world; for it could play any tune that was called for; Carlo pulling in and out the ivory knobs at one side, and so manufacturing melody at pleasure.

True, some censorious gentlemen cabin-passengers protested, that such or such an air, was not precisely according to Handel or Mozart; and some ladies, whom I overheard talking about throwing their nosegays to Malibran at Covent Garden, assured the attentive Captain Riga, that Carlo's organ was a most wretched affair, and made a horrible din.

"Yes, ladies," said the captain, bowing, "by your leave, I think Carlo's organ must have lost its mother, for it squeals like a pig running after its dam."

Harry was incensed at these criticisms; and yet these cabin-people were all ready enough to dance to poor Carlo's music.

"Carlo"—said I, one night, as he was marching forward from the quarter-deck, after one of these sea-quadrilles, which took place during my watch on deck:—"Carlo"—said I, "what do the gentlemen and ladies give you for playing?"

"Look!"—and he showed me three copper medals of Britannia and her shield—three English pennies.

Now, whenever we discover a dislike in us, toward any one, we should ever be a little suspicious of ourselves. It may be, therefore, that the natural antipathy with which almost all seamen and steerage-passengers, regard the inmates of the cabin, was one cause at least, of my not feeling very charitably disposed toward them, myself.

Yes: that might have been; but nevertheless, I will let nature have her own way for once; and here declare roundly, that, however it was, I cherished a feeling toward these cabin-passengers, akin to contempt. Not because they happened to be cabin-passengers: not at all: but only because they seemed the most finical, miserly, mean men and women, that ever stepped over the Atlantic.

One of them was an old fellow in a robust looking coat, with broad skirts; he had a nose like a bottle of port-wine; and would stand for a whole hour, with his legs straddling apart, and his hands deep down in his breeches pockets, as if he had two mints at work there, coining guineas. He was an abominable looking old fellow, with cold, fat, jelly-like eyes; and avarice, heartlessness, and sensuality stamped all over him. He seemed all the time going through some process of mental arithmetic; doing sums with dollars and cents: his very mouth, wrinkled and drawn up at the corners, looked like a purse. When he dies, his skull ought to be turned into a savings box, with the till-hole between his teeth.

Another of the cabin inmates, was a middle-aged Londoner, in a comical Cockney-cut coat, with a pair of semicircular tails: so that he looked as if he were sitting in a swing. He wore a spotted neckerchief; a short, little, fiery-red vest; and striped pants, very thin in the calf, but very full about the waist. There was nothing describable about him but his dress; for he had such a meaningless face, I can not remember it; though I have a vague impression, that it looked at the time, as if its owner was laboring under the mumps.

Then there were two or three buckish looking young fellows, among the rest; who were all the time playing at cards on the poop, under the lee of the *spanker;* or smoking cigars on the taffrail; or sat quizzing the emigrant women with opera-glasses, leveled through the windows of the upper cabin. These sparks frequently called for the steward to help them to brandy and water, and talked about going on to Washington, to see Niagara Falls.

There was also an old gentleman, who had brought with him three or four heavy files of the *London Times,* and other papers; and he spent all his hours in reading them, on the shady side of the deck, with one leg crossed over the other; and without crossed legs, he never read at all. That was indispensable to the proper understanding of what he studied. He growled terribly, when disturbed by the sailors, who now and then were obliged to move him to get at the ropes.

As for the ladies, I have nothing to say concerning them; for ladies are like creeds; if you can not speak well of them, say nothing.

CHAPTER LII
THE EMIGRANTS' KITCHEN

I have made some mention of the "galley," or great stove for the steerage passengers, which was planted over the main hatches.

During the outward-bound passage, there were so few occupants of the steerage, that they had abundant room to do their cooking at this galley. But it was otherwise now; for we had four or five hundred in the steerage; and all their cooking was to be done by one fire; a pretty large one, to be sure, but, nevertheless, small enough, considering the number to be accommodated, and the fact that the fire was only to be kindled at certain hours.

For the emigrants in these ships are under a sort of martial-law; and in all their affairs are regulated by the despotic ordinances of the captain. And though it is evident, that to a certain extent this is necessary, and even indispensable; yet, as at sea no appeal lies beyond the captain, he too often makes unscrupulous use of his power. And as for going to law with him at the end of the voyage, you might as well go to law with the Czar of Russia.

At making the fire, the emigrants take turns; as it is often very disagreeable work, owing to the pitching of the ship, and the heaving of the spray over the uncovered "galley." Whenever I had the morning watch, from four to eight, I was sure to see some poor fellow crawling up from below about daybreak, and go to groping over the deck after bits of rope-yarn, or tarred canvas, for kindling-stuff. And no sooner would the fire be fairly made, than up came the old women, and men, and children; each armed with an iron pot or saucepan; and invariably a great tumult ensued, as to whose turn to cook came next; sometimes the more quarrelsome would fight, and upset each other's pots and pans.

Once, an English lad came up with a little coffee-pot, which he managed to crowd in between two pans. This done, he went below. Soon after a great strapping Irishman, in knee-breeches and bare calves, made his appearance; and eying the row of things on the fire, asked whose coffee-pot that was; upon being told, he removed it, and put his own in its place; saying something about that individual place belonging to him; and with that, he turned aside.

Not long after, the boy came along again; and seeing his pot removed, made a violent exclamation, and replaced it; which the Irishman no sooner perceived, than he rushed at him, with his fists doubled. The boy snatched up the boiling coffee, and spirted its contents all about the fellow's bare legs; which incontinently began to dance involuntary hornpipes and fandangoes, as a preliminary to giving chase to the boy, who by this time, however, had decamped.

Many similar scenes occurred every day; nor did a single day pass, but scores of the poor people got no chance whatever to do their cooking.

This was bad enough; but it was a still more miserable thing, to see these poor emigrants wrangling and fighting together for the want of the most ordinary accommodations. But thus it is, that the very hardships to which such beings are subjected, instead of uniting them, only tends, by imbittering their tempers, to set them against each other; and thus they themselves drive the strongest rivet into the chain, by which their social superiors hold them subject.

It was with a most reluctant hand, that every evening in the second dog-watch, at the mate's command, I would march up to the fire, and giving notice to the assembled crowd, that the time was come to extinguish it, would dash it out with my bucket of salt water; though many, who had long waited for a chance to cook, had now to go away disappointed.

The staple food of the Irish emigrants was oatmeal and water, boiled into what is sometimes called *mush;* by the Dutch is known as *supaan;* by sailors *burgoo;* by the New Englanders *hasty-pudding;* in which hasty-pudding, by the way, the poet Barlow found the materials for a sort of epic.

Some of the steerage passengers, however, were provided with sea-biscuit, and other perennial food, that was eatable all the year round, fire or no fire.

There were several, moreover, who seemed better to do in the world than the rest; who were well furnished with hams, cheese, Bologna sausages, Dutch herrings, alewives, and other delicacies adapted to the contingencies of a voyager in the steerage.

There was a little old Englishman on board, who had been a grocer ashore, whose greasy trunks seemed all pantries; and he was constantly using himself for a cupboard, by transferring their contents into his own interior. He was a little light of head, I always thought. He particularly doated on his long strings of sausages; and would sometimes take them out, and play with them, wreathing them round him, like an Indian juggler with charmed snakes. What with this diversion, and eating his cheese, and helping himself from an inexhaustible junk bottle, and smoking his pipe, and meditating, this crack-pated grocer made time jog along with him at a tolerably easy pace.

But by far the most considerable man in the steerage, in point of pecuniary circumstances at least, was a slender little pale-faced English tailor, who it seemed had engaged a passage for himself and wife in some imaginary section of the ship, called the *second cabin*, which was feigned to combine the comforts of the first cabin with the cheapness of the steerage. But it turned out that this second cabin was comprised in the after part of the steerage itself, with nothing intervening but a name. So to his no small disgust, he found himself herding with the rabble; and his complaints to the captain were unheeded.

This luckless tailor was tormented the whole voyage by his wife, who was young and handsome; just such a beauty as farmers'-boys fall in love with; she had bright eyes, and red cheeks, and looked plump and happy.

She was a sad coquette; and did not turn away, as she was bound to do, from the dandy glances of the cabin bucks, who ogled her through their double-barreled opera glasses. This enraged the tailor past telling; he would remonstrate with his wife, and scold her; and lay his matrimonial commands upon her, to go below instantly, out of sight. But the lady was not to be tyrannized over; and so she told him. Meantime, the bucks would be still framing her in their lenses, mightily enjoying the fun. The last resources of the poor tailor would be, to start up, and make a dash at the rogues, with clenched fists; but upon getting as far as the mainmast, the mate would accost him from over the rope that divided them, and beg leave to communicate the fact, that he could come no further. This unfortunate tailor was also a fiddler; and when fairly baited into desperation, would rush for his instrument, and try to get rid of his wrath by playing the most savage, remorseless airs he could think of.

While thus employed, perhaps his wife would accost him—

"Billy, my dear;" and lay her soft hand on his shoulder.

But Billy, he only fiddled harder.

"Billy, my love!"

The bow went faster and faster.

"Come, now, Billy, my dear little fellow, let's make it all up;" and she bent over his knees, looking bewitchingly up at him, with her irresistible eyes.

Down went fiddle and bow; and the couple would sit together for an hour or two, as pleasant and affectionate as possible.

But the next day, the chances were, that the old feud would be renewed, which was certain to be the case at the first glimpse of an opera-glass from the cabin.

CHAPTER LIII
THE HORATII AND CURIATII

With a slight alteration, I might begin this chapter after the manner of Livy, in the 24th section of his first book:—"It *happened, that in each family were three twin brothers, between whom there was little disparity in point of age or of strength.*"

Among the steerage passengers of the Highlander, were two women from Armagh, in Ireland, widows and sisters, who had each three twin sons, born, as they said, on the same day.

They were ten years old. Each three of these six cousins were as like as the mutually reflected figures in a kaleidoscope; and like the forms seen in a kaleidoscope, together, as well as separately, they seemed to form a complete figure. But, though besides this fraternal likeness, all six boys bore a strong cousin-german resemblance to each other; yet, the O'Briens were in disposition quite the reverse of the O'Regans. The former were a timid, silent trio, who used to revolve around their mother's waist, and seldom quit the maternal orbit; whereas, the O'Regans were "broths of boys," full of mischief and fun, and given to all manner of devilment, like the tails of the comets.

Early every morning, Mrs. O'Regan emerged from the steerage, driving her spirited twins before her, like a riotous herd of young steers; and made her way to the capacious deck-tub, full of salt water, pumped up from the sea, for the purpose of washing down the ship. Three splashes, and the three boys were ducking and diving together in the brine; their mother engaged in *shampooing* them, though it was haphazard sort of work enough; a rub here, and a scrub there, as she could manage to fasten on a stray limb.

"Pat, ye divil, hould still while I wash ye. Ah! but it's you, Teddy, you rogue. Arrah, now, Mike, ye spalpeen, don't be mixing your legs up with Pat's."

The little rascals, leaping and scrambling with delight, enjoyed the sport mightily; while this indefatigable, but merry matron, manipulated them all over, as if it were a matter of conscience.

Meanwhile, Mrs. O'Brien would be standing on the boatswain's locker—or rope and tar-pot pantry in the vessel's bows—with a large old quarto Bible, black with age, laid before her between the knight-heads, and reading aloud to her three meek little lambs.

The sailors took much pleasure in the deck-tub performances of the O'Regans, and greatly admired them always for their archness and activity; but the tranquil O'Briens they did not fancy so much. More especially they disliked the grave matron herself; hooded in rusty black; and they had a bitter grudge against her book. To that, and the incantations muttered over it, they ascribed the head winds that haunted us; and Blunt, our Irish cockney, really believed that Mrs. O'Brien purposely came on deck every morning, in order to secure a foul wind for the next ensuing twenty-four hours.

At last, upon her coming forward one morning, Max the Dutchman accosted her, saying he was sorry for it, but if she went between the knight-heads again with her book, the crew would throw it overboard for her.

Now, although contrasted in character, there existed a great warmth of affection between the two families of twins, which upon this occasion was curiously manifested.

Notwithstanding the rebuke and threat of the sailor, the widow silently occupied her old place; and with her children clustering round her, began her low, muttered reading, standing right in the extreme bows of the ship, and slightly leaning over them, as if addressing the multitudinous waves from a floating pulpit. Presently Max came behind her, snatched the book from her hands, and threw it overboard. The widow gave a wail, and her boys set up a cry. Their cousins, then ducking in the water close by, at once saw the cause of the cry; and springing from the tub, like so many dogs, seized Max by the legs, biting and striking at him: which, the before timid little O'Briens no sooner perceived, than they, too, threw themselves on the enemy, and the amazed seaman found himself baited like a bull by all six boys.

And here it gives me joy to record one good thing on the part of the mate. He saw the fray, and its beginning; and rushing forward, told Max that he would harm the boys at his peril; while he cheered them on, as if rejoiced at their giving the fellow such a tussle. At last Max, sorely scratched, bit, pinched, and every way aggravated, though of course without a serious bruise, cried out "enough!" and the assailants were ordered to quit him; but though the three O'Briens obeyed, the three O'Regans hung on to him like leeches, and had to be dragged off.

"There now, you rascal," cried the mate, "throw overboard another Bible, and I'll send you after it without a bowline."

This event gave additional celebrity to the twins throughout the vessel. That morning all six were invited to the quarter-deck, and reviewed by the cabin-passengers, the ladies manifesting particular interest in them, as they always do concerning twins, which some of them show in public parks and gardens, by stopping to look at them, and questioning their nurses.

"And were you all born at one time?" asked an old lady, letting her eye run in wonder along the even file of white heads.

"Indeed, an' we were," said Teddy; "wasn't we, mother?"

Many more questions were asked and answered, when a collection was taken up for their benefit among these magnanimous cabin-passengers, which resulted in starting all six boys in the world with a penny apiece.

I never could look at these little fellows without an inexplicable feeling coming over me; and though there was nothing so very remarkable or unprecedented about them, except the singular coincidence of two sisters simultaneously making the world such a generous present; yet, the mere fact of there being twins always seemed curious; in fact, to me at least, all twins are prodigies; and still I hardly know why this should be; for all of us in our own persons furnish numerous examples of the same phenomenon. Are not our thumbs twins? A regular Castor and Pollux? And all of our fingers? Are not our arms, hands, legs, feet, eyes, ears, all twins; born at one birth, and as much alike as they possibly can be?

Can it be, that the Greek grammarians invented their dual number for the particular benefit of twins?

CHAPTER LIV
SOME SUPERIOR OLD NAIL-ROD AND PIG-TAIL

It has been mentioned how advantageously my shipmates disposed of their tobacco in Liverpool; but it is to be related how those nefarious commercial speculations of theirs reduced them to sad extremities in the end.

True to their improvident character, and seduced by the high prices paid for the weed in England, they had there sold off by far the greater portion of what tobacco they had; even inducing the mate to surrender the portion he had secured under lock and key by command of the Custom-house officers. So that when the crew were about two weeks out, on the homeward-bound passage, it became sorrowfully evident that tobacco was at a premium.

Now, one of the favorite pursuits of sailors during a dogwatch below at sea is cards; and though they do not understand whist, cribbage, and games of that kidney, yet they are adepts at what is called *"High-low-Jack-and-the-game,"* which name, indeed, has a Jackish and nautical flavor. Their stakes are generally so many plugs of tobacco, which, like rouleaux of guineas, are piled on their chests when they play. Judge, then, the wicked zest with which the Highlander's crew now shuffled and dealt the pack; and how the interest curiously and invertedly increased, as the stakes necessarily became less and less; and finally resolved themselves into *"chaws."*

So absorbed, at last, did they become at this business, that some of them, after being hard at work during a nightwatch on deck, would rob themselves of rest below, in order to have a brush at the cards. And as it is very difficult sleeping in the presence of gamblers; especially if they chance to be sailors, whose conversation at all times is apt to be boisterous; these fellows would often be driven out of the forecastle by those who desired to rest. They were obliged to repair on deck, and make a card-table of it; and invariably, in such cases, there was a great deal of contention, a great many ungentlemanly charges of nigging and cheating; and, now and then, a few parenthetical blows were exchanged.

But this was not so much to be wondered at, seeing they could see but very little, being provided with no light but that of a midnight sky; and the cards, from long wear and rough usage, having become exceedingly torn and tarry, so much so, that several members of the four suits might have seceded from their respective clans, and formed into a fifth tribe, under the name of *"Tar-spots."*

Every day the tobacco grew scarcer and scarcer; till at last it became necessary to adopt the greatest possible economy in its use. The modicum constituting an ordinary *"chaw,"* was made to last a whole day; and at night, permission being had from the cook, this self-same *"chaw"* was placed in the oven of the stove, and there dried; so as to do duty in a pipe.

In the end not a plug was to be had; and deprived of a solace and a stimulus, on which sailors so much rely while at sea, the crew became absent, moody, and sadly tormented with the hypos. They were something like opium-smokers, suddenly cut off from their drug. They would sit on their chests, forlorn and moping; with a steadfast sadness, eying the forecastle lamp, at which they had lighted so many a pleasant pipe. With touching eloquence they recalled those happier evenings—the time of smoke and vapor; when, after a whole day's delectable *"chawing,"* they beguiled themselves with their genial, and most companionable puffs.

One night, when they seemed more than usually cast down and disconsolate, Blunt, the Irish cockney, started up suddenly with an idea in his head—"Boys, let's search under the bunks!" Bless you, Blunt! what a happy conceit! Forthwith, the chests were dragged out; the dark places explored; and two sticks of *nail-rod* tobacco, and several old *"chaws,"* thrown aside by sailors on some previous voyage, were their cheering reward. They were impartially divided by Jackson, who, upon this occasion, acquitted himself to the satisfaction of all.

Their mode of dividing this tobacco was the rather curious one generally adopted by sailors, when the highest possible degree of impartiality is desirable. I will describe it, recommending its earnest consideration to all heirs, who may hereafter divide an inheritance; for if they adopted this nautical method, that universally slanderous aphorism of Lavater would be forever rendered nugatory—"*Expect not to understand any man till you have divided with him an inheritance.*"

The *nail-rods* they cut as evenly as possible into as many parts as there were men to be supplied; and this operation having been performed in the presence of all, Jackson, placing the tobacco before him, his face to the wall, and back to the company, struck one of the bits of weed with his knife, crying out, "Whose is this?" Whereupon a respondent, previously pitched upon, replied, at a venture, from the opposite corner of the forecastle, "Blunt's;" and to Blunt it went; and so on, in like manner, till all were served.

I put it to you, lawyers—shade of Blackstone, I invoke you—if a more impartial procedure could be imagined than this?

But the nail-rods and last-voyage *"chaws"* were soon gone, and then, after a short interval of comparative gayety, the men again drooped, and relapsed into gloom.

They soon hit upon an ingenious device, however—but not altogether new among seamen—to allay the severity of the depression under which they languished. Ropes were unstranded, and the yarns picked apart; and, cut up into small bits, were used as a substitute for the weed. Old ropes were preferred; especially those which had long lain in the hold, and had contracted an epicurean dampness, making still richer their ancient, cheese-like flavor.

In the middle of most large ropes, there is a straight, central part, round which the exterior strands are twisted. When in picking oakum, upon various occasions, I have chanced, among the old junk used at such times, to light upon a fragment of this species of rope, I have ever taken, I know not what kind of strange, nutty delight in untwisting it slowly, and gradually coming upon its deftly hidden and aromatic *"heart;"* for so this central piece is denominated.

It is generally of a rich, tawny, Indian hue, somewhat inclined to luster; is exceedingly agreeable to the touch; diffuses a pungent odor, as of an old dusty bottle of Port, newly opened above ground; and, altogether, is an object which no man, who enjoys his dinners, could refrain from hanging over, and caressing.

Nor is this delectable morsel of *old junk* wanting in many interesting, mournful, and tragic suggestions. Who can say in what gales it may have been; in what remote seas it may have sailed? How many stout masts of seventy-fours and frigates it may have staid in the tempest? How deep it may have lain, as a hawser, at the bottom of strange harbors? What outlandish fish may have nibbled at it in the water, and what un-catalogued sea-fowl may have pecked at it, when forming part of a lofty stay or a shroud?

Now, this particular part of the rope, this nice little "cut" it was, that among the sailors was the most eagerly sought after. And getting hold of a foot or two of old cable, they would cut into it lovingly, to see whether it had any *"tenderloin."*

For my own part, nevertheless, I can not say that this tit-bit was at all an agreeable one in the mouth; however pleasant to the sight of an antiquary, or to the nose of an epicure in nautical fragrancies. Indeed, though possibly I might have been mistaken, I thought it had rather an astringent, acrid taste; probably induced by the tar, with which the flavor of all ropes is more or less vitiated. But the sailors seemed to like it, and at any rate nibbled at it with great gusto. They converted one pocket of their trowsers into a junk-shop, and when solicited by a shipmate for a *"chaw,"* would produce a small coil of rope.

Another device adopted to alleviate their hardships, was the substitution of dried tea-leaves, in place of tobacco, for their pipes. No one has ever supped in a forecastle at sea, without having been struck by the prodigious residuum of tea-leaves, or cabbage stalks, in his tin-pot of bohea. There was no lack of material to supply every pipe-bowl among us.

I had almost forgotten to relate the most noteworthy thing in this matter; namely, that notwithstanding the general scarcity of the genuine weed, Jackson was provided with a supply; nor did it give out, until very shortly previous to our arrival in port.

In the lowest depths of despair at the loss of their precious solace, when the sailors would be seated inconsolable as the Babylonish captives, Jackson would sit cross-legged in his bunk, which was an upper one, and enveloped in a cloud of tobacco smoke, would look down upon the mourners below, with a sardonic grin at their forlornness.

He recalled to mind their folly in selling for filthy lucre, their supplies of the weed; he painted their stupidity; he enlarged upon the sufferings they had brought upon themselves; he exaggerated those sufferings, and every way derided, reproached, twitted, and hooted at them. No one dared to return his scurrilous animadversions, nor did any presume to ask him to relieve their necessities out of his fullness. On the contrary, as has been just related, they divided with him the *nail-rods* they found.

The extraordinary dominion of this one miserable Jackson, over twelve or fourteen strong, healthy tars, is a riddle, whose solution must be left to the philosophers.

CHAPTER LV
DRAWING NIGH TO THE LAST SCENE IN JACKSON'S CAREER

The closing allusion to Jackson in the chapter preceding, reminds me of a circumstance—which, perhaps, should have been mentioned before—that after we had been at sea about ten days, he pronounced himself too unwell to do duty, and accordingly went below to his bunk. And here, with the exception of a few brief intervals of sunning himself in fine weather, he remained on his back, or seated cross-legged, during the remainder of the homeward-bound passage.

Brooding there, in his infernal gloom, though nothing but a castaway sailor in canvas trowsers, this man was still a picture, worthy to be painted by the dark, moody hand of Salvator. In any of that master's lowering sea-pieces, representing the desolate crags of Calabria, with a midnight shipwreck in the distance, this Jackson's would have been the face to paint for the doomed vessel's figurehead, seamed and blasted by lightning.

Though the more sneaking and cowardly of my shipmates whispered among themselves, that Jackson, sure of his wages, whether on duty or off, was only feigning indisposition, nevertheless it was plain that, from his excesses in Liverpool, the malady which had long fastened its fangs in his flesh, was now gnawing into his vitals.

His cheek became thinner and yellower, and the bones projected like those of a skull. His snaky eyes rolled in red sockets; nor could he lift his hand without a violent tremor; while his racking cough many a time startled us from sleep. Yet still in his tremulous grasp he swayed his scepter, and ruled us all like a tyrant to the last.

The weaker and weaker he grew, the more outrageous became his treatment of the crew. The prospect of the speedy and unshunable death now before him, seemed to exasperate his misanthropic soul into madness; and as if he had indeed sold it to Satan, he seemed determined to die with a curse between his teeth.

I can never think of him, even now, reclining in his bunk, and with short breaths panting out his maledictions, but I am reminded of that misanthrope upon the throne of the world—the diabolical Tiberius at Caprese; who even in his self-exile, imbittered by bodily pangs, and unspeakable mental terrors only known to the damned on earth, yet did not give over his blasphemies but endeavored to drag down with him to his own perdition, all who came within the evil spell of his power. And though Tiberius came in the succession of the Caesars, and though unmatchable Tacitus has embalmed his carrion, yet do I account this Yankee Jackson full as dignified a personage as he, and as well meriting his lofty gallows in history; even though he was a nameless vagabond without an epitaph, and none, but I, narrate what he was. For there is no dignity in wickedness, whether in purple or rags; and hell is a democracy of devils, where all are equals. There, Nero howls side by side with his own malefactors. If Napoleon were truly but a martial murderer, I pay him no more homage than I would a felon. Though Milton's Satan dilutes our abhorrence with admiration, it is only because he is not a genuine being, but something altered from a genuine original. We gather not from the four gospels alone, any high-raised fancies concerning this Satan; we only know him from thence as the personification of the essence of evil, which, who but pickpockets and burglars will admire? But this takes not from the merit of our high-priest of poetry; it only enhances it, that with such unmitigated evil for his material, he should build up his most goodly structure. But in historically canonizing on earth the condemned below, and lifting up and lauding the illustrious damned, we do but make examples of wickedness; and call upon ambition to do some great iniquity, and be sure of fame.

CHAPTER LVI
UNDER THE LEE OF THE LONG-BOAT, REDBURN AND HARRY HOLD CONFIDENTIAL COMMUNION

A sweet thing is a song; and though the Hebrew captives hung their harps on the willows, that they could not sing the melodies of Palestine before the haughty beards of the Babylonians; yet, to themselves, those melodies of other times and a distant land were as sweet as the June dew on Hermon.

And poor Harry was as the Hebrews. He, too, had been carried away captive, though his chief captor and foe was himself; and he, too, many a night, was called upon to sing for those who through the day had insulted and derided him.

His voice was just the voice to proceed from a small, silken person like his; it was gentle and liquid, and meandered and tinkled through the words of a song, like a musical brook that winds and wantons by pied and pansied margins.

"*I* can't sing to-night"—sadly said Harry to the Dutchman, who with his watchmates requested him to while away the middle watch with his melody—"I can't sing to-night. But, Wellingborough," he whispered,—and I stooped my ear,— "come *you* with me under the lee of the long-boat, and there I'll hum you an air."

It was *The Banks of the Blue Moselle*.

Poor, poor Harry! and a thousand times friendless and forlorn! To be singing that thing, which was only meant to be warbled by falling fountains in gardens, or in elegant alcoves in drawing-rooms,—to be singing it *here*—*here*, as I live, under the tarry lee of our long-boat.

But he sang, and sang, as I watched the waves, and peopled them all with sprites, and cried *"chassez!" "hands across!"* to the multitudinous quadrilles, all danced on the moonlit, musical floor.

But though it went so hard with my friend to sing his songs to this ruffian crew, whom he hated, even in his dreams, till the foam flew from his mouth while he slept; yet at last I prevailed upon him to master his feelings, and make them subservient to his interests. For so delighted, even with the rudest minstrelsy, are sailors, that I well knew Harry possessed a spell over them, which, for the time at least, they could not resist; and it might induce them to treat with more deference the being who was capable of yielding them such delight. Carlo's organ they did not so much care for; but the voice of my Bury blade was an accordion in their ears.

So one night, on the windlass, he sat and sang; and from the ribald jests so common to sailors, the men slid into silence at every verse. Hushed, and more hushed they grew, till at last Harry sat among them like Orpheus among the charmed leopards and tigers. Harmless now the fangs with which they were wont to tear my zebra, and backward curled in velvet paws; and fixed their once glaring eyes in fascinated and fascinating brilliancy. Ay, still and hissingly all, for a time, they relinquished their prey.

Now, during the voyage, the treatment of the crew threw Harry more and more upon myself for companionship; and few can keep constant company with another, without revealing some, at least, of their secrets; for all of us yearn for sympathy, even if we do not for love; and to be intellectually alone is a thing only tolerable to genius, whose cherisher and inspirer is solitude.

But though my friend became more communicative concerning his past career than ever he had been before, yet he did not make plain many things in his hitherto but partly divulged history, which I was very curious to know; and especially he never made the remotest allusion to aught connected with our trip to London; while the oath of secrecy by which he had bound me held my curiosity on that point a captive. However, as it was, Harry made many very interesting disclosures; and if he did not gratify me more in that respect, he atoned for it in a measure, by dwelling upon the future, and the prospects, such as they were, which the future held out to him.

He confessed that he had no money but a few shillings left from the expenses of our return from London; that only by selling some more of his clothing, could he pay for his first week's board in New York; and that he was altogether without any regular profession or business, upon which, by his own exertions, he could securely rely for support. And yet, he told me that he was determined never again to return to England; and that somewhere in America he must work out his temporal felicity.

"I have forgotten England," he said, "and never more mean to think of it; so tell me, Wellingborough, what am I to do in America?"

It was a puzzling question, and full of grief to me, who, young though I was, had been well rubbed, curried, and ground down to fine powder in the hopper of an evil fortune, and who therefore could sympathize with one in similar circumstances. For though we may look grave and behave kindly and considerately to a friend in calamity; yet, if we have never actually experienced something like the woe that weighs him down, we can not with the best grace proffer our sympathy. And perhaps there is no true sympathy but between equals; and it may be, that we should distrust that man's sincerity, who stoops to condole with us.

So Harry and I, two friendless wanderers, beguiled many a long watch by talking over our common affairs. But inefficient, as a benefactor, as I certainly was; still, being an American, and returning to my home; even as he was a stranger, and hurrying from his; therefore, I stood toward him in the attitude of the prospective doer of the honors of my country; I accounted him the nation's guest. Hence, I esteemed it more befitting, that I should rather talk with him, than he with me: that *his* prospects and plans should engage our attention, in preference to my own.

Now, seeing that Harry was so brave a songster, and could sing such bewitching airs: I suggested whether his musical talents could not be turned to account. The thought struck him most favorably—"Gad, my boy, you have hit it, you have," and then he went on to mention, that in some places in England, it was customary for two or three young men of highly respectable families, of undoubted antiquity, but unfortunately in lamentably decayed circumstances, and thread-bare coats—it was customary for two or three young gentlemen, so situated, to obtain their livelihood by their voices: coining their silvery songs into silvery shillings.

They wandered from door to door, and rang the bell—Are *the ladies and gentlemen in?* Seeing them at least gentlemanly looking, if not sumptuously appareled, the servant generally admitted them at once; and when the people entered to greet them, their spokesman would rise with a gentle bow, and a smile, and say, *We come, ladies and gentlemen, to sing you a song: we are singers, at your service.* And so, without waiting reply, forth they burst into song; and having most mellifluous voices, enchanted and transported all auditors; so much so, that at the conclusion of the entertainment, they very seldom failed to be well recompensed, and departed with an invitation to return again, and make the occupants of that dwelling once more delighted and happy.

"Could not something of this kind now, be done in New York?" said Harry, "or are there no parlors with ladies in them, there?" he anxiously added.

Again I assured him, as I had often done before, that New York was a civilized and enlightened town; with a large population, fine streets, fine houses, nay, plenty of omnibuses; and that for the most part, he would almost think himself in England; so similar to England, in essentials, was this outlandish America that haunted him.

I could not but be struck—and had I not been, from my birth, as it were, a cosmopolite—I had been amazed at his skepticism with regard to the civilization of my native land. A greater patriot than myself might have resented his insinuations. He seemed to think that we Yankees lived in wigwams, and wore bear-skins. After all, Harry was a spice of a Cockney, and had shut up his Christendom in London.

Having then assured him, that I could see no reason, why he should not play the troubadour in New York, as well as elsewhere; he suddenly popped upon me the question, whether I would not join him in the enterprise; as it would be quite out of the question to go alone on such a business.

Said I, "My dear Bury, I have no more voice for a ditty, than a dumb man has for an oration. Sing? Such Macadamized lungs have I, that I think myself well off, that I can talk; let alone nightingaling."

So that plan was quashed; and by-and-by Harry began to give up the idea of singing himself into a livelihood.

"No, I won't sing for my mutton," said he—"what would Lady Georgiana say?"

"If I could see her ladyship once, I might tell you, Harry," returned I, who did not exactly doubt him, but felt ill at ease for my bosom friend's conscience, when he alluded to his various noble and right honorable friends and relations.

"But surely, Bury, my friend, you must write a clerkly hand, among your other accomplishments; and *that* at least, will be sure to help you."

"I *do* write a hand," he gladly rejoined—"there, look at the implement!—do you not think, that such a hand as *that* might dot an *i*, or cross a *t*, with a touching grace and tenderness?"

Indeed, but it did betoken a most excellent penmanship. It was small; and the fingers were long and thin; the knuckles softly rounded; the nails hemispherical at the base; and the smooth palm furnishing few characters for an Egyptian fortune-teller to read. It was not as the sturdy farmer's hand of Cincinnatus, who followed the plough and guided the state; but it was as the perfumed hand of Petronius Arbiter, that elegant young buck of a Roman, who once cut great Seneca dead in the forum.

His hand alone, would have entitled my Bury blade to the suffrages of that Eastern potentate, who complimented Lord Byron upon his feline fingers, declaring that they furnished indubitable evidence of his noble birth. And so it did: for Lord Byron was as all the rest of us—the son of a *man*. And so are the dainty-handed, and wee-footed half-cast paupers in Lima; who, if their hands and feet were entitled to consideration, would constitute the oligarchy of all Peru.

Folly and foolishness! to think that a gentleman is known by his finger-nails, like Nebuchadnezzar, when his grew long in the pasture: or that the badge of nobility is to be found in the smallness of the foot, when even a fish has no foot at all!

Dandies! amputate yourselves, if you will; but know, and be assured, oh, democrats, that, like a pyramid, a great man stands on a broad base. It is only the brittle porcelain pagoda, that tottles on a toe.

But though Harry's hand was lady-like looking, and had once been white as the queen's cambric handkerchief, and free from a stain as the reputation of Diana; yet, his late pulling and hauling of halyards and clew-lines, and his occasional dabbling in tar-pots and slush-shoes, had somewhat subtracted from its original daintiness.

Often he ruefully eyed it.

Oh! hand! thought Harry, ah, hand! what have you come to? Is it seemly, that you should be polluted with pitch, when you once handed countesses to their coaches? Is *this* the hand I kissed to the divine Georgiana? with which I pledged Lady Blessington, and ratified my bond to Lord Lovely?

This the hand that Georgiana clasped to her bosom, when she vowed she was mine?—Out of sight, recreant and apostate!—deep down—disappear in this foul monkey-jacket pocket where I thrust you!

After many long conversations, it was at last pretty well decided, that upon our arrival at New York, some means should be taken among my few friends there, to get Harry a place in a mercantile house, where he might flourish his pen, and gently exercise his delicate digits, by traversing some soft foolscap; in the same way that slim, pallid ladies are gently drawn through a park for an airing.

CHAPTER LVII
ALMOST A FAMINE

"Mammy! mammy! come and see the sailors eating out of little troughs, just like our pigs at home." Thus exclaimed one of the steerage children, who at dinner-time was peeping down into the forecastle, where the crew were assembled, helping themselves from the "kids," which, indeed, resemble hog-troughs not a little.

"Pigs, is it?" coughed Jackson, from his bunk, where he sat presiding over the banquet, but not partaking, like a devil who had lost his appetite by chewing sulphur.—"Pigs, is it?—and the day is close by, ye spalpeens, when you'll want to be after taking a sup at our troughs!"

This malicious prophecy proved true.

As day followed day without glimpse of shore or reef, and head winds drove the ship back, as hounds a deer; the improvidence and shortsightedness of the passengers in the steerage, with regard to their outfits for the voyage, began to be followed by the inevitable results.

Many of them at last went aft to the mate, saying that they had nothing to eat, their provisions were expended, and they must be supplied from the ship's stores, or starve.

This was told to the captain, who was obliged to issue a ukase from the cabin, that every steerage passenger, whose destitution was demonstrable, should be given one sea-biscuit and two potatoes a day; a sort of substitute for a muffin and a brace of poached eggs.

But this scanty ration was quite insufficient to satisfy their hunger: hardly enough to satisfy the necessities of a healthy adult. The consequence was, that all day long, and all through the night, scores of the emigrants went about the decks, seeking what they might devour. They plundered the chicken-coop; and disguising the fowls, cooked them at the public galley. They made inroads upon the pig-pen in the boat, and carried off a promising young shoat: *him* they devoured raw, not venturing to make an incognito of his carcass; they prowled about the cook's caboose, till he threatened them with a ladle of scalding water; they waylaid the steward on his regular excursions from the cook to the cabin; they hung round the forecastle, to rob the bread-barge; they beset the sailors, like beggars in the streets, craving a mouthful in the name of the Church.

At length, to such excesses were they driven, that the Grand Russian, Captain Riga, issued another ukase, and to this effect: Whatsoever emigrant is found guilty of stealing, the same shall be tied into the rigging and flogged.

Upon this, there were secret movements in the steerage, which almost alarmed me for the safety of the ship; but nothing serious took place, after all; and they even acquiesced in, or did not resent, a singular punishment which the captain caused to be inflicted upon a culprit of their clan, as a substitute for a flogging. For no doubt he thought that such rigorous discipline as *that* might exasperate five hundred emigrants into an insurrection.

A head was fitted to one of the large deck-tubs—the half of a cask; and into this head a hole was cut; also, two smaller holes in the bottom of the tub. The head—divided in the middle, across the diameter of the orifice—was now fitted round the culprit's neck; and he was forthwith coopered up into the tub, which rested on his shoulders, while his legs protruded through the holes in the bottom.

It was a burden to carry; but the man could walk with it; and so ridiculous was his appearance, that spite of the indignity, he himself laughed with the rest at the figure he cut.

"Now, Pat, my boy," said the mate, "fill that big wooden belly of yours, if you can."

Compassionating his situation, our old "doctor" used to give him alms of food, placing it upon the cask-head before him; till at last, when the time for deliverance came, Pat protested against mercy, and would fain have continued playing Diogenes in the tub for the rest of this starving voyage.

CHAPTER LVIII
THOUGH THE HIGHLANDER PUTS INTO NO HARBOR AS YET; SHE HERE AND THERE LEAVES MANY OF HER PASSENGERS BEHIND

Although fast-sailing ships, blest with prosperous breezes, have frequently made the run across the Atlantic in eighteen days; yet, it is not uncommon for other vessels to be forty, or fifty, and even sixty, seventy, eighty, and ninety days, in making the same passage. Though in the latter cases, some signal calamity or incapacity must occasion so great a detention. It is also true, that generally the passage out from America is shorter than the return; which is to be ascribed to the prevalence of westerly winds.

We had been outside of Cape Clear upward of twenty days, still harassed by head-winds, though with pleasant weather upon the whole, when we were visited by a succession of rain storms, which lasted the greater part of a week.

During the interval, the emigrants were obliged to remain below; but this was nothing strange to some of them; who, not recovering, while at sea, from their first attack of seasickness, seldom or never made their appearance on deck, during the entire passage.

During the week, now in question, fire was only once made in the public galley. This occasioned a good deal of domestic work to be done in the steerage, which otherwise would have been done in the open air. When the lulls of the rain-storms would intervene, some unusually cleanly emigrant would climb to the deck, with a bucket of slops, to toss into the sea. No experience seemed sufficient to instruct some of these ignorant people in the simplest, and most elemental principles of ocean-life. Spite of all lectures on the subject, several would continue to shun the leeward side of the vessel, with their slops. One morning, when it was blowing very fresh, a simple fellow pitched over a gallon or two of something to windward. Instantly it flew back in his face; and also, in the face of the chief mate, who happened to be standing by at the time. The offender was collared, and shaken on the spot; and ironically commanded, never, for the future, to throw any thing to windward at sea, but fine ashes and scalding hot water.

During the frequent *hard blows* we experienced, the hatchways on the steerage were, at intervals, hermetically closed; sealing down in their noisome den, those scores of human beings. It was something to be marveled at, that the shocking fate, which, but a short time ago, overtook the poor passengers in a Liverpool steamer in the Channel, during similar stormy weather, and under similar treatment, did not overtake some of the emigrants of the Highlander.

Nevertheless, it was, beyond question, this noisome confinement in so close, unventilated, and crowded a den: joined to the deprivation of sufficient food, from which many were suffering; which, helped by their personal uncleanliness, brought on a malignant fever.

The first report was, that two persons were affected. No sooner was it known, than the mate promptly repaired to the medicine-chest in the cabin: and with the remedies deemed suitable, descended into the steerage. But the medicines proved of no avail; the invalids rapidly grew worse; and two more of the emigrants became infected.

Upon this, the captain himself went to see them; and returning, sought out a certain alleged physician among the cabin-passengers; begging him to wait upon the sufferers; hinting that, thereby, he might prevent the disease from extending into the cabin itself. But this person denied being a physician; and from fear of contagion—though he did not confess that to be the motive—refused even to enter the steerage. The cases increased: the utmost alarm spread through the ship: and scenes ensued, over which, for the most part, a veil must be drawn; for such is the fastidiousness of some readers, that, many times, they must lose the most striking incidents in a narrative like mine.

Many of the panic-stricken emigrants would fain now have domiciled on deck; but being so scantily clothed, the wretched weather—wet, cold, and tempestuous—drove the best part of them again below. Yet any other human beings, perhaps, would rather have faced the most outrageous storm, than continued to breathe the pestilent air of the steerage. But some of these poor people must have been so used to the most abasing calamities, that the atmosphere of a lazar-house almost seemed their natural air.

The first four cases happened to be in adjoining bunks; and the emigrants who slept in the farther part of the steerage, threw up a barricade in front of those bunks; so as to cut off communication. But this was no sooner reported to the captain, than he ordered it to be thrown down; since it could be of no possible benefit; but would only make still worse, what was already direful enough.

It was not till after a good deal of mingled threatening and coaxing, that the mate succeeded in getting the sailors below, to accomplish the captain's order.

The sight that greeted us, upon entering, was wretched indeed. It was like entering a crowded jail. From the rows of rude bunks, hundreds of meager, begrimed faces were turned upon us; while seated upon the chests, were scores of unshaven men, smoking tea-leaves, and creating a suffocating vapor. But this vapor was better than the native air of the place, which from almost unbelievable causes, was fetid in the extreme. In every corner, the females were huddled together, weeping and lamenting; children were asking bread from their mothers, who had none to give; and old men, seated upon the floor, were leaning back against the heads of the water-casks, with closed eyes and fetching their breath with a gasp.

At one end of the place was seen the barricade, hiding the invalids; while—notwithstanding the crowd—in front of it was a clear area, which the fear of contagion had left open.

"That bulkhead must come down," cried the mate, in a voice that rose above the din. "Take hold of it, boys."

But hardly had we touched the chests composing it, when a crowd of pale-faced, infuriated men rushed up; and with terrific howls, swore they would slay us, if we did not desist.

"Haul it down!" roared the mate.

But the sailors fell back, murmuring something about merchant seamen having no pensions in case of being maimed, and they had not shipped to fight fifty to one. Further efforts were made by the mate, who at last had recourse to entreaty; but it would not do; and we were obliged to depart, without achieving our object.

About four o'clock that morning, the first four died. They were all men; and the scenes which ensued were frantic in the extreme. Certainly, the bottomless profound of the sea, over which we were sailing, concealed nothing more frightful.

Orders were at once passed to bury the dead. But this was unnecessary. By their own countrymen, they were torn from the clasp of their wives, rolled in their own bedding, with ballast-stones, and with hurried rites, were dropped into the ocean.

At this time, ten more men had caught the disease; and with a degree of devotion worthy all praise, the mate attended them with his medicines; but the captain did not again go down to them.

It was all-important now that the steerage should be purified; and had it not been for the rains and squalls, which would have made it madness to turn such a number of women and children upon the wet and unsheltered decks, the steerage passengers would have been ordered above, and their den have been given a thorough cleansing. But, for the present, this was out of the question. The sailors peremptorily refused to go among the defilements to remove them; and so besotted were the greater part of the emigrants themselves, that though the necessity of the case was forcibly painted to them, they would not lift a hand to assist in what seemed their own salvation.

The panic in the cabin was now very great; and for fear of contagion to themselves, the cabin passengers would fain have made a prisoner of the captain, to prevent him from going forward beyond the mainmast. Their clamors at last induced him to tell the two mates, that for the present they must sleep and take their meals elsewhere than in their old quarters, which communicated with the cabin.

On land, a pestilence is fearful enough; but there, many can flee from an infected city; whereas, in a ship, you are locked and bolted in the very hospital itself. Nor is there any possibility of escape from it; and in so small and crowded a place, no precaution can effectually guard against contagion.

Horrible as the sights of the steerage now were, the cabin, perhaps, presented a scene equally despairing. Many, who had seldom prayed before, now implored the merciful heavens, night and day, for fair winds and fine weather. Trunks were opened for Bibles; and at last, even prayer-meetings were held over the very table across which the loud jest had been so often heard.

Strange, though almost universal, that the seemingly nearer prospect of that death which any body at any time may die, should produce these spasmodic devotions, when an everlasting Asiatic Cholera is forever thinning our ranks; and die by death we all must at last.

On the second day, seven died, one of whom was the little tailor; on the third, four; on the fourth, six, of whom one was the Greenland sailor, and another, a woman in the cabin, whose death, however, was afterward supposed to have been purely induced by her fears. These last deaths brought the panic to its height; and sailors, officers, cabin-passengers, and emigrants—all looked upon each other like lepers. All but the only true leper among us—the mariner Jackson, who seemed elated with the thought, that for *him*—already in the deadly clutches of another disease—no danger was to be apprehended from a fever which only swept off the comparatively healthy. Thus, in the midst of the despair of the healthful, this incurable invalid was not cast down; not, at least, by the same considerations that appalled the rest.

And still, beneath a gray, gloomy sky, the doomed craft beat on; now on this tack, now on that; battling against hostile blasts, and drenched in rain and spray; scarcely making an inch of progress toward her port.

On the sixth morning, the weather merged into a gale, to which we stripped our ship to a storm-stay-sail. In ten hours' time, the waves ran in mountains; and the Highlander rose and fell like some vast buoy on the water. Shrieks and lamentations were driven to leeward, and drowned in the roar of the wind among the cordage; while we gave to the gale the blackened bodies of five more of the dead.

But as the dying departed, the places of two of them were filled in the rolls of humanity, by the birth of two infants, whom the plague, panic, and gale had hurried into the world before their time. The first cry of one of these infants, was almost simultaneous with the splash of its father's body in the sea. Thus we come and we go. But, surrounded by death, both mothers and babes survived.

At midnight, the wind went down; leaving a long, rolling sea; and, for the first time in a week, a clear, starry sky.

In the first morning-watch, I sat with Harry on the windlass, watching the billows; which, seen in the night, seemed real hills, upon which fortresses might have been built; and real valleys, in which villages, and groves, and gardens, might have nestled. It was like a landscape in Switzerland; for down into those dark, purple glens, often tumbled the white foam of the wave-crests, like avalanches; while the seething and boiling that ensued, seemed the swallowing up of human beings.

By the afternoon of the next day this heavy sea subsided; and we bore down on the waves, with all our canvas set; stun'-sails alow and aloft; and our best steersman at the helm; the captain himself at his elbow;—bowling along, with a fair, cheering breeze over the taffrail.

The decks were cleared, and swabbed bone-dry; and then, all the emigrants who were not invalids, poured themselves out on deck, snuffing the delightful air, spreading their damp bedding in the sun, and regaling themselves with the generous charity of the captain, who of late had seen fit to increase their allowance of food. A detachment of them now joined a band of the crew, who proceeding into the steerage, with buckets and brooms, gave it a thorough cleansing, sending on deck, I know not how many bucketsful of defilements. It was more like cleaning out a stable, than a retreat for men and women. This day we buried three; the next day one, and then the pestilence left us, with seven convalescent; who, placed near the opening of the hatchway, soon rallied under the skillful treatment, and even tender care of the mate.

But even under this favorable turn of affairs, much apprehension was still entertained, lest in crossing the Grand Banks of Newfoundland, the fogs, so generally encountered there, might bring on a return of the fever. But, to the joy of all hands, our fair wind still held on; and we made a rapid run across these dreaded shoals, and southward steered for New York.

Our days were now fair and mild, and though the wind abated, yet we still ran our course over a pleasant sea. The steerage-passengers—at least by far the greater number—wore a still, subdued aspect, though a little cheered by the genial air, and the hopeful thought of soon reaching their port. But those who had lost fathers, husbands, wives, or children, needed no crape, to reveal to others, who they were. Hard and bitter indeed was their lot; for with the poor and desolate, grief is no indulgence of mere sentiment, however sincere, but a gnawing reality, that eats into their vital beings; they have no kind condolers, and bland physicians, and troops of sympathizing friends; and they must toil, though to-morrow be the burial, and their pallbearers throw down the hammer to lift up the coffin.

How, then, with these emigrants, who, three thousand miles from home, suddenly found themselves deprived of brothers and husbands, with but a few pounds, or perhaps but a few shillings, to buy food in a strange land?

As for the passengers in the cabin, who now so jocund as they? drawing nigh, with their long purses and goodly portmanteaus to the promised land, without fear of fate. One and all were generous and gay, the jelly-eyed old gentleman, before spoken of, gave a shilling to the steward.

The lady who had died, was an elderly person, an American, returning from a visit to an only brother in London. She had no friend or relative on board, hence, as there is little mourning for a stranger dying among strangers, her memory had been buried with her body.

But the thing most worthy of note among these now light-hearted people in feathers, was the gay way in which some of them bantered others, upon the panic into which nearly all had been thrown.

And since, if the extremest fear of a crowd in a panic of peril, proves grounded on causes sufficient, they must then indeed come to perish;—

therefore it is, that at such times they must make up their minds either to die, or else survive to be taunted by their fellow-men with their fear. For except in extraordinary instances of exposure, there are few living men, who, at bottom, are not very slow to admit that any other living men have ever been very much nearer death than themselves. Accordingly, *craven* is the phrase too often applied to any one who, with however good reason, has been appalled at the prospect of sudden death, and yet lived to escape it. Though, should he have perished in conformity with his fears, not a syllable of *craven* would you hear. This is the language of one, who more than once has beheld the scenes, whence these principles have been deduced. The subject invites much subtle speculation; for in every being's ideas of death, and his behavior when it suddenly menaces him, lies the best index to his life and his faith. Though the Christian era had not then begun, Socrates died the death of the Christian; and though Hume was not a Christian in theory, yet he, too, died the death of the Christian,—humble, composed, without bravado; and though the most skeptical of philosophical skeptics, yet full of that firm, creedless faith, that embraces the spheres. Seneca died dictating to posterity; Petronius lightly discoursing of essences and love-songs; and Addison, calling upon Christendom to behold how calmly a Christian could die; but not even the last of these three, perhaps, died the best death of the Christian.

The cabin passenger who had used to read prayers while the rest kneeled against the transoms and settees, was one of the merry young sparks, who had occasioned such agonies of jealousy to the poor tailor, now no more. In his rakish vest, and dangling watch-chain, this same youth, with all the awfulness of fear, had led the earnest petitions of his companions; supplicating mercy, where before he had never solicited the slightest favor. More than once had he been seen thus engaged by the observant steersman at the helm: who looked through the little glass in the cabin bulk-head.

But this youth was an April man; the storm had departed; and now he shone in the sun, none braver than he.

One of his jovial companions ironically advised him to enter into holy orders upon his arrival in New York.

"Why so?" said the other, "have I such an orotund voice?"

"No;" profanely returned his friend—"but you are a coward—just the man to be a parson, and pray."

However this narrative of the circumstances attending the fever among the emigrants on the Highland may appear; and though these things happened so long ago; yet just such events, nevertheless, are perhaps taking place to-day. But the only account you obtain of such events, is generally contained in a newspaper paragraph, under the shipping-head. *There* is the obituary of the destitute dead, who die on the sea. They die, like the billows that break on the shore, and no more are heard or seen. But in the events, thus merely initialized in the catalogue of passing occurrences, and but glanced at by the readers of news, who are more taken up with paragraphs of fuller flavor; what a world of life and death, what a world of humanity and its woes, lies shrunk into a three-worded sentence!

You see no plague-ship driving through a stormy sea; you hear no groans of despair; you see no corpses thrown over the bulwarks; you mark not the wringing hands and torn hair of widows and orphans:—all is a blank. And one of these blanks I have but filled up, in recounting the details of the Highlander's calamity.

Besides that natural tendency, which hurries into oblivion the last woes of the poor; other causes combine to suppress the detailed circumstances of disasters like these. Such things, if widely known, operate unfavorably to the ship, and make her a bad name; and to avoid detention at quarantine, a captain will state the case in the most palliating light, and strive to hush it up, as much as he can.

In no better place than this, perhaps, can a few words be said, concerning emigrant ships in general.

Let us waive that agitated national topic, as to whether such multitudes of foreign poor should be landed on our American shores; let us waive it, with the one only thought, that if they can get here, they have God's right to come; though they bring all Ireland and her miseries with them. For the whole world is the patrimony of the whole world; there is no telling who does not own a stone in the Great Wall of China. But we waive all this; and will only consider, how best the emigrants can come hither, since come they do, and come they must and will.

Of late, a law has been passed in Congress, restricting ships to a certain number of emigrants, according to a certain rate. If this law were enforced, much good might be done; and so also might much good be done, were the English law likewise enforced, concerning the fixed supply of food for every emigrant embarking from Liverpool. But it is hardly to be believed, that either of these laws is observed.

But in all respects, no legislation, even nominally, reaches the hard lot of the emigrant. What ordinance makes it obligatory upon the captain of a ship, to supply the steerage-passengers with decent lodgings, and give them light and air in that foul den, where they are immured, during a long voyage across the Atlantic? What ordinance necessitates him to place the *galley*, or steerage-passengers' stove, in a dry place of shelter, where the emigrants can do their cooking during a storm, or wet weather? What ordinance obliges him to give them more room on deck, and let them have an occasional run fore and aft?—There is no law concerning these things. And if there was, who but some Howard in office would see it enforced? and how seldom is there a Howard in office!

We talk of the Turks, and abhor the cannibals; but may not some of *them,* go to heaven, before some of *us?* We may have civilized bodies and yet barbarous souls. We are blind to the real sights of this world; deaf to its voice; and dead to its death. And not till we know, that one grief outweighs ten thousand joys, will we become what Christianity is striving to make us.

CHAPTER LIX
THE LAST END OF JACKSON

"Off Cape Cod!" said the steward, coming forward from the quarter-deck, where the captain had just been taking his noon observation; sweeping the vast horizon with his quadrant, like a dandy circumnavigating the dress-circle of an amphitheater with his glass.

Off Cape Cod! and in the shore-bloom that came to us— even from that desert of sand-hillocks—methought I could almost distinguish the fragrance of the rose-bush my sisters and I had planted, in our far inland garden at home. Delicious odors are those of our mother Earth; which like a flower-pot set with a thousand shrubs, greets the eager voyager from afar.

The breeze was stiff, and so drove us along that we turned over two broad, blue furrows from our bows, as we plowed the watery prairie. By night it was a reef-topsail-breeze; but so impatient was the captain to make his port before a shift of wind overtook us, that even yet we carried a main-topgallant-sail, though the light mast sprung like a switch.

In the second dog-watch, however, the breeze became such, that at last the order was given to douse the top-gallant-sail, and clap a reef into all three top-sails.

While the men were settling away the halyards on deck, and before they had begun to haul out the reef-tackles, to the surprise of several, Jackson came up from the forecastle, and, for the first time in four weeks or more, took hold of a rope.

Like most seamen, who during the greater part of a voyage, have been off duty from sickness, he was, perhaps, desirous, just previous to entering port, of reminding the captain of his existence, and also that he expected his wages; but, alas! his wages proved the wages of sin.

At no time could he better signalize his disposition to work, than upon an occasion like the present; which generally attracts every soul on deck, from the captain to the child in the steerage.

His aspect was damp and death-like; the blue hollows of his eyes were like vaults full of snakes; and issuing so unexpectedly from his dark tomb in the forecastle, he looked like a man raised from the dead.

Before the sailors had made fast the reef-tackle, Jackson was tottering up the rigging; thus getting the start of them, and securing his place at the extreme weather-end of the topsail-yard—which in reefing is accounted the post of honor. For it was one of the characteristics of this man, that though when on duty he would shy away from mere dull work in a calm, yet in tempest-time he always claimed the van, and would yield it to none; and this, perhaps, was one cause of his unbounded dominion over the men.

Soon, we were all strung along the main-topsail-yard; the ship rearing and plunging under us, like a runaway steed; each man gripping his reef-point, and sideways leaning, dragging the sail over toward Jackson, whose business it was to confine the reef corner to the yard.

His hat and shoes were off; and he rode the yard-arm end, leaning backward to the gale, and pulling at the earing-rope, like a bridle. At all times, this is a moment of frantic exertion with sailors, whose spirits seem then to partake of the commotion of the elements, as they hang in the gale, between heaven and earth; and *then* it is, too, that they are the most profane.

"Haul out to windward!" coughed Jackson, with a blasphemous cry, and he threw himself back with a violent strain upon the bridle in his hand. But the wild words were hardly out of his mouth, when his hands dropped to his side, and the bellying sail was spattered with a torrent of blood from his lungs.

As the man next him stretched out his arm to save, Jackson fell headlong from the yard, and with a long seethe, plunged like a diver into the sea.

It was when the ship had rolled to windward, which, with the long projection of the yard-arm over the side, made him strike far out upon the water. His fall was seen by the whole upward-gazing crowd on deck, some of whom were spotted with the blood that trickled from the sail, while they raised a spontaneous cry, so shrill and wild, that a blind man might have known something deadly had happened.

Clutching our reef-points, we hung over the stick, and gazed down to the one white, bubbling spot, which had closed over the head of our shipmate; but the next minute it was brewed into the common yeast of the waves, and Jackson never arose. We waited a few minutes, expecting an order to descend, haul back the fore-yard, and man the boat; but instead of that, the next sound that greeted us was, "Bear a hand, and reef away, men!" from the mate.

Indeed, upon reflection, it would have been idle to attempt to save Jackson; for besides that he must have been dead, ere he struck the sea—and if he had not been dead then, the first immersion must have driven his soul from his lacerated lungs—our jolly-boat would have taken full fifteen minutes to launch into the waves.

And here it should be said, that the thoughtless security in which too many sea-captains indulge, would, in case of some sudden disaster befalling the Highlander, have let us all drop into our graves.

Like most merchant ships, we had but two boats: the longboat and the jolly-boat. The long boat, by far the largest and stoutest of the two, was permanently bolted down to the deck, by iron bars attached to its sides. It was almost as much of a fixture as the vessel's keel. It was filled with pigs, fowls, firewood, and coals. Over this the jolly-boat was capsized without a *thole-pin* in the gunwales; its bottom bleaching and cracking in the sun.

Judge, then, what promise of salvation for us, had we shipwrecked; yet in this state, one merchant ship out of three, keeps its boats. To be sure, no vessel full of emigrants, by any possible precautions, could in case of a fatal disaster at sea, hope to save the tenth part of the souls on board; yet provision should certainly be made for a handful of survivors, to carry home the tidings of her loss; for even in the worst of the calamities that befell patient Job, some *one* at least of his servants escaped to report it.

In a way that I never could fully account for, the sailors, in my hearing at least, and Harry's, never made the slightest allusion to the departed Jackson. One and all they seemed tacitly to unite in hushing up his memory among them. Whether it was, that the severity of the bondage under which this man held every one of them, did really corrode in their secret hearts, that they thought to repress the recollection of a thing so degrading, I can not determine; but certain it was, that *his* death was *their* deliverance; which they celebrated by an elevation of spirits, unknown before. Doubtless, this was to be in part imputed, however, to their now drawing near to their port.

CHAPTER LX
HOME AT LAST

Next day was Sunday; and the mid-day sun shone upon a glassy sea.

After the uproar of the breeze and the gale, this profound, pervading calm seemed suited to the tranquil spirit of a day, which, in godly towns, makes quiet vistas of the most tumultuous thoroughfares.

The ship lay gently rolling in the soft, subdued ocean swell; while all around were faint white spots; and nearer to, broad, milky patches, betokening the vicinity of scores of ships, all bound to one common port, and tranced in one common calm. Here the long, devious wakes from Europe, Africa, India, and Peru converged to a line, which braided them all in one.

Full before us quivered and danced, in the noon-day heat and mid-air, the green heights of New Jersey; and by an optical delusion, the blue sea seemed to flow under them.

The sailors whistled and whistled for a wind; the impatient cabin-passengers were arrayed in their best; and the emigrants clustered around the bows, with eyes intent upon the long-sought land.

But leaning over, in a reverie, against the side, my Carlo gazed down into the calm, violet sea, as if it were an eye that answered his own; and turning to Harry, said, "This America's skies must be down in the sea; for, looking down in this water, I behold what, in Italy, we also behold overhead. Ah! after all, I find my Italy somewhere, wherever I go. I even found it in rainy Liverpool."

Presently, up came a dainty breeze, wafting to us a white wing from the shore—the pilot-boat! Soon a monkey-jacket mounted the side, and was beset by the captain and cabin people for news. And out of bottomless pockets came bundles of newspapers, which were eagerly caught by the throng.

The captain now abdicated in the pilot's favor, who proved to be a tiger of a fellow, keeping us hard at work, pulling and hauling the braces, and trimming the ship, to catch the least *cat's-paw* of wind.

When, among sea-worn people, a strange man from shore suddenly stands among them, with the smell of the land in his beard, it conveys a realization of the vicinity of the green grass, that not even the distant sight of the shore itself can transcend.

The steerage was now as a bedlam; trunks and chests were locked and tied round with ropes; and a general washing and rinsing of faces and hands was beheld. While this was going on, forth came an order from the quarter-deck, for every bed, blanket, bolster, and bundle of straw in the steerage to be committed to the deep.—A command that was received by the emigrants with dismay, and then with wrath. But they were assured, that this was indispensable to the getting rid of an otherwise long detention of some weeks at the quarantine. They therefore reluctantly complied; and overboard went pallet and pillow. Following them, went old pots and pans, bottles and baskets. So, all around, the sea was strewn with stuffed bed-ticks, that limberly floated on the waves—couches for all mermaids who were not fastidious. Numberless things of this sort, tossed overboard from emigrant ships nearing the harbor of New York, drift in through the Narrows, and are deposited on the shores of Staten Island; along whose eastern beach I have often walked, and speculated upon the broken jugs, torn pillows, and dilapidated baskets at my feet.

A second order was now passed for the emigrants to muster their forces, and give the steerage a final, thorough cleaning with sand and water. And to this they were incited by the same warning which had induced them to make an offering to Neptune of their bedding. The place was then fumigated, and dried with pans of coals from the galley; so that by evening, no stranger would have imagined, from her appearance, that the Highlander had made otherwise than a tidy and prosperous voyage. Thus, some sea-captains take good heed that benevolent citizens shall not get a glimpse of the true condition of the steerage while at sea.

That night it again fell calm; but next morning, though the wind was somewhat against us, we set sail for the Narrows; and making short tacks, at last ran through, almost bringing our jib-boom over one of the forts.

An early shower had refreshed the woods and fields, that glowed with a glorious green; and to our salted lungs, the land breeze was spiced with aromas. The steerage passengers almost neighed with delight, like horses brought back to spring pastures; and every eye and ear in the Highlander was full of the glad sights and sounds of the shore.

No more did we think of the gale and the plague; nor turn our eyes upward to the stains of blood, still visible on the topsail, whence Jackson had fallen; but we fixed our gaze on the orchards and meads, and like thirsty men, drank in all their dew.

On the Staten Island side, a white staff displayed a pale yellow flag, denoting the habitation of the quarantine officer; for as if to symbolize the yellow fever itself, and strike a panic and premonition of the black vomit into every beholder, all quarantines all over the world, taint the air with the streamings of their fever-flag.

But though the long rows of white-washed hospitals on the hill side were now in plain sight, and though scores of ships were here lying at anchor, yet no boat came off to us; and to our surprise and delight, on we sailed, past a spot which every one had dreaded. How it was that they thus let us pass without boarding us, we never could learn.

Now rose the city from out the bay, and one by one, her spires pierced the blue; while thick and more thick, ships, brigs, schooners, and sail boats, thronged around. We saw the Hartz Forest of masts and black rigging stretching along the East River; and northward, up the stately old Hudson, covered with white sloop-sails like fleets of swans, we caught a far glimpse of the purple Palisades.

Oh! he who has never been afar, let him once go from home, to know what home is. For as you draw nigh again to your old native river, he seems to pour through you with all his tides, and in your enthusiasm, you swear to build altars like mile-stones, along both his sacred banks.

Like the Czar of all the Russias, and Siberia to boot, Captain Riga, telescope in hand, stood on the poop, pointing out to the passengers, Governor's Island, Castle Garden, and the Battery.

"And *that*" said he, pointing out a vast black hull which, like a shark, showed tiers of teeth, "*that*, ladies, is a line-of-battle-ship, the North Carolina."

"Oh, dear!"—and "Oh my!"—ejaculated the ladies, and—"Lord, save us," responded an old gentleman, who was a member of the Peace Society.

Hurra! hurra! and ten thousand times hurra! down goes our old anchor, fathoms down into the free and independent Yankee mud, one handful of which was now worth a broad manor in England.

The Whitehall boats were around us, and soon, our cabin passengers were all off, gay as crickets, and bound for a late dinner at the Astor House; where, no doubt, they fired off a salute of champagne corks in honor of their own arrival. Only a very few of the steerage passengers, however, could afford to pay the high price the watermen demanded for carrying them ashore; so most of them remained with us till morning. But nothing could restrain our Italian boy, Carlo, who, promising the watermen to pay them with his music, was triumphantly rowed ashore, seated in the stern of the boat, his organ before him, and something like "Hail Columbia!" his tune. We gave him three rapturous cheers, and we never saw Carlo again.

Harry and I passed the greater part of the night walking the deck, and gazing at the thousand lights of the city.

At sunrise, we *warped* into a berth at the foot of Wall-street, and knotted our old ship, stem and stern, to the pier. But that knotting of *her*, was the unknotting of the bonds of the sailors, among whom, it is a maxim, that the ship once fast to the wharf, they are free. So with a rush and a shout, they bounded ashore, followed by the tumultuous crowd of emigrants, whose friends, day-laborers and housemaids, stood ready to embrace them.

But in silent gratitude at the end of a voyage, almost equally uncongenial to both of us, and so bitter to one, Harry and I sat on a chest in the forecastle. And now, the ship that we had loathed, grew lovely in our eyes, which lingered over every familiar old timber; for the scene of suffering is a scene of joy when the suffering is past; and the silent reminiscence of hardships departed, is sweeter than the presence of delight.

CHAPTER LXI
REDBURN AND HARRY, ARM IN ARM, IN HARBOR

There we sat in that tarry old den, the only inhabitants of the deserted old ship, but the mate and the rats.

At last, Harry went to his chest, and drawing out a few shillings, proposed that we should go ashore, and return with a supper, to eat in the forecastle. Little else that was eatable being for sale in the paltry shops along the wharves, we bought several pies, some doughnuts, and a bottle of ginger-pop, and thus supplied we made merry. For to us, whose very mouths were become pickled and puckered, with the continual flavor of briny beef, those pies and doughnuts were most delicious. And as for the ginger-pop, why, that ginger-pop was divine! I have reverenced ginger-pop ever since.

We kept late hours that night; for, delightful certainty! placed beyond all doubt—like royal landsmen, we were masters of the watches of the night, and no *starb-o-leens ahoy!* would annoy us again.

"All night in! think of *that*, Harry, my friend!"

"Ay, Wellingborough, it's enough to keep me awake forever, to think I may now sleep as long as I please."

We turned out bright and early, and then prepared for the shore, first stripping to the waist, for a toilet.

"I shall never get these confounded tar-stains out of my fingers," cried Harry, rubbing them hard with a bit of oakum, steeped in strong suds. "No! they will *not* come out, and I'm ruined for life. Look at my hand once, Wellingborough!"

It was indeed a sad sight. Every finger nail, like mine, was dyed of a rich, russet hue; looking something like bits of fine tortoise shell.

"Never mind, Harry," said I—"You know the ladies of the east steep the tips of their fingers in some golden dye."

"And by Plutus," cried Harry—"I'd steep mine up to the armpits in gold; since you talk about *that*. But never mind, I'll swear I'm just from Persia, my boy."

We now arrayed ourselves in our best, and sallied ashore; and, at once, I piloted Harry to the sign of a Turkey Cock in Fulton-street, kept by one Sweeny, a place famous for cheap Souchong, and capital buckwheat cakes.

"Well, gentlemen, what will you have?"—said a waiter, as we seated ourselves at a table.

"*Gentlemen!*" whispered Harry to me—"*gentlemen!*—hear him!—I say now, Redburn, they didn't talk to us that way on board the old Highlander. By heaven, I begin to feel my straps again:—Coffee and hot rolls," he added aloud, crossing his legs like a lord, "and fellow—come back—bring us a venison-steak."

"Haven't got it, gentlemen."

"Ham and eggs," suggested I, whose mouth was watering at the recollection of that particular dish, which I had tasted at the sign of the Turkey Cock before. So ham and eggs it was; and royal coffee, and imperial toast.

But the butter!

"Harry, did you ever taste such butter as this before?"

"Don't say a word,"—said Harry, spreading his tenth slice of toast "I'm going to turn dairyman, and keep within the blessed savor of butter, so long as I live."

We made a breakfast, never to be forgotten; paid our bill with a flourish, and sallied into the street, like two goodly galleons of gold, bound from Acapulco to Old Spain.

"Now," said Harry, "lead on; and let's see something of these United States of yours. I'm ready to pace from Maine to Florida; ford the Great Lakes; and jump the River Ohio, if it comes in the way. Here, take my arm;—lead on."

Such was the miraculous change, that had now come over him. It reminded me of his manner, when we had started for London, from the sign of the Golden Anchor, in Liverpool.

He was, indeed, in most wonderful spirits; at which I could not help marveling; considering the cavity in his pockets; and that he was a stranger in the land.

By noon he had selected his boarding-house, a private establishment, where they did not charge much for their board, and where the landlady's butcher's bill was not very large.

Here, at last, I left him to get his chest from the ship; while I turned up town to see my old friend Mr. Jones, and learn what had happened during my absence.

With one hand, Mr. Jones shook mine most cordially; and with the other, gave me some letters, which I eagerly devoured. Their purport compelled my departure homeward; and I at once sought out Harry to inform him.

Strange, but even the few hours' absence which had intervened; during which, Harry had been left to himself, to stare at strange streets, and strange faces, had wrought a marked change in his countenance. He was a creature of the suddenest impulses. Left to himself, the strange streets seemed now to have reminded him of his friendless condition; and I found him with a very sad eye; and his right hand groping in his pocket.

"Where am I going to dine, this day week?"—he slowly said. "What's to be done, Wellingborough?"

And when I told him that the next afternoon I must leave him; he looked downhearted enough. But I cheered him as well as I could; though needing a little cheering myself; even though I *had* got home again. But no more about that.

Now, there was a young man of my acquaintance in the city, much my senior, by the name of Goodwell; and a good natured fellow he was; who had of late been engaged as a clerk in a large forwarding house in South-street; and it occurred to me, that he was just the man to befriend Harry, and procure him a place. So I mentioned the thing to my comrade; and we called upon Goodwell.

I saw that he was impressed by the handsome exterior of my friend; and in private, making known the case, he faithfully promised to do his best for him; though the times, he said, were quite dull.

That evening, Goodwell, Harry, and I, perambulated the streets, three abreast:—Goodwell spending his money freely at the oyster-saloons; Harry full of allusions to the London Clubhouses: and myself contributing a small quota to the general entertainment.

Next morning, we proceeded to business.

Now, I did not expect to draw much of a salary from the ship; so as to retire for life on the profits of *my first voyage;* but nevertheless, I thought that a dollar or two might be coming. For dollars are valuable things; and should not be overlooked, when they are owing. Therefore, as the second morning after our arrival, had been set apart for paying off the crew, Harry and I made our appearance on ship-board, with the rest. We were told to enter the cabin; and once again I found myself, after an interval of four months, and more, surrounded by its mahogany and maple.

Seated in a sumptuous arm-chair, behind a lustrous, inlaid desk, sat Captain Riga, arrayed in his City Hotel suit, looking magisterial as the Lord High Admiral of England. Hat in hand, the sailors stood deferentially in a semicircle before him, while the captain held the ship-papers in his hand, and one by one called their names; and in mellow bank notes—beautiful sight!—paid them their wages.

Most of them had less than ten, a few twenty, and two, thirty dollars coming to them; while the old cook, whose piety proved profitable in restraining him from the expensive excesses of most seafaring men, and who had taken no pay in advance, had the goodly round sum of seventy dollars as his due.

Seven ten dollar bills! each of which, as I calculated at the time, was worth precisely one hundred dimes, which were equal to one thousand cents, which were again subdivisible into fractions. So that he now stepped into a fortune of seventy thousand American *"mitts."* Only seventy dollars, after all; but then, it has always seemed to me, that stating amounts in sounding fractional sums, conveys a much fuller notion of their magnitude, than by disguising their immensity in such aggregations of value, as doubloons, sovereigns, and dollars. Who would not rather be worth 125,000 francs in Paris, than only £5000 in London, though the intrinsic value of the two sums, in round numbers, is pretty much the same.

With a scrape of the foot, and such a bow as only a negro can make, the old cook marched off with his fortune; and I have no doubt at once invested it in a grand, underground oyster-cellar.

The other sailors, after counting their cash very carefully, and seeing all was right, and not a bank-note was dog-eared, in which case they would have demanded another: for they are not to be taken in and cheated, your sailors, and they know their rights, too; at least, when they are at liberty, after the voyage is concluded:— the sailors also salaamed, and withdrew, leaving Harry and me face to face with the Paymaster-general of the Forces.

We stood awhile, looking as polite as possible, and expecting every moment to hear our names called, but not a word did we hear; while the captain, throwing aside his accounts, lighted a very fragrant cigar, took up the morning paper—I think it was the Herald—threw his leg over one arm of the chair, and plunged into the latest intelligence from all parts of the world.

I looked at Harry, and he looked at me; and then we both looked at this incomprehensible captain.

At last Harry hemmed, and I scraped my foot to increase the disturbance.

The Paymaster-general looked up.

"Well, where do you come from? Who are *you,* pray? and what do you want? Steward, show these young gentlemen out."

"I want my money," said Harry.

"My wages are due," said I.

The captain laughed. Oh! he was exceedingly merry; and taking a long inspiration of smoke, removed his cigar, and sat sideways looking at us, letting the vapor slowly wriggle and spiralize out of his mouth.

"Upon my soul, young gentlemen, you astonish me. Are your names down in the City Directory? have you any letters of introduction, young gentlemen?"

"Captain Riga!" cried Harry, enraged at his impudence—"I tell you what it is, Captain Riga; this won't do—where's the rhino?"

"Captain Riga," added I, "do you not remember, that about four months ago, my friend Mr. Jones and myself had an interview with you in this very cabin; when it was agreed that I was to go out in your ship, and receive three dollars per month for my services? Well, Captain Riga, I have gone out with you, and returned; and now, sir, I'll thank you for my pay."

"Ah, yes, I remember," said the captain. *"Mr. Jones!* Ha! ha! I remember Mr. Jones: a very gentlemanly gentleman; and stop—*you,* too, are the son of a wealthy French importer; and—let me think—was not your great-uncle a barber?"

"No!" thundered I.

"Well, well, young gentleman, really I beg your pardon. Steward, chairs for the young gentlemen—be seated, young gentlemen. And now, let me see," turning over his accounts— "Hum, hum!—yes, here it is: Wellingborough Redburn, at three dollars a month. Say four months, that's twelve dollars; less three dollars advanced in Liverpool—that makes it nine dollars; less three hammers and two scrapers lost overboard— that brings it to four dollars and a quarter. I owe you four dollars and a quarter, I believe, young gentleman?"

"So it seems, sir," said I, with staring eyes.

"And now let me see what you owe me, and then well be able to square the yards, Monsieur Redburn."

Owe *him!* thought I—what do I owe him but a grudge, but I concealed my resentment; and presently he said, "By running away from the ship in Liverpool, you forfeited your wages, which amount to twelve dollars; and as there has been advanced to you, in money, hammers, and scrapers, seven dollars and seventy-five cents, you are therefore indebted to me in precisely that sum. Now, young gentleman, I'll thank you for the money;" and he extended his open palm across the desk.

"Shall I pitch into him?" whispered Harry.

I was thunderstruck at this most unforeseen announcement of the state of my account with Captain Riga; and I began to understand why it was that he had till now ignored my absence from the ship, when Harry and I were in London. But a single minute's consideration showed that I could not help myself; so, telling him that he was at liberty to begin his suit, for I was a bankrupt, and could not pay him, I turned to go.

Now, here was this man actually turning a poor lad adrift without a copper, after he had been slaving aboard his ship for more than four mortal months. But Captain Riga was a bachelor of expensive habits, and had run up large wine bills at the City Hotel. He could not afford to be munificent. Peace to his dinners.

"Mr. Bolton, I believe," said the captain, now blandly bowing toward Harry. "Mr. Bolton, *you* also shipped for three dollars per month: and you had one month's advance in Liverpool; and from dock to dock we have been about a month and a half; so I owe you just one dollar and a half, Mr. Bolton; and here it is;" handing him six two-shilling pieces.

"And this," said Harry, throwing himself into a tragical attitude, "*this* is the reward of my long and faithful services!"

Then, disdainfully flinging the silver on the desk, he exclaimed, "There, Captain Riga, you may keep your tin! It has been in *your* purse, and it would give me the itch to retain it. Good morning, sir."

"Good morning, young gentlemen; pray, call again," said the captain, coolly bagging the coins. His politeness, while in port, was invincible.

Quitting the cabin, I remonstrated with Harry upon his recklessness in disdaining his wages, small though they were; I begged to remind him of his situation; and hinted that every penny he could get might prove precious to him. But he only cried *Pshaw!* and that was the last of it.

Going forward, we found the sailors congregated on the forecastle-deck, engaged in some earnest discussion; while several carts on the wharf, loaded with their chests, were just in the act of driving off, destined for the boarding-houses uptown. By the looks of our shipmates, I saw very plainly that they must have some mischief under weigh; and so it turned out.

Now, though Captain Riga had not been guilty of any particular outrage against the sailors; yet, by a thousand small meannesses—such as indirectly causing their allowance of bread and beef to be diminished, without betraying any appearance of having any inclination that way, and without speaking to the sailors on the subject—by this, and kindred actions, I say, he had contracted the cordial dislike of the whole ship's company; and long since they had bestowed upon him a name unmentionably expressive of their contempt.

The voyage was now concluded; and it appeared that the subject being debated by the assembly on the forecastle was, how best they might give a united and valedictory expression of the sentiments they entertained toward their late lord and master. Some emphatic symbol of those sentiments was desired; some unmistakable token, which should forcibly impress Captain Riga with the justest possible notion of their feelings.

It was like a meeting of the members of some mercantile company, upon the eve of a prosperous dissolution of the concern; when the subordinates, actuated by the purest gratitude toward their president, or chief, proceed to vote him a silver pitcher, in token of their respect. It was something like this, I repeat—but with a material difference, as will be seen.

At last, the precise manner in which the thing should be done being agreed upon, Blunt, the "Irish cockney," was deputed to summon the captain. He knocked at the cabin-door, and politely requested the steward to inform Captain Riga, that some gentlemen were on the pier-head, earnestly seeking him; whereupon he joined his comrades.

In a few moments the captain sallied from the cabin, and found the *gentlemen* alluded to, strung along the top of the bulwarks, on the side next to the wharf. Upon his appearance, the row suddenly wheeled about, presenting their backs; and making a motion, which was a polite salute to every thing before them, but an abominable insult to all who happened to be in their rear, they gave three cheers, and at one bound, cleared the ship.

True to his imperturbable politeness while in port, Captain Riga only lifted his hat, smiled very blandly, and slowly returned into his cabin.

Wishing to see the last movements of this remarkable crew, who were so clever ashore and so craven afloat, Harry and I followed them along the wharf, till they stopped at a sailor retreat, poetically denominated "The Flashes." And here they all came to anchor before the bar; and the landlord, a lantern-jawed landlord, bestirred himself behind it, among his villainous old bottles and decanters. He well knew, from their looks, that his customers were "flush," and would spend their money freely, as, indeed, is the case with most seamen, recently paid off.

It was a touching scene.

"Well, maties," said one of them, at last—"I spose we shan't see each other again:—come, let's splice the main-brace all round, and drink to *the last voyage!*"

Upon this, the landlord danced down his glasses, on the bar, uncorked his decanters, and deferentially pushed them over toward the sailors, as much as to say—"*Honorable gentlemen, it is not for me to allowance your liquor;—help yourselves, your honors.*"

And so they did; each glass a bumper; and standing in a row, tossed them all off; shook hands all round, three times three; and then disappeared in couples, through the several doorways; for *"The Flashes"* was on a corner.

If to every one, life be made up of farewells and greetings, and a *"Good-by, God bless you,"* is heard for every *"How d'ye do, welcome, my boy"*—then, of all men, sailors shake the most hands, and wave the most hats. They are here and then they are there; ever shifting themselves, they shift among the shifting: and like rootless sea-weed, are tossed to and fro.

As, after shaking our hands, our shipmates departed, Harry and I stood on the corner awhile, till we saw the last man disappear.

"They are gone," said I.

"Thank heaven!" said Harry.

CHAPTER LXII
THE LAST THAT WAS EVER HEARD OF HARRY BOLTON

That same afternoon, I took my comrade down to the Battery; and we sat on one of the benches, under the summer shade of the trees.

It was a quiet, beautiful scene; full of promenading ladies and gentlemen; and through the foliage, so fresh and bright, we looked out over the bay, varied with glancing ships; and then, we looked down to our boots; and thought what a fine world it would be, if we only had a little money to enjoy it. But that's the everlasting rub—oh, who can cure an empty pocket?

"I have no doubt, Goodwell will take care of you, Harry," said I, "he's a fine, good-hearted fellow; and will do his best for you, I know."

"No doubt of it," said Harry, looking hopeless.

"And I need not tell you, Harry, how sorry I am to leave you so soon."

"And I am sorry enough myself," said Harry, looking very sincere.

"But I will be soon back again, I doubt not," said I.

"Perhaps so," said Harry, shaking his head. "How far is it off?"

"Only a hundred and eighty miles," said I.

"A hundred and eighty miles!" said Harry, drawing the words out like an endless ribbon. "Why, I couldn't walk that in a month."

"Now, my dear friend," said I, "take my advice, and while I am gone, keep up a stout heart; never despair, and all will be well."

But notwithstanding all I could say to encourage him, Harry felt so bad, that nothing would do, but a rush to a neighboring bar, where we both gulped down a glass of ginger-pop; after which we felt better.

He accompanied me to the steamboat, that was to carry me homeward; he stuck close to my side, till she was about to put off; then, standing on the wharf, he shook me by the hand, till we almost counteracted the play of the paddles; and at last, with a mutual jerk at the arm-pits, we parted. I never saw Harry again.

I pass over the reception I met with at home; how I plunged into embraces, long and loving:—I pass over this; and will conclude *my first voyage* by relating all I know of what overtook Harry Bolton.

Circumstances beyond my control, detained me at home for several weeks; during which, I wrote to my friend, without receiving an answer.

I then wrote to young Goodwell, who returned me the following letter, now spread before me.

"Dear Redburn—Your poor friend, Harry, I can not find any where. After you left, he called upon me several times, and we walked out together; and my interest in him increased every day. But you don't know how dull are the times here, and what multitudes of young men, well qualified, are seeking employment in counting-houses. I did my best; but could not get Harry a place. However, I cheered him. But he grew more and more melancholy, and at last told me, that he had sold all his clothes but those on his back to pay his board. I offered to loan him a few dollars, but he would not receive them. I called upon him two or three times after this, but he was not in; at last, his landlady told me that he had permanently left her house the very day before. Upon my questioning her closely, as to where he had gone, she answered, that she did not know, but from certain hints that had dropped from our poor friend, she feared he had gone on a whaling voyage. I at once went to the offices in South-street, where men are shipped for the Nantucket whalers, and made inquiries among them; but without success. And this, I am heartily grieved to say, is all I know of our friend. I can not believe that his melancholy could bring him to the insanity of throwing himself away in a whaler; and I still think, that he must be somewhere in the city. You must come down yourself, and help me seek him out."

This letter gave me a dreadful shock. Remembering our adventure in London, and his conduct there; remembering how liable he was to yield to the most sudden, crazy, and contrary impulses; and that, as a friendless, penniless foreigner in New York, he must have had the most terrible incitements to committing violence upon himself; I shuddered to think, that even now, while I thought of him, he might no more be living. So strong was this impression at the time, that I quickly glanced over the papers to see if there were any accounts of suicides, or drowned persons floating in the harbor of New York.

I now made all the haste I could to the seaport, but though I sought him all over, no tidings whatever could be heard.

To relieve my anxiety, Goodwell endeavored to assure me, that Harry must indeed have departed on a whaling voyage. But remembering his bitter experience on board of the Highlander, and more than all, his nervousness about going aloft, it seemed next to impossible.

At last I was forced to give him up.

Years after this, I found myself a sailor in the Pacific, on board of a whaler. One day at sea, we spoke another whaler, and the boat's crew that boarded our vessel, came forward among us to have a little sea-chat, as is always customary upon such occasions.

Among the strangers was an Englishman, who had shipped in his vessel at Callao, for the cruise. In the course of conversation, he made allusion to the fact, that he had now been in the Pacific several years, and that the good craft Huntress of Nantucket had had the honor of originally bringing him round upon that side of the globe. I asked him why he had abandoned her; he answered that she was the most unlucky of ships.

"We had hardly been out three months," said he, "when on the Brazil banks we lost a boat's crew, chasing a whale after sundown; and next day lost a poor little fellow, a countryman of mine, who had never entered the boats; he fell over the side, and was jammed between the ship, and a whale, while we were cutting the fish in. Poor fellow, he had a hard time of it, from the beginning; he was a gentleman's son, and when you could coax him to it, he sang like a bird."

"What was his name?" said I, trembling with expectation; "what kind of eyes did he have? what was the color of his hair?"

"Harry Bolton was not your brother?" cried the stranger, starting.

Harry Bolton! it was even he!

But yet, I, Wellingborough Redburn, chance to survive, after having passed through far more perilous scenes than any narrated in this, *My First Voyage*—which here I end.